The EVERYTHING.
Sugar-Free Cookbook

Dear Reader,

When I was trying to quit smoking, I learned to quickly envision some other sensory image whenever a craving for a cigarette struck me. "What does Chanel No. 5 smell like?" I'd ask myself, and the scent of one of my least-favorite perfumes would occupy my senses. After a very few seconds, the cigarette craving would go away. If I couldn't imagine a scent, I'd try a visual image. Images of yellow chickens and pink pigs made me smile and lessened my cravings. Over time, the cravings became more and more rare and of shorter duration. The same principle applies to leading a sugar-free life. Just line up some things for yourself to visualize or recall when you want something sweet.

Go for it! Have an apple, a banana, a diet soda, or a dish of sugar-free ice cream! Or make some of the recipes in this book, and soon you'll find you have lost interest in eating sugar.

Nancy T. Maar

Welcome to the EVERYTHING® Series!

These handy, accessible books give you all you need to tackle a difficult project, gain a new hobby, comprehend a fascinating topic, prepare for an exam, or even brush up on something you learned back in school but have since forgotten.

You can read an *Everything*® book from cover to cover or just pick out the information you want from our four useful boxes: e-questions, e-facts, e-alerts, e-ssentials. We give you everything you need to know on the subject, but throw in a lot of fun stuff along the way, too.

We now have more than 400 *Everything*® books in print, spanning such wide-ranging categories as weddings, pregnancy, cooking, music instruction, foreign language, crafts, pets, New Age, and so much more. When you're done reading them all, you can finally say you know *Everything*®!

QUESTIONS?
Answers to
common questions

FACTS
Important snippets
of information

ALERTS!
Urgent
warnings

ESSENTIALS
Quick
handy tips

Editorial

Director of Innovation: Paula Munier

Editorial Director: Laura M. Daly

Executive Editor, Series Books: Brielle K. Matson

Associate Copy Chief: Sheila Zwiebel

Acquisitions Editor: Kerry Smith

Development Editor: Elizabeth Kassab

Production Editor: Casey Ebert

Production

Director of Manufacturing: Susan Beale

Production Project Manager: Michelle Roy Kelly

Prepress: Erick DaCosta, Matt LeBlanc

Design Manager: Heather Blank

Interior Layout: Heather Barrett, Brewster Brownville, Colleen Cunningham

Visit the entire Everything® series at www.everything.com

THE
EVERYTHING®
SUGAR-FREE
COOKBOOK

Satisfy your sweet tooth with
elegant entrees and decadent
desserts your family will crave!

Nancy T. Maar
Technical Review by Julie Negrin, M.S.

Avon, Massachusetts

DISCLAIMER: Although the American Diabetes Association states that it is safe for diabetics to eat sucralose, it's always a good idea for diabetics to consult with a doctor when making dietary changes.

This book does not use ingredients such as refined white sugar, raw sugar, honey, or molasses. But some recipes do use ingredients that contain naturally occurring fruit sugars. Fruit, vegetables, fresh fruit juice, and unique ingredients like tamarind all fall into this category. When possible, freshly squeezed juice is recommended rather than store bought. Other ingredients like dried fruits, fruit juice, jams, and yogurts should specify "no added sugars" on the packaging. Most of these products contain added sugars but can be easily bought without added sugars at most health food stores.

An Everything® Series Book.
Everything® and everything.com® are registered trademarks of F+W Publications, Inc.

Published by Adams Media, an F+W Publications Company
57 Littlefield Street, Avon, MA 02322. U.S.A.
www.adamsmedia.com

ISBN 10: 1-59869-408-1
ISBN 13: 978-1-59869-408-6
Printed in the United States of America.

J I H G F E D C B A

Library of Congress Cataloging-in-Publication Data
available from publisher.

This publication is designed to provide accurate and authoritative information with regard to the subject matter covered. It is sold with the understanding that the publisher is not engaged in rendering legal, accounting, or other professional advice. If legal advice or other expert assistance is required, the services of a competent professional person should be sought.
—From a *Declaration of Principles* jointly adopted by a Committee of the American Bar Association and a Committee of Publishers and Associations

Many of the designations used by manufacturers and sellers to distinguish their products are claimed as trademarks. Where those designations appear in this book and Adams Media was aware of a trademark claim, the designations have been printed with initial capital letters.

This book is available at quantity discounts for bulk purchases. For information, please call 1-800-289-0963.

Contents

Introduction • x

1 Living Sugar-Free • 1

Knowing Friend from Enemy • 2

Sugar and the Human Body • 3

Following a Sugar-Free Diet • 7

Mealtime Options • 8

Snacking Smart • 11

Choose an Active Life • 13

2 Breakfast Breads and Muffins • 15

3 Breakfast Meats, Eggs, and Fruits • 31

4 Thick and Tasty Winter Soups • 45

5 Light and Satisfying Summer Soups • 63

6 Poultry • 77

7 Beef and Veal • 95

8 Lamb • 111

9 Pork • 125

10 Shrimp and Lobster • 139

11 Clams, Oysters, and Mussels • 151

12 Entrée Salads • 163

13 Side Salads • 181

14 Vegetables • 195

15 Rice, Risotto, and Wild Rice • 209

16 Potatoes and Pasta • 223

17 Dressings and Sauces • 237

18 Snacks • 251

19 Desserts • 263

20 Fun Family Snacks and Meals • 277

Appendix A:
Resources • 292

Appendix B:
Sugar-Free Menus • 294

Index • 296

Dedication

This is for my sister, Jamie Glade, and for all of those with both diabetes and cravings for sweets. Try these recipes to assuage your sweet tooth.

Acknowledgments

I am grateful to my editor, Kerry Smith, for her patience and juggling abilities in getting through not one but two cookbooks, which I wrote more or less (mostly more) simultaneously! I deeply appreciate the good offices of my agent, June Clark, and her efforts on my behalf. Thank you, Kerry and June!

Introduction

Artificial sweeteners, a great boon to diabetics and dieters alike, are finally coming into their own. New developments have improved the taste and quality of artificial sweetners, eliminating the nasty aftertaste of early versions.

The history of artificial sweeteners is full of unintentional discoveries. Dirty hands inadvertently led two scientists at the Johns Hopkins University to discover saccharin in 1879. Professor Ira Remsen had been working with coal-tar derivatives before eating dinner. He touched his food without washing his hands and found his meal curiously sweet. Constantine Fahlberg, a research fellow in Remsen's lab, tasted the same sweetness in his lunch. The coal-tar derivative on his hands made his sandwich sweeter.

Saccharin is 300 times as sweet as sugar and in high doses has a bitter or metallic aftertaste. The offensive aftertaste can't be masked by adding fruit flavors, vanilla, or chocolate. However, saccharin remains stable under high heat and it is not affected by acids in cooking.

Another artificial sweetener, aspartame, was also discovered accidentally. In 1965, a scientist at G.D. Searle named James Schlatter found the sweetener when working on an anti-ulcer drug. Today, aspartame is marketed under the brand names Nutrasweet and Equal and is used in about 6,000 products marketed in the United States. Unfortunately for bakers, its molecules break down when subjected to heat.

Then came Splenda, a mixture of maltodextrin and sucralose. Maltodextrin is a by-product derived from cornstarch. Sucralose was discovered by accident in 1976 by Leslie Hough and Shashikant Phadnis, researchers at Tate & Lyle, now part of King's College in London. The team had been working on the compound when Hough asked Phadnis to test the substance. He thought she said "taste," so he tasted it and discovered its incredible sweetness. With different properties and composition than aspartame, Splenda holds up well when heated, so it's fine for cooking and baking.

The creative part of a sugar-free diet is working out ways to cook delicious three- to four-course meals that are totally free of refined sugar. This book lays the foundations for you to start making recipes of your own. Use your favorite foods and invent ways to add wonderful, sugar-free notes to each dish.

Work with herbs and spices to add flavors that enhance the food naturally. For example, most vinaigrette recipes call for a pinch of sugar. Instead, use a pinch of Splenda or make the dressing with extra oil or freshly squeezed orange juice and skip the sweetness. The same method works when you try to cut back on salt. Wean yourself from it, and soon you'll find you won't miss either sugar or salt.

The health benefits of a sugar-free diet are myriad. The trick is to make the food taste as good as or better than you're used to. The beautiful part is that this can be done—and it's not difficult! It's delicious, fun, and healthy to change your cooking style to reduce or totally eliminate refined sugar.

Chapter 1
Living Sugar-Free

Sugar plays an integral part in the human body's functioning, but eating too much of it can result in major health problems. Complex starches, known as carbohydrates, are essential to producing energy, maintaining internal organs, facilitating brain function, and aiding overall health. The goal of this book is to help you use naturally occurring sugars while avoiding artificially processed sugars. You can live happily and healthily on a diet of natural sugars.

Knowing Friend from Enemy

The body converts sugars into energy to help the body function; excess sugar is converted into fat to be stored and used later. Sugars are naturally found in fruit, vegetables, and starchy foods such as unprocessed rice, potatoes, whole grains, and legumes. The recipes in this book take advantage of natural sugars and avoid refined sugar.

Good Sugar

Complex carbohydrates are the friendly sugars. They are found naturally in unprocessed foods and have long, complex strands of molecules. The digestive system needs more time to process complex sugars than simple sugars, so the release of complex sugars into the body is spread out over a longer period of time.

Lactose is the natural sugar in milk and dairy. Fructose is a natural sugar from fruit. Glucose occurs in varying quantities in tubers, legumes, grains, and some green, yellow, and red vegetables.

Buy fresh foods at your grocery store or market. When it comes to fruit and vegetables, eat raw food as much as possible. Fresh fruits and vegetables will provide the carbs and complex sugars you need for energy and good health. They will leave you feeling full so you won't be tempted by empty-calorie snacks.

Bad Sugar

Simple sugars contain one powerfully sweet molecule, called a saccharide. Saccharides come from beets and sugar cane and have been reduced to their simplest form through processing. This type of sugar is nutritionally empty and creates spikes in blood sugar as it races through the digestive system. Simple sugar, also known as sucrose or table sugar, is used as a flavor-enhancer in baked products and candy. It is also found in high-fructose corn syrup and other synthetic sweeteners. White sugar, brown sugar, and confectioner's sugar are all easily recognized examples of bad sugars.

ALERT!

Simple sugars are used to preserve canned and frozen foods. Read food labels when you grocery shop and buy products with no sugar added, but this won't help you avoid all unnecessary and unhealthy sugars. To resolve this problem, buy fresh ingredients and make your own mayonnaise, salad dressing, chili sauce, spaghetti sauce, and mustard using the sugar-free recipes in this book. Do not buy foods packed in heavy, medium, or light syrup.

Although they are much more natural than refined sugar, it is still true that honey, maple sugar and syrup, jams, and jellies also contain simple sugars and should be limited or avoided. Products like honey, maple syrup, and molasses have natural sugars, but they are highly concentrated and do not offer the same nutritional benefits as the natural sugars in fruits and vegetables.

Sugar and the Human Body

The human body needs sugar. It recognizes sweet tastes and craves them, but modern diets contain too much sugar. Sugar needs to be converted into energy or stored as fat, and consuming too much of it strains your body's resources and can lead to serious health problems, including diabetes, obesity, and heart disease. By cutting refined sugar out of your diet, you can prevent many diseases or control existing ones. Fruits, which contain some naturally occurring sugars that you will need to take into account, and the sugar substitute Splenda will be used to add sweetness to the recipes in this book.

Sugar and Obesity

Obesity, an excessive buildup of body fat, is caused by poor diet and inactivity. Sugars, starches, proteins, and fats that have not been burned for energy are stored as glycogen and body fat. The U.S. Centers for Disease

Control (CDC) report a widespread rise in obesity in the last twenty years, and the media has declared the problem epidemic. Diet change is a major part of controlling obesity. Health experts recommend a diet that is high in complex carbohydrates and fiber and low in fat and sugar.

According to the CDC, in all fifty states, less than 20 percent of the population was obese in 1995. In 2005, only four states reported obesity rates less than 20 percent.

Obesity is linked to increased risk of heart disease, stroke, diabetes, and certain types of cancer. Other painful effects of obesity include stress and damage to the body structure. Carrying excess weight puts stress on the back, hip joints, knees, ankles, and feet. This stress on the joints produces a great deal of pain and leads to arthritis.

Sugar and Diabetes

How can sugar contribute to disease? In the simplest of terms, overconsumption of sugar stresses the pancreas, the organ responsible for making insulin. After years of eating too much sugar, a person's pancreas rebels and stops doing its job. Without as much insulin, which helps the body process sugar, the body is unable to get energy from sugar, and sugar builds up in the bloodstream. The result is type 2 diabetes.

The American Diabetes Association (ADA) estimates 20.8 million Americans—7 percent of the total population—have diabetes. The ADA contends that up to a third of American diabetics have not been diagnosed. In addition, the ADA classifies 54 million Americans as prediabetics, which means they have elevated blood sugar levels but do not yet have diabetes.

There are two types of diabetes:

- **Type 2 diabetes** accounts for up to 95 percent of all diabetes cases. It is typically diagnosed in middle-aged patients, but experts have recorded a recent surge in childhood cases. There are many reasons why people become diabetic, and a poor diet is one factor that elevates the risk of type 2 diabetes. There is no cure for type 2 diabetes, but it can be controlled through diet, exercise, and occasionally medication.
- **Type 1 diabetes** is classified as an auto-immune condition and occurs in people with a genetic predisposition to the disease. In type 1 diabetes, the body's immune system attacks insulin-producing cells and impairs the pancreas's ability to produce insulin. Type 1 diabetes is not connected with eating too much sugar. Type 1 diabetics need to monitor their blood sugar levels and must be given insulin.

ALERT!

According to the National Institutes of Health (NIH), diabetes is the leading cause of adult kidney failure, blindness, and amputations. Diabetes is also linked to heart disease and strokes.

In prediabetes, the body's ability to control sugar levels in the bloodstream is impaired. People with prediabetes are at greater risk for developing type 2 diabetes and all of the health issues associated with it. Eating a healthy diet and exercising regularly are crucial for diabetics and prediabetics alike.

Sugar and Tooth Decay

Sugar reacts with the natural bacteria in your mouth to create acid. Over time, the acid eats away at tooth enamel and results in tooth decay. Reducing the amount of sugar in your diet can help slow this process. Brushing your teeth after meals or chewing sugar-free gum cleanses your mouth and helps remove sugar before it can interact with the bacteria.

Children and Sugar

The same sugar-related problems that affect adults are also affecting record numbers of children. The NIH estimates that as many as one in five children is overweight, and doctors are reporting increased numbers of children with type 2 diabetes. They attribute these health problems to childrens' diet and lack of exercise.

Sugar does have a deservedly bad reputation, but there is one condition it's incorrectly blamed for: hyperactivity. Studies published in the *Journal of the American Medical Association* have shown there is no link between sugar consumption and children's behavior.

Why Cut Back on Sugar?

There are many health reasons for cutting back on the amount of sugar in your diet. You can reduce your risk of diabetes, heart disease, and tooth decay. Reducing your sugar intake can be beneficial to your immediate well-being as well as your long-term health. Many people find they have more energy when they adhere to a sugar-free diet. Eating less sugar can help you lose weight and feel healthier. Cutting back on the empty-calorie sugary foods that fill you up will leave room for more nutrious options.

Eating too much sugar in the morning can throw off blood sugar levels all day long. Both children and adults should avoid breakfasting on sugary treats. Drinks and beverages that are high in sugar cause a spike in energy, which quickly leads to low sugar levels once the sugar has been digested. People tend to reach for more sugar when this happens, and the cycle continues for the rest of the day.

Following a Sugar-Free Diet

The first step in reducing the amount of sugar you eat is to identify where it appears in your diet. From there, you can plot a new diet for yourself. Pinpoint the areas that need to change and decide on sugar-free alternatives.

Fresh Food

Always stock up on the freshest ingredients you can find. Most fresh foods have a natural sweetness, so you won't need to add extra sugar. Look for brightly colored fruits and vegetables. If you normally snack on sugar-loaded sweets during the day, make a conscious effort to munch on some fruits and vegetables instead. You can also use them to add some sweetness and color to your meals.

Many parts of the country have farms where you can pick your own berries, tomatoes, or peppers, as well as orchards where you can pick your own peaches, apples, pears, and plums. Nothing is quite as good as eating a piece of fruit right off the tree.

Shop the perimeter of the supermarket. That's where the fresh, raw food is displayed. Go to the market with a list that includes the ingredients for sugar-free menus (see Appendix B). Buying what's in season makes sense both economically and nutritionally. Fresh fruits are seasonal, as are many vegetables, so look for organically grown food, free of pesticides and chemical fertilizers. Frequent a farm stand or green market; many of these advertise organically grown food that are fresher than foods that have been shipped.

Read Labels

It's easy to avoid the obvious sugar-rich foods—candy, cakes, doughnuts, cookies, brownies, breads and muffins, snack foods, regular soda, and fruit juices. But refined sugar can be found in an enormous number of commercial products that don't strictly require sweetening. Get into the habit of reading labels when you go grocery shopping to select the products with the least sugar.

Excess sugar is added to items that you wouldn't expect to have added sugars. Cold cereals, brown-sugar flavored oatmeal, fruit-flavored yogurt, fat-free ice cream, whole-grain cereals and crackers, corn and bran muffins, and whole-grain breads are a few of the unlikely culprits. You may also find sugar in sauces such as salsa or added to fruit juice.

Many multigrain breads have a touch of sugar in them to enhance the dry flavor and consistency of the complex carbs of grains. This bit of sugar may be mitigated by the immense amount of fiber and complex carbohydrates in the bread. In other words, the fiber greatly slows down the absorption of the sugar. However, if you are a diabetic, you must read every label.

Once a week, plan out all of your meals and snacks for the coming week. Write a list of the ingredients you need, and do not deviate from what you've written once you get to the grocery store. Planning will help you avoid overeating and stick to the correct amount of complex sugars for your body to burn as energy during normal activities and exercise.

Make Your Own

Your diet inventory may have turned up store-bought condiments, sauces, or dressings that contain sugar. Mayonnaise, mustard, barbecue sauce, and many dressings contain added sugar. Take a little time to follow the recipes in this book and make your own. This is the only sure way you have of knowing—and better yet, controlling—how much sugar is in your dressings and sauces.

Mealtime Options

Fast does not have to mean *fat*. With a little planning, you can have healthy, sugar-free meals that are just as convenient as fast or frozen food. You can control your family's intake of simple sugars and starches by cooking at home.

Following the recipes in this book will help you to regulate and restrict the quantities of what your family eats.

Nutrition Planning

Plan your menus around delicious tastes as well as nutrition. There should be some salad or a vegetable at lunch and dinner. These should be brightly colored and attractive as well as very delicious and healthful. A serving of protein such as fish, chicken, or meat is in order, and a very small side of potatoes or pasta will satisfy almost any eater. Portion control is the key to weight control. You can feel satisfied without being stuffed, and it's important to eat foods that will stay with you.

Breakfast on the Go

Who has time to make breakfast? You don't, but the smiling faces behind the counter at McDonald's do. Conveniently enough, you probably pass several fast-food joints on your way to work, all of which are more than happy to hand you some sugar and fat thinly disguised as a tasty breakfast patty. Frozen breakfast sandwiches are more of the same—processed fast food that in this case happens to come from your own freezer. There's a problem here, and the solution is simpler than you might think. Making a healthy, sugar-free breakfast takes no more time or effort than standing in line for an egg, bacon, and cheese sandwich.

Before you go grocery shopping, think about your breakfast options. Buy the ingredients and make items ahead of time if necessary:

- Fresh fruit of any kind can ride shotgun on the ride to work with absolutely no preparation.
- Whip up a smoothie in the blender and throw it into a travel-safe mug.
- Instant oatmeal is just that—instant.
- Mix plain yogurt, fruit, nuts, and high-quality granola or cereal for another instant meal.
- Bake muffins in advance and freeze them for quick breakfasts.

What to Munch for Lunch

Lunch needs to sustain the body without adding undue sugars and fats to the diet. It might sound a little backwards, but you can eat dinner for lunch. Freeze dinner leftovers in lunch-sized portions that you can easily carry with you. It takes even less time out of your day to reheat them than it does to cook a high-sugar frozen meal. Cook more food than you know you'll eat at dinner so you will always have leftovers to freeze. Salads make nutritious lunches. Buy a bag of prewashed salad at the grocery store, dress it at work, and add some fruit, leftover chicken, or a small can of tuna fish for a fine sugar-free lunch.

People who work from home or stay at home have the blessing and the curse of close proximity to a fully stocked kitchen all day. You have more choices, but it's easy to reach for quick, unhealthy lunches when you are pressed for time. Resist the temptation by having equally quick nutritious lunches on hand.

For children, school cafeteria lunches have become toxic. Except for a few school districts, most school lunches are mass-produced meals that are high in sugar, fat, and calories. Vending machines allow children to supplement their unhealthy lunches with equally unhealthy candies, chips, and soft drinks.

In 2005, British chef Jamie Oliver spearheaded the Feed Me Better Campaign. His mission was to show that schools could provide a nutritious meal for the cost of a bag of potato chips. Using one school system of 15,000 students, he exposed the unhealthy food Britain's schoolchildren were eating and created a series of new nutritious menus. In March 2006, Prime Minister Tony Blair pledged £280,000 (roughly $573,000) to overhaul British school lunches.

If your kids head to school for a fast-food meal, it's important to change the agenda. Get your PTA behind a healthy food program for the school cafeteria. Start by sending your child or children off to school with homemade lunches, which won't take any more time than the lunch you pack for yourself. Keep in mind that schools won't have microwaves or refrigerators, so only pack food that can be eaten as is. Take two slices of one of the breads in this book, such as pumpkin bread, spread with some low-fat cream cheese. Add little bag of salad and some fruit for dessert. Well nourished, your child will get through the afternoon's study and sports with flying colors.

The Ever-Changing Dinner Table

The advent of frozen-food technology revolutionized dinner. The family meal used to be full of fresh food, and leftovers went into a pot of soup, constantly simmering on the back of the stove. Then came frozen veggies, TV dinners, and many precooked meals in plastic bags. Frozen and precooked meals tend to be chock full of sugar and other preservatives and flavor enhancers. Making dinner yourself with fresh ingredients cuts down on the amount of sugar you ingest. Not only do you know exactly what you're eating, you can control it.

Relaxing at mealtime aids digestion, makes families happier, and provides positive and highly valuable communication time. The dinner table is a great place to bring everyone together and set a sugar-free example for your family.

Fortunately, cooking a fresh dinner doesn't have to be a long drawn-out affair. The recipes in this book show you how effortless cooking a sugar-free meal can be. Chapters 6 through 12 offer dozens of equally nutritious and delicious entrée choices. Rice and pasta have their own chapters, but they are meant to be used primarily for side dishes. Starches are good, to a point. If you decide to make pasta or rice as a main course, add lots of vegetables and toss in a bit of seafood, poultry, or meat.

Snacking Smart

Take your lifestyle into account when you plan your snacks. Chasing after a toddler requires more energy than sitting behind a desk, so account for it in your snack choices. No snacks should be sugary or fatty starches, such as cookies or doughnuts.

Snacking for Dieters

Even if you are on a strict sugar-free diet, you can still enjoy snacktime. Make your own oatmeal cookies with the sugar substitute Splenda. Eat cut-up veggies, such as gorgeous red and yellow peppers, broccoli florets, carrots, celery, and cherry tomatoes. Mix minced veggies and salad dressing with plain low-fat yogurt.

Smoothies are an excellent quick source of energy that also make you feel full. You can make your own frozen sugar-free yogurt treats in ice-cube trays by mixing fruit with plain yogurt and a bit of Splenda. Big smoothies made with natural fruit sugar, protein, fat from milk or yogurt, and some kashi or whey to add long-term energy will keep an athlete going.

Good snacks include things like hardboiled eggs, sugar-free cereal bars, fresh and dried fruits, cheese sandwiches on whole-wheat bread, and small sandwiches of roast beef and tomato on thinly sliced whole-grain bread.

Eating is often an unconscious reaction to boredom. Learn to recognize whether your hunger pangs are coming from your stomach or your brain. If your stomach is satisfied, chew on some sugar-free gum and let the flavors distract your brain. To avoid the temptation of the vending machine, always carry some sugar-free snacks, such as nuts or dried fruit, for those inevitable occasions when you are truly hungry.

Sugar-Free Snacks

Sugar-free snacks help you to handle your hunger when you are in the mood for something sweet. Try some sugar-free candies, cakes, and cookies available in the market. Keep fresh fruits and vegetables nearby or make some of the sugar-free quick breads from the recipes in this book and have a slice with a bit of cream cheese. Herbal teas are warm and soothing and don't have added calories.

Sugar Substitutes

The sugar substitute market has expanded over the years. There are many sugar substitutes. Total and Sweet 'n Low come in small packets, suitable for a cup of tea, coffee, or cocoa. Splenda and DiabetiSweet can be used in cooking as well as in drinks. It's brown version has no real sugar in it. However, Splenda also has a product for baking and a brown sugar substitute. These are not recommended for diabetics because they are half white or brown sugar and half Splenda.

Sugar substitutes add sweetness to foods without raising the body's blood sugar levels. They have no nutritional value themselves, but they do not have the calories of table sugar. There have been concerns about the safety of artificial sweeteners, but the U.S. Food and Drug Administration stands by its approval of these substances.

However, they are valuable for nondiabetics who want to make an occasional treat. Sugar substitutes do not work so well when used in baking. Real sugar adds moisture, texture, and flavor to baked foods, which most sugar substitutes cannot duplicate.

Choose an Active Life

Exercise burns recently ingested sugars and carbs as well as stored fat. Exercise is essential for losing weight, keeping weight down, and maintaining your health. The most basic exercise is walking. Incorporate more walking into your daily life by parking your car farther from the store you are visiting. Better yet, leave your car at home and walk to the store. Join a gym or get friends together for an early morning walking group. If you make exercise a part of your daily schedule, you'll come to enjoy it and to need it more and more.

Play Time for Adults

Get out and play, whether you have kids or not. Walking, biking, and roller-blading are good solitary activities, but you can also do them with your kids for some active family bonding time. If you do have children, they'll love you for getting involved in games and sports with them. Go to the playground together, and jog next to a child who's on a skateboard. Go swimming and skiing as a family.

If you don't have children, you can still embrace your inner twelve-year-old. Join a local Ultimate Frisbee, soccer, or dodgeball league. Plan a water-side barbecue with friends or family. Set up a volleyball net, and rent canoes to paddle around in.

Nutritional needs vary according a person's age, level of activity, individual metabolic rate, and lifestyle. Thus, it is important to analyze your needs and lifestyle to create an individual diet. Always check in with a doctor or a nutritionist to find out what your individual needs are before starting a new diet.

Let It Grow

Plant a garden, if you have a yard, or grow herbs or cherry tomatoes on your windowsill. If you have a deck or patio, you can fill big planters with very easy-to-grow herbs and miniature vegetables. Maintaining a garden takes work and burns calories; it's a form of exercise. Growing your own food also gives you more control over what you eat.

Chapter 2
Breakfast Breads and Muffins

Caramelized-Onion and Gorgonzola Bread 16

Savory Summer-Squash Bread 17

Swedish Coffee Bread 18

Hot Corn Bread with Cherry Peppers 19

Oatmeal-Walnut Bread 20

Chestnut Bread 21

Cheese-and-Herb Bread 21

Banana and Tart-Apple Bread 22

Bran Muffins 23

Blueberry Muffins 24

Autumn Muffins 25

Muffins with Sun-Dried Tomatoes and Pine Nuts 26

Corn-and-Ham Muffins 27

Zucchini-Spice Muffins 28

Polenta Griddle Cakes 29

Buttermilk Volcano Biscuits 29

Strawberry-Stuffed French Toast 30

Caramelized-Onion and Gorgonzola Bread

*This is a uniquely delectable combination. Serve as
a side with soup, salad, or with your dinner entrée.*

∽

**Yields 1 loaf; serving
size 1 slice**

Calories: 91.57
Protein: 3.94 grams
Carbohydrates: 12.32 grams
Sugar: 1.21 grams
Fat: 3.66 grams

*2 tablespoons olive oil
1 Vidalia or other sweet
    onion, thinly sliced
2 eggs
⅔ cup skim milk
¼ cup Splenda
2 cups all-purpose or whole-
    wheat flour
1 teaspoon salt
1 teaspoon baking powder
½ teaspoon baking soda
1 teaspoon dried oregano
⅔ cup Gorgonzola cheese,
    crumbled*

1. Preheat oven to 350°F. Prepare a standard loaf pan with nonstick spray.

2. Heat the oil in a nonstick pan. Add onions and cook over very low heat until caramelized. Set aside.

3. In a large bowl, beat the eggs, milk, and Splenda until smooth. Add the onions, flour, salt, baking powder, baking soda, oregano, and cheese. Mix well, and pour into the loaf pan.

4. Bake for 60 minutes on a rack in the middle of the oven. Remove the bread from the oven and set on a cooling rack. Slice and serve warm or at room temperature.

Savory Summer-Squash Bread

You can make several batches of this bread and freeze them to enjoy that fresh, summery taste in any season.

◦√◦

Yields 1 loaf; serving size 1 slice

Calories: 60.62
Protein: 2.25 grams
Carbohydrates: 9.48 grams
Sugar: 0.90 gram
Fat: 1.60 grams

1. Preheat oven to 350°F. Prepare a standard loaf pan with nonstick spray. Whisk the eggs and milk together in a blender. Add the grated squash, green onions, and unsalted butter and blend till combined.

2. Combine celery salt, pepper, Splenda, parsley, savory, baking powder, baking soda, and flours in a separate bowl. Add to moist ingredients and mix thoroughly.

3. Pour into the loaf pan and bake for 60 minutes. Remove the pan from the oven and cool loaf on a rack. This recipe is excellent with whipped cream cheese.

2 eggs
½ cup milk
1 cup zucchini or yellow summer squash, trimmed and grated
2 green onions, finely chopped
1 tablespoon melted unsalted butter
1 teaspoon celery salt
½ teaspoon freshly ground black pepper
1 teaspoon Splenda
¼ cup Italian flat-leaf parsley, minced
2 teaspoons chopped fresh summer savory, or 1 teaspoon dried savory
1 teaspoon baking powder
1 teaspoon baking soda
1 cup all-purpose flour
½ cup whole-wheat flour

Herbs Make Food Savory

You can do a lot with herbs to make even the plainest dishes more appealing. For added zing, mix sweet and savory flavors. Most supermarkets carry a good selection of fresh herbs. You can also grow your own on a sunny windowsill or in your backyard and pick them as you need them.

Swedish Coffee Bread

This braided bread is a sweet Scandinavian delicacy.
It is particularly popular around the holiday season.

⌒⌒⌒

Yields 1 loaf; serving size 1 slice

Calories: 47.4
Protein: 1.18 grams
Carbohydrates: 6.51 grams
Sugar: 1.33 grams
Fat: 2.20 grams

1 ounce live yeast, crumbled
½ cup warm milk
½ cup unsalted butter
1 cup Splenda, divided
1 teaspoon salt
3 eggs, divided
½ cup cold milk
2 cups all-purpose flour,
2 cups whole wheat flour plus
   extra for sprinkling
1 tablespoon ground
   cardamom
1 tablespoon ground
   cinnamon
1 cup raisins without added
   sugar
1 cup chopped pecans or
   walnuts

1. In a small bowl, mix the yeast and warm milk. Set aside. In a large bowl, mix the unsalted butter, Splenda, and salt. Beat in two of the eggs and cold milk. Add the yeast and set aside for 10 minutes. Stir in the flour, mix well, cover, and let rise in a warm place for 60 minutes.

2. Sprinkle a flat surface with flour and roll the dough out onto it. Knead the dough until it is smooth and elastic. Roll into a long rope, about 18" long and ⅓" thick.

3. Mix the Splenda, cardamom, and cinnamon in a small bowl. Sprinkle the dough with the Splenda and spice mixture, then spread the raisins and nuts on top. Spray a cookie sheet with nonstick spray.

4. Cut the dough in three 6" pieces. Braid the pieces together and place on the cookie sheet.

5. Cover and let rise for 60 minutes. When the dough has doubled in size, heat oven to 350°F. Beat the remaining egg. Brush the dough with egg and bake for 25 to 30 minutes.

Hot Corn Bread with Cherry Peppers

Cherry peppers are mild to moderately hot; jalapeños tend to be hotter.
Try different varieties of hot peppers to see what your palate prefers.
The seeds and veins have a great deal of added heat,
so you may want to clean away these elements.

1. In a small saucepan, heat the oil and sauté the peppers and chives over medium heat for about 5 minutes. Set aside. The oil will serve as shortening for your bread.

2. Preheat oven to 350°F, and prepare a standard loaf pan with nonstick spray. In a bowl, whisk the eggs and buttermilk together. Slowly beat in the rest of the ingredients, then fold in the peppers, chives, and oil mixture.

3. Pour into the loaf pan and bake for 60 minutes in the middle of the oven. Let cool slightly before turning out and cutting. Serve with sugar-free jalapeño jelly.

Too Hot Is Dangerous!

Every time you burn your mouth on hot peppers, you kill some of your taste buds. That's why people who get used to hot food want it progressively hotter. Most—but not all—taste buds will regenerate in time.

Yields 1 loaf; serving size 1 slice

Calories: 76.03
Protein: 2.80 grams
Carbohydrates: 12.98 grams
Sugar: 0.91 gram
Fat: 1.68 grams

1 tablespoon cooking oil
2 cherry or jalapeño peppers, stemmed, seeded, deveined, and minced
1 tablespoon fresh chives, snipped with kitchen scissors
2 eggs, lightly beaten
1 cup buttermilk
1 teaspoon dried oregano
1 teaspoon baking powder
1 teaspoon baking soda
1 cup cornmeal
1 cup all-purpose or whole-wheat flour
2 tablespoons Splenda

Oatmeal-Walnut Bread

This quick and easy breakfast bread is excellent with eggs.
It also works well as an afternoon snack.

Yields 1 loaf; serving size 1 slice

Calories: 111.5
Protein: 3.31 grams
Carbohydrates: 9.08 grams
Sugar: 1.04 grams
Fat: 7.39 grams

2 eggs
1 cup milk
2 tablespoons melted unsalted butter
2 tablespoons Splenda
1 teaspoon salt
1 teaspoon vanilla extract
1 teaspoon baking soda
1 teaspoon baking powder
1 teaspoon cinnamon
½ cup rice or tapioca flour
1 cup uncooked old-fashioned or Irish oatmeal
1 cup walnut pieces, toasted

1. Preheat oven to 350°F. Prepare a standard bread loaf pan with nonstick spray. In a large bowl, beat the eggs, milk, butter, Splenda, salt, and vanilla extract together.

2. Stir in the rest of the ingredients and mix thoroughly.

3. Bake for 60 minutes on a rack in the middle of the oven. Remove the bread from the oven and set on a cooling rack. Slice and serve warm or at room temperature.

Chestnut Bread

This is one of the most elegant quick breads. You can use imported French chestnuts in cans or jars. Be sure not to get sugared chestnuts or those packed in sugar syrup.

✣

1. Preheat oven to 350°F. Prepare a loaf pan with nonstick spray.

2. Combine the egg, milk, chestnuts, butter, and Splenda in a blender and purée.

3. Pour the puréed mixture into a large bowl. Stir in the flour, salt, baking powder, and baking soda. Fold in the egg whites.

4. Bake for 60 minutes on a rack in the middle of the oven. Remove bread from the oven and set on a cooling rack. Slice and serve warm or at room temperature.

Yields 1 loaf; serving size 1 slice

Calories: 57.49
Protein: 2.54 grams
Carbohydrates: 8.92 grams
Sugar: 1.93 grams
Fat: 1.48 grams

1 egg
⅔ cup milk
1 cup canned chestnuts, drained, rinsed, and dried
1 tablespoon unsalted butter, melted
2 tablespoons Splenda
2¼ cups chestnut flour
1 teaspoon salt
1 teaspoon baking powder
1 teaspoon baking soda
2 egg whites, beaten stiff

Cheese-and-Herb Bread

This easy and excellent bread is delicious when served hot with soup for lunch or a light supper.

✣

1. Preheat oven to 350°F. Prepare a standard loaf pan with nonstick spray.

2. Whisk the eggs, milk, and oil together in a large bowl.

3. Beat in the flour, baking powder, salt, oregano, and rosemary. Spread half of the batter in the loaf pan. Sprinkle with cheese and spread the rest of the batter on top.

4. Bake for 45 to 50 minutes. Serve hot so that cheese is still melted inside.

Yields 1 loaf; serving size 1 slice

Calories: 112.60
Protein: 3.95 grams
Carbohydrates: 14.83 grams
Sugar: 0.92 gram
Fat: 4.07 grams

2 eggs
1 cup skim milk
1 tablespoon walnut oil
2 cups rice or corn flour
1 tablespoon baking powder
1 teaspoon salt
2 teaspoons dried oregano
1 tablespoon dried rosemary
1 cup grated cheddar cheese

Banana and Tart-Apple Bread

This healthful and delicious recipe is great with afternoon tea or milk.
Double the recipe and freeze the extra loaf for a quick breakfast.

అఁ

Yields 1 loaf; serving
size 1 slice

Calories: 97.35
Protein: 2.6 grams
Carbohydrates: 16.25 grams
Sugar: 53.87 grams
Fat: 3.11 grams

1 ripe banana, peeled and
*   sliced*
1 tart green apple, peeled,
*   cored, and quartered*
2 eggs
⅔ cup milk
3 tablespoons unsalted
*   butter, melted*
½ cup Splenda
2 cups all-purpose or whole-
*   wheat flour*
1 teaspoon salt
1 teaspoon baking powder
½ teaspoon baking soda
1 teaspoon ground mace

1. Preheat oven to 350°F. Prepare a standard loaf pan with nonstick spray.

2. Combine the banana, apple, eggs, milk, and butter in a food processor, adding ingredients one at a time until smooth. Mix the Splenda, flour, salt, baking powder, baking soda, and mace in a large bowl. Add the liquids and blend well. Pour into the loaf pan.

3. Bake for 60 minutes on a rack in the middle of the oven. Remove the bread from the oven and cool on a rack. Slice and serve warm or at room temperature.

Bran Muffins

Freshly baked muffins please everyone. Enhance the recipe by adding a handful of nuts, dried currants, or raisins.

∾

1. Preheat oven to 350°F. In a large bowl, beat together the eggs, salt, milk, and butter.

2. Mix in the flours, bran, Splenda, and baking powder. Prepare muffin tin with nonstick spray. Fill each cup halfway.

3. Bake for 20 minutes. Cool, remove from tin, and serve with unsalted butter or sugar-free jam.

The Versatile Muffin

You can add many different things to muffins and quick breads. Try different kinds of nuts. You can also add sugar-free dried fruits, such as apples and apricots, either soaked until soft in water or left chewy. These make great afternoon snacks and can be frozen for a fast breakfast.

Yields 12 muffins; serving size 1 muffin

Calories: 86
Protein: 4 grams
Carbohydrates: 15 grams
Sugar: 1.35 grams
Fat: 3.2 grams

2 eggs, beaten
1 teaspoon salt
1 cup milk
1 tablespoon unsalted butter, melted
½ cup rice or corn flour
½ cup whole-wheat flour
1 cup oat or wheat bran
¼ cup Splenda
1 tablespoon baking powder

Blueberry Muffins

*These muffins freeze beautifully, so make a double batch
and reheat leftovers for a quick breakfast treat. Make extras
when blueberries are in season, plentiful, and inexpensive.*

**Yields 12 muffins;
serving size 1 muffin**

Calories: 128.83
Protein: 4.56 grams
Carbohydrates: 24 grams
Sugar: 2.73 grams
Fat: 3.06 grams

*2 eggs
1 teaspoon salt
1 cup milk
1 tablespoon unsalted butter,
 melted
1½ cups whole-wheat flour
1 cup coarse cornmeal
1 tablespoon baking powder
½ cup Splenda
1 cup fresh or frozen
 blueberries, rinsed and
 dried*

1. Preheat oven to 350°F.

2. Whisk the eggs, salt, milk, and butter together until light and fluffy. Stir in the flour, cornmeal, baking powder, and Splenda. Gently fold in the berries.

3. Prepare a muffin tin with nonstick spray. Fill each cup halfway with batter. Bake for 15 to 20 minutes.

Fresh Berries

Make sure you dry fresh berries before you add them to muffin batter. If they are wet, the added moisture will throw off your recipe. If the berries are super juicy, you can always add more flour.

Autumn Muffins

The same combination of herbs traditionally used to flavor turkey stuffing makes these muffins especially delicious. They're very good with a chicken dinner, too!

✧

1. Preheat oven to 350°F. Prepare a muffin tin with nonstick spray. Melt the butter in a pan. Sauté the onions and celery over medium heat until softened. Set aside.

2. In a large bowl, beat the eggs and milk together. Stir in remaining ingredients and mix thoroughly. Fill each cup halfway with batter. Bake for 20 to 25 minutes.

Dried Fruits

Dried fruits make an excellent addition to both sweet and savory breads and muffins. Try dried cherries and raisins. Before buying, make sure there's no sugar added commercially to the dried fruit.

Yields 12 muffins; serving size 1 muffin

Calories: 131.06
Protein: 3.66 grams
Carbohydrates: 22.73 grams
Sugar: 5.52 grams
Fat: 2.59 grams

1 tablespoon unsalted butter
¼ cup minced onion
½ cup finely minced celery
2 eggs
1 cup milk
1 teaspoon baking soda
1 teaspoon baking powder
1 tablespoon Splenda
1 teaspoon dried thyme
1 teaspoon dried sage
1 cup flour
1 cup cornmeal
⅔ cup sugar-free dried cranberries

Muffins with Sun-Dried Tomatoes and Pine Nuts

The flavors really sing in these delectable muffins.

**Yields 14 muffins;
serving size 1 muffin**

Calories: 129.94
Protein: 4.59 grams
Carbohydrates: 17.44 grams
Sugar: 1.25 grams
Fat: 4.88 grams

2 eggs
1 cup buttermilk
*1 tablespoon unsalted butter,
  melted*
1 teaspoon Splenda
1 teaspoon salt
½ cup fresh parsley, minced
1 teaspoon dried oregano
1 cup cornmeal
*1 cup unbleached all-purpose
  flour*
1 teaspoon baking powder
1 teaspoon baking soda
*½ cup pine nuts, lightly
  toasted*
*½ cup sun-dried tomatoes,
  chopped*

1. Preheat oven to 350°F. Prepare muffin tins with nonstick spray.

2. Whisk together the first seven ingredients. Slowly beat in the remaining ingredients one at a time. Fill the cups halfway with batter.

3. Bake for 20 minutes in the middle of the oven. Cool, turn out, and serve.

Corn-and-Ham Muffins

*These hearty and wonderful muffins are the perfect complement
to split pea soup. They also go well with eggs for breakfast.*

1. Preheat oven to 350°F. In a large bowl, beat the eggs, buttermilk, butter, and ham together. Stir in the baking powder, baking soda, Splenda, cloves, flour, and cornmeal, and blend well.

2. Prepare the muffin tin with nonstick spray. Fill each cup halfway with batter. Bake for 20 to 25 minutes.

3. Place a teaspoon of cheese on each muffin, and return to oven just long enough to melt.

**Yields 12 muffins;
serving size 1 muffin**

Calories: 116
Protein: 5.97 grams
Carbohydrates: 16.73 grams
Sugar: 1.45 grams
Fat: 3.37 grams

2 eggs
1 cup buttermilk
1 tablespoon unsalted butter, melted
4 ounces smoked Virginia ham, finely chopped
1 teaspoon baking powder
1 teaspoon baking soda
2 tablespoons Splenda
¼ teaspoon ground cloves
1 cup whole-wheat flour
1 cup cornmeal or corn flour
4 tablespoons sharp Cheddar cheese, grated

Zucchini-Spice Muffins

**Yields 16 muffins;
serving size 1 muffin**

Calories: 94.73
Protein: 2.7 grams
Carbohydrates: 17.85 grams
Sugar: 1.03 grams
Fat: 2.07 grams

2 eggs
1 teaspoon salt
1 cup milk
1 tablespoon unsalted butter, melted
1½ cups rice flour
½ cup whole-wheat flour
1 tablespoon baking powder
1 teaspoon salt
12 teaspoons ground cloves
1 teaspoon ground cinnamon
½ teaspoon ground allspice
½ cup Splenda
1 cup zucchini, grated

Zucchini is the base ingredient for many delicious cakes, breads, and muffins. Try mixing it with grated carrots and apples for a different texture and flavor.

✴

1. Preheat oven to 350°F. Prepare muffin tin with nonstick spray. Whisk the eggs, salt, milk, and butter together. Add the rest of the ingredients one at a time, mixing thoroughly between additions.

2. Fill each up halfway with batter. Bake for 20 minutes or until nicely brown.

Endless Options

The possibilities for sugar-free quick breads and muffins are only limited by your imagination. Go to your market or grocery store and check out fruits and vegetables. Don't be afraid to use different cheeses in your muffin and bread recipes.

Polenta Griddle Cakes

These griddle cakes have a creamy consistency with a touch of sweetness.

❧

1. In a large pot, bring the water to a boil and add the salt. Slowly add the cornmeal. Reduce heat and let cook until thick, stirring constantly. Allow to cool slightly.

2. Stir in the Splenda. Whisk the eggs, milk, and nutmeg together in a separate bowl and mix them with the polenta, blending well.

3. Heat the unsalted butter or oil on a griddle over medium flame. Drop spoonfuls of batter on the griddle. Cook until well browned. Flip each griddle cake with a spatula and brown the reverse side.

4. Serve hot topped with applesauce or jam or with fresh berries on the side.

Serves 6; serving size 1 cake

Calories: 147.05
Protein: 4.43 grams
Carbohydrates: 17.68 grams
Sugar: 1.47 grams
Fat: 7.01 grams

3 cups water
1 teaspoon salt
1 cup coarsely ground
  cornmeal
1 tablespoon Splenda
2 eggs, beaten
⅔ cup milk
½ teaspoon nutmeg
2 tablespoons unsalted butter
  or canola oil
Sugar-free applesauce, jam,
  or fresh berries

Buttermilk Volcano Biscuits

To make a wild-looking shortbread, prepare this recipe and serve topped with berries and cream.

❧

1. Preheat oven to 400°F. Prepare a cookie sheet with nonstick spray. Mix the flour, baking powder, Splenda, and salt in a large bowl. Add the milk and mix until stiff.

2. Use a spoon to drop the biscuit dough on the cookie sheet. Twist your spoon as you drop each biscuit to make the volcano shape. If you want lava, make a double biscuit with a dollop of sugar-free jam in the middle.

3. Bake for 15 to 20 minutes or until golden.

Yields 12 biscuits; serving size 1 biscuit

Calories: 97.12
Protein: 3.13 grams
Carbohydrates: 20.70 grams
Sugar: 1.5 grams
Fat: 0.98 gram

2 cups corn or rice flour
4 teaspoons baking powder
1 tablespoon Splenda
1 teaspoon salt
1 cup unsalted buttermilk

Strawberry-Stuffed French Toast

Strawberries add natural sugar to this breakfast favorite. Their sweetness means you don't need to add powdered sugar or maple syrup.

∿

1. Combine the strawberries, Splenda, and cream cheese. Set aside.

2. Whisk the eggs, milk, and orange zest together. Soak the bread in the egg mixture.

3. Melt the buttery spread in a large skillet over medium flame. Add all four pieces of bread to the skillet.

4. Flip the toast after the first side is browned and brown second side. Remove from pan and spread strawberry mixture on two of the slices. Make sandwiches with the strawberries and cheese mixture in the center.

5. Sprinkle the top of sandwiches with extra strawberries.

Yields 2 servings; serving size 2 pieces of toast

Calories: 313.38
Protein: 12.60 grams
Carbohydrates: 29.63 grams
Sugar: 6.91 grams
Fat: 18.82 grams

⅔ cup strawberries, chopped
1 tablespoon Splenda
2 heaping tablespoons
    cream cheese at room
    temperature
2 eggs
¼ cup milk
1 teaspoon orange zest
4 slices very thin wheat bread
1 tablespoon buttery spread
    or margarine
Whole strawberries for
    garnish

Chapter 3
Breakfast Meats, Eggs, and Fruits

Smoked Bacon Breakfast Sandwiches 32

Breakfast Sausage 33

Salt-and-Sugar Cured Salmon 34

High-Flying Poached Eggs in Tomato Sauce 34

Picnic Breakfast Stuffed Hard-Boiled Eggs 35

Egg-and-Cheese Wraps 36

Smoked-Ham and Peach Omelet 37

Family Frittata with Onions, Potatoes, and Sausage . . . 38

Mixed-Berry–Filled Omelet 39

Salsa-and-Cheddar Omelet 40

Tomato-Basil Omelet 41

Muesli 41

Lime-Banana Smoothie 42

Peach Melba Smoothie 42

Prosciutto with Melon 43

Baked Grapefruit 43

Grilled Peaches with Cream Cheese 44

Smoked Bacon Breakfast Sandwiches

Yields 2 servings; serving size 1 sandwich

Calories: 456.68
Protein: 15.31 grams
Carbohydrates: 32.28 grams
Sugar: 4.28 grams
Fat: 31.2 grams

4 slices smoked bacon
4 slices sugar-free whole-wheat bread
2 teaspoons mayonnaise
Dijon mustard to taste
2 medium-sized tomatoes, sliced
8 fresh basil leaves
2 ounces sharp cheddar cheese, grated
Freshly ground black pepper to taste
2 tablespoons butter or cholesterol-free margarine

You'll soon become very educated in the art of reading labels if you're on a sugar-free diet. You'll also start making sugar substitutions in your own recipes.

❦

1. Wrap bacon in paper towels and microwave until crisp.

2. Spread half of the bread slices with mayonnaise and mustard. Add the bacon, tomato, basil, and cheese. Sprinkle with pepper. Top with remaining bread slices.

3. Melt the butter over medium heat in a large frying pan. Pan-grill the sandwiches until cheese melts and they are brown on both sides.

Breakfast Sausage

*Whether you are making a holiday breakfast or brunch
or a special family morning meal, you will find that
your guests will rave over homemade sausages.*

**Yields 6 servings; serving
size 4½ ounces each patty**

Calories: 273
Protein: 20.42 grams
Carbohydrates: 0.65 grams
Sugar: 0 grams
Fat: 20.6 grams

1 pound lean ground pork
½ pound ground veal
*¼ pound ground sirloin or
    chuck*
*2 tablespoons fresh shredded
    sage leaves or 1
    tablespoon dried sage*
¼ teaspoon ground nutmeg
¼ teaspoon ground cloves
1 teaspoon Splenda Brown
*1 teaspoon Worcestershire
    sauce*
1 teaspoon fine sea salt
*1 teaspoon coarsely ground
    black pepper*
*2 tablespoons canola or
    peanut oil*

1. Thoroughly mix all of the ingredients except for the canola oil. Form the meat and seasonings into patties. Heat the oil over medium heat and fry the sausages for about 4 minutes per side.

Homemade Sausage

You can vary the meats you use to make your sausage, but pork is a traditional staple. You can change the spices, using more or less cloves or nutmeg or adding a pinch of cinnamon. You can also make the sausage even more savory by adding some onion and fresh garlic.

Salt-and-Sugar Cured Salmon

This classic Scandinavian dish takes on a luscious Oriental twist with the addition of fresh ginger. The salt acts as a curing agent that "cooks" the fish.

1. Place the salmon in a glass baking dish. Combine remaining ingredients in a separate bowl. Spread over the salmon.

2. Cover with foil or plastic wrap. Refrigerate for 6 hours. Turn the fish and refrigerate for 6 hours. Repeat process for 48 hours. Scrape off the salt mixture. Slice thinly. Serve on rye toast or crackers.

Yields 12 servings; serving size ¼ pound

Calories: 216
Protein: 30 grams
Carbohydrates: 3 grams
Sugar: 0 grams
Fat: 9.6 grams

3-pound filet of salmon, skin on, scaled, and halved laterally
⅓ cup kosher salt
½ cup Splenda
1 large bunch dill weed
1 teaspoon freshly ground or coarsely crushed black pepper
1 inch gingerroot, peeled and chopped

High-Flying Poached Eggs in Tomato Sauce

Poaching the eggs directly in the tomato sauce not only adds great flavor, it makes cleanup a snap. Use hearty artisan-style country bread to soak up the sauce and make a breakfast dish worth remembering.

1. Heat the olive oil in a large frying pan. Sauté the onion and garlic. Add the Splenda, tomatoes, rosemary, basil, salt, and pepper.

2. Bring the sauce to a simmer and cover. Cook for 10 minutes. Make the toast and place on warm plates.

3. Break the eggs into the simmering sauce. Poach for 2–3 minutes. Spoon eggs and sauce over toast.

Yields 2 servings; serving size 2 eggs

Calories: 446.2
Protein: 18.6 grams
Carbohydrates: 38.8 grams
Sugar: 5.8 grams
Fat: 25.62 grams

2 tablespoons olive oil
½ cup onion, minced
1 clove garlic, chopped
1 teaspoon Splenda
2 cups crushed tomatoes
1 tablespoon fresh rosemary, chopped
4 fresh basil leaves, torn
Salt and pepper to taste
4 slices toast
4 eggs

Picnic Breakfast Stuffed Hard-Boiled Eggs

These stuffed eggs travel beautifully and make any picnic special.
Enjoy them anywhere—at the beach, on a mountain-top, or in the car.

∿

1. Mix the carbmeat, mayonnaise, lemon juice, and Old Bay seasoning or chili powder.

2. Set cooked egg white halves on a serving platter. Mash the egg yolks together. Using a fork, mix them with the crabmeat salad, Worcestershire sauce. Sprinkle with dill weed, and pepper. Pile on the egg whites.

3. Wrap stuffed eggs individually with foil if packing for picnic. Or serve on a platter, with cucumber slices separating stuffed eggs to keep them from rolling around.

Perfect Hard-Boiled Eggs

Start with very fresh eggs. Using a pin, make a very small hole in the larger end of each egg. Place the eggs in cold water. Start them over high flame. When they come to a boil, reduce heat to very low. Let cook for 5 minutes. Turn off heat. Let eggs sit for another 4–5 minutes. Run pan of eggs under cold water. Crack and peel as soon as possible.

Yields 6 servings;
serving size 1 egg

Calories: 93
Protein: 7.8 grams
Carbohydrates: 1.7 grams
Sugar: 0.5 grams
Fat: 5.8 grams

¼ pound crabmeat
¼ cup homemade mayonnaise
Juice of ½ lemon
½ teaspoon Old Bay seasonings or chili powder
6 hardboiled eggs, halved, yolks removed from whites
1 teaspoon Worcestershire sauce
½ teaspoon dried dill weed
Freshly ground black pepper to taste

Egg-and-Cheese Wraps

This dish is easy and very popular with kids. It also makes a nice weekend treat, one that's tasty while leaving you a little extra time to relax.

Yields 2 servings; serving size 2 wraps

Calories: 485.29
Protein: 21.75 grams
Carbohydrates: 42.14 grams
Sugar: 3.2 grams
Fat: 25.16 grams

*1 tablespoon butter or
    buttery spread
4 6-inch flour or corn tortillas
4 tablespoons salsa
4 eggs
4 tablespoons grated
    Monterey Jack or Pepper
    Jack cheese*

1. Melt the butter in a nonstick frying pan. Set the broiler to 350°F. Put the tortillas on a cookie sheet and run them under the broiler until toasted on one side.

2. While the tortillas are toasting, break eggs into frying pan and fry. Drizzle the untoasted side of tortillas with salsa. Place an egg on each tortilla.

3. Spoon the cheese on top of the eggs. Fold each wrap and serve. If you like, you can also warm wraps in a 350° oven for 4–5 minutes.

Wrap and Roll

You can serve wraps whole or halved at mealtime, or you can slice them into pretty little discs to serve as snacks or appetizers. Try stuffing your wraps with all kinds of goodies. You can mix various kinds of cheeses, meats, and fruits into spreads to make nutritious little surprises.

Smoked-Ham and Peach Omelet

Ham and fruit are excellent together. You can also make this omelet with fresh or frozen nectarines, apricots, or raspberries. For an added variation, try making this omelet with different spices, such as cinnamon or nutmeg.

1. Sprinkle the sliced peaches with lemon juice, tossing to coat. Combine Splenda and cloves and mix with peaches. Let macerate for 10 minutes.

2. Heat margarine in a skillet over medium heat.

3. Whisk eggs and milk together. Pour into the skillet. Sprinkle with salt and pepper. Drain the juice from the peaches into a bowl. Spread the ham and peaches over one side of the omelet.

4. Flip the omelet when the bottom is browned.

5. Finish cooking and cut in half. Slide onto plates. Heat the reserved peach juice in skillet and pour over the omelet.

Yields 2 servings; serving size 1 omelet

Calories: 271
Protein: 18 grams
Carbohydrates: 16 grams
Sugar: 11.5 grams
Fat: 15.72 grams

2 ripe peaches, blanched, peeled, and sliced, or ½ cup frozen sliced peaches
1 tablespoon lemon juice
1 tablespoon Splenda
¼ teaspoon ground cloves
1 tablespoon buttery spread or margarine
4 eggs, well beaten
¼ cup lowfat milk
Salt and pepper to taste
½ cup smoked ham, chopped

Family Frittata with Onions, Potatoes, and Sausage

This is an excellent breakfast or light supper dish. As with most egg dishes, the quantities of sausage and other fillings can be adjusted according to your taste. You can substitute other herbs and have fun with the variations.

1. Line up the sausage, onion, and potatoes next to the stove.

2. Beat the eggs and add the milk, continuing to whisk until well combined. Set aside.

3. Melt the butter or heat the olive oil in a large 12" frying pan over medium-high heat. Brown the potatoes. Add the onions, and cook until they caramelize.

4. Pour in the egg-milk combination. Sprinkle with sausage, salt, pepper, and thyme. Reduce heat, cover, and let cook for about 10 minutes or until the eggs are set.

Yields 4 servings; serving size ¼ frittata

Calories: 525.5
Protein: 23.25 grams
Carbohydrates: 26.58 grams
Sugar: 8 grams
Fat: 37.4 grams

2 Breakfast Sausage patties (page 33)
1 cup sweet onion, peeled and sliced into thin rings
4 large or 8 small new potatoes, parboiled and sliced thin
8 eggs, well beaten
½ cup milk
2 tablespoons buttery spread or olive oil
1 tablespoon fresh thyme or 1 teaspoon dried thyme
Salt and pepper to taste

Mixed-Berry–Filled Omelet

You can vary the berries you choose by season and availability in the market. Blackberries make a nice change. After the berries have macerated in the sugar, they will give up some juice, which you can use as a sauce on your omelet.

1. Mix the berries, Splenda, and orange zest. Let macerate for 30 minutes. Heat the buttery spread or margarine in a nonstick pan over medium flame.

2. Whisk the eggs and milk together. Pour into the hot pan and cook until the mixture just begins to set.

3. Spoon the berries in a strip down the middle of the omelet and flip the sides over the berries. Let cook until set. Split the omelet in half and serve, using the berry juice as a sauce.

Macerating Fruits

Macerating is the act of softening an object by soaking it in liquid. The principle is similar to marinating meats.

**Yields 2 servings;
serving size ½ omelet**

Calories: 185.5
Protein: 12.3 grams
Carbohydrates: 8.6 grams
Sugar: 5.3 grams
Fat: 12 grams

¼ cup fresh blueberries
¼ cup fresh raspberries
1 tablespoon Splenda
1 teaspoon grated orange zest
1 teaspoon buttery spread or margarine
4 eggs
¼ cup milk
Salt and freshly ground black pepper

Salsa-and-Cheddar Omelet

This is a delectable omelet, especially when served with some crunchy taco chips and a pile of black bean salad on the side. Be sure to make your own condiments if you are on a sugar-free diet.

✺

1. Set the warmed salsa and grated cheese next to the stove. Heat the oil or margarine over medium heat and sauté the onion.

2. Whisk the egg and milk together and pour over the onion. When the omelet just begins to set, spread half with the salsa and cheese. Flip the other side up and over to cover.

3. Cook until the omelet reaches the desired level of firmness. Garnish with a dollop of sour cream and a sprig of cilantro or parsley.

Yields 2 servings; serving size ½ omelet

Calories: 351.69
Protein: 20.4 grams
Carbohydrates: 12.17 grams
Sugar: 6 grams
Fat: 24.86 grams

½ cup Tomato Salsa (page 250), warmed
½ cup sharp white Cheddar cheese, coarsely grated
2 teaspoons buttery spread or olive oil
½ cup sweet onion, chopped
4 eggs, well beaten
¼ cup low-fat milk
Low-fat sour cream for garnish
Fresh cilantro or parsley for garnish

Tomato-Basil Omelet

This is tastier than a commercial egg-and-cheese sandwich, and it's much better for you! The creative use of cheese gives extra flavor and richness.

1. Set the tomato slices and basil leaves next to the stove. Heat the olive oil in a nonstick pan over medium heat.

2. Mix the egg, milk, and Parmesan cheese. Pour into the pan. Arrange the tomatoes and basil down the center. Sprinkle with salt and pepper.

3. Fold over the sides of the omelet. Place the cheese on top and run the omelet under the broiler until the cheese melts. Cut in half and serve.

Yields 2 servings; serving size ½ omelet

Calories: 272.3 grams
Protein: 20.4 grams
Carbohydrates: 7.1 grams
Sugar: 5.26 grams
Fat: 17.76 grams

1 medium tomato, cored and thinly sliced
8 fresh basil leaves, shredded, or 1 teaspoon dried basil
2 teaspoons olive oil
4 eggs, beaten
¼ cup low-fat milk
¼ cup Parmesan cheese, grated
Salt and pepper to taste
2 slices white American cheese

Muesli

Muesli was devised by a Swiss doctor as a restorative for his patients. It tastes like a cool pudding.

1. Soak the rolled oats in warm water for 15 minutes. Add the apple, Splenda Brown, yogurt, and lemon juice. Microwave for 4 minutes to serve hot or store in the refrigerator to serve cold at your convenience.

Yields 1 serving; serving size ½ cup

Calories: 153.27
Protein: 4 grams
Carbohydrates: 31.95 grams
Sugar: 19.34 grams
Fat: 3 grams

2 tablespoons rolled oats
3 tablespoons warm water
1 apple, peeled and grated
2 teaspoons Splenda Brown
¼ cup yogurt
1 tablespoon lemon juice

Lime-Banana Smoothie

Smoothies are a wonderfully refreshing way to start any day,
but they're particularly good on a hot and sultry morning.

✺

1. Add all ingredients but the mint to blender. Blend until smooth. Pour into frosty glasses. Garnish with a sprig of fresh mint in each smoothie.

Yields 2 servings; serving size 1 cup

Calories: 173
Protein: 7 grams
Carbohydrates: 26 grams
Sugar: 19.7 grams
Fat: 6 grams

Juice of 1 lime
1½ cups plain yogurt
1 cup cracked ice
1 banana
1 tablespoon Splenda
½ teaspoon lime zest
Fresh mint for garnish

Peach Melba Smoothie

This pretty and delicious breakfast smoothie is a
take-off on the classic dessert, Peach Melba.

✺

1. Add all ingredients but the raspberries to blender. Blend until smooth. Pour into frosty glasses and garnish with a few raspberries on top of each smoothie.

Yields 2 servings; serving size 1 foaming cup

Calories: 130.5
Protein: 5 grams
Carbohydrates: 20 grams
Sugar: 14.78 grams
Fat: 4.12 grams

2 fresh, ripe peaches, peeled
and sliced, or 1 cup frozen
peaches
1 teaspoon lemon juice
1 cup plain yogurt
2 tablespoons sugar-free
raspberry jam or jelly
2 teaspoons Splenda
1 teaspoon pure vanilla
extract
1 cup crushed ice or ice chips
Fresh raspberries for garnish

Prosciutto with Melon

This is an excellent summery taste for the first course in a big eggy breakfast.

༚ঔ

1. Arrange the melon on a platter. Sprinkle with lime juice, wrap with prosciutto, and serve with extra lime slices and plenty of pepper.

The Breakfast Rut
It's easy to keep serving the same old things for breakfast in the morning, when you're usually short on time, because you don't have to think about what to cook. However, introducing some variety to your diet is more healthful than staying in a rut.

Yields 4 servings; serving size ¼ melon

Calories: 69
Protein: 6 grams
Carbohydrates: 8.5 grams
Sugar: 5.6 grams
Fat: 1.4 grams

½ cantaloupe or ¼ honeydew melon, skinned and cut into 4 slices
Juice of ½ lime
4 paper-thin slices prosciutto
4 slices fresh lime
Coarsely ground black pepper

Baked Grapefruit

Honey is the traditional sweetener for this treat. However, the grapefruit is just as tasty with Splenda Brown caramelized on top.

༚ঔ

1. Preheat oven to 400°F. Place the grapefruit halves on a pan. Sprinkle with Splenda Brown, dot with buttery spread, and bake for 10 minutes. Garnish with strawberries.

Grilled, Baked, and Broiled Fruit
You can create excellent side dishes by cooking fruit in either a sweet or a savory manner. Add green grapes to your poached chicken or pears to your duckling. Aside from being delicious, fruit is good for you!

Yields 2 servings; serving size ½ grapefruit

Calories: 92.5
Protein: 1.2 grams
Carbohydrates: 17.7 grams
Sugar: 12.45 grams
Fat: 4 grams

1 large grapefruit, halved and sectioned
2 tablespoons Splenda Brown
2 teaspoons buttery spread
Whole strawberries for garnish

Grilled Peaches with Cream Cheese

Lemon juice and cream cheese contrast refreshingly with
sweet peaches, and the cinnamon adds a little jolt.

1. Sprinkle the peaches with lemon juice.

2. Place the peaches cut side down on a grill over medium flame.

3. Grill peach halves for about 4 minutes. Meanwhile, combine cream cheese and Splenda. Turn the peaches and divide the cheese between the halves.

4. Let grill for another 2–3 minutes. Sprinkle with cinnamon and serve hot.

Yields 4 servings; serving size 1 peach

Calories: 107.59
Protein: 1.95 grams
Carbohydrates: 1.91 grams
Sugar: 14.20 grams
Fat: 3.94 grams

4 large peaches, halved and pitted
4 teaspoons lemon juice
3 tablespoons cream cheese at room temperature
1 tablespoon Splenda
4 pinches cinnamon

Chapter 4
Thick and Tasty Winter Soups

Spicy Ham and Bean Soup 46

Chicken and Wild Rice Soup with Cranberries 47

Chili-Spiced Beef and Black Bean Soup 48

Quick Italian Sausage for Soups, Meatballs, and Sauces . 49

Zucchini and Sausage Soup 50

Italian Escarole, Sausage, and Bean Soup 51

Spanish Garlic and Sausage Soup 52

Creamy Fish Soup 53

Sicilian Mussel Soup 54

Lobster-and-Corn Chowder 55

Creamed Broccoli and Cheddar Soup 56

Creamy Puréed Mushroom Soup 57

Irish Leek-and-Potato Soup 58

White Bean and Tomato Soup 59

Tomato Bisque with Sour Cream 60

Herb Crackers 61

Spicy Cheese Twists 62

Spicy Ham and Bean Soup

*The ham hocks add a tremendous amount of flavor
to the soup, but be sure to skim off the fat!*

1. Boil ham hocks in water (2 quarts or enough to cover) until meat is falling off the bone. Cool and remove skin, fat, and bone. Chop and save meat. Return broth to a boil and reduce by half (to measure 1 quart). Cool broth and skim fat from top.

2. Heat the oil in a large soup pot over medium heat. Sauté the onion, red pepper, and garlic.

3. Stir in the Splenda, cloves, salt and pepper to taste, and crushed red pepper. Add the chicken broth, tomatoes, beans, ham meat, and reduced ham broth.

4. Bring to a boil. Reduce heat to a simmer. Cover and cook for 2 hours. Stir in chopped parsley just before serving.

**Yields 10 servings;
serving size 12 ounces**

Calories: 133.90
Protein: 6.47 grams
Carbohydrates: 14.09 grams
Sugar: 1.20 grams
Fat: 5.96 grams

*2 smoked ham hocks
2 quarts water
2 tablespoons olive oil
½ large sweet onion,
    chopped
1 sweet red pepper, stemmed,
    seeded, and chopped
4 cloves garlic, chopped
2 tablespoons Splenda
¼ teaspoon ground cloves
Salt and freshly ground black
    pepper to taste
1 tablespoon red pepper
    flakes or to taste
1½ quarts chicken broth
1 cup canned sugar-free
    crushed tomatoes
2 13-ounce cans white kidney
    beans, drained and rinsed
½ bunch parsley leaves,
    chopped*

Chicken and Wild Rice Soup with Cranberries

Eliminating sugar from a recipe also eliminates a great deal of flavor, which is why we use the Splenda sugar substitute. Remember that wild rice takes a very long time to cook, and cranberries are very bitter. Thus, the Splenda is essential! The tiny bit of anchovy paste gives this dish the dark flavor you'd get with Worcestershire sauce with none of the sugar.

✦

1. Place the cranberries, 2 cups of water, and Splenda in a small saucepan and bring to a boil. Reduce heat and simmer until the berries pop. Remove from heat and set aside.

2. Heat the oil in a large soup pot over medium heat. Add the onion and celery. Cook for 5 minutes, stirring constantly. Stir in the rice. Add the remaining 2 cups of water, beef and chicken broth, soy sauce, anchovy paste, thyme, and sage. Pour in the cranberries. Cover pot and let simmer.

3. Meanwhile, heat the butter in a saucepan over medium heat. Add the chicken and cook for 5 minutes, stirring constantly. Set aside.

5. Keep soup at simmer for 2 hours, or until wild rice grains have bloomed. Add chicken, salt, and pepper. Cover and simmer for another 10 minutes. Serve hot.

Yields 12 servings; serving size 10 ounces

Calories: 159.2
Protein: 12.17 grams
Carbohydrates: 10.08 grams
Sugar: 2.37 grams
Fat: 8.12 grams

1 cup fresh cranberries
4 cups water, divided
¼ cup Splenda
2 tablespoons olive oil
1 cup red Spanish onion, finely chopped
2 stalks celery with leaves, minced
½ cup wild rice
1 quart beef broth
2 quarts chicken broth
2 teaspoons soy sauce
1 teaspoon anchovy paste
1 teaspoon dried thyme leaves
6 fresh sage leaves, torn, or 1 teaspoon dried sage
1 tablespoon unsalted butter
1 pound boneless, skinless chicken breasts, cut in slivers
Salt and freshly ground pepper to taste

Chili-Spiced Beef and Black Bean Soup

Use dollops of sour cream or shredded cheddar cheese to garnish this dish.
Freeze the leftovers—if there are any!

Calories: 196.55
Protein: 14.42 grams
Carbohydrates: 21.58 grams
Sugar: 2.44 grams
Fat: 8.45 grams

2 tablespoons olive oil
1 large onion, chopped
4 cloves garlic, chopped
1 sweet red bell pepper,
*   stemmed, seeded,*
*   deveined, and chopped*
1 sweet green bell pepper,
*   stemmed, seeded,*
*   deveined, and chopped*
2 jalapeño peppers,
*   stemmed, seeded,*
*   deveined, and chopped*
½ pound lean ground sirloin
½ pound lean ground pork
2 tablespoons Splenda
2 13-ounce cans beef broth
2 tablespoons chili powder
¼ teaspoon ground cloves
¼ teaspoon cinnamon
1 teaspoon unsweetened
*   cocoa powder*
1 28-ounce can crushed
*   Italian plum tomatoes*
3 13-ounce cans black beans,
*   drained*
Salt and freshly ground black
*   pepper to taste*
Juice of 1 lime

1. Heat the olive oil in a large kettle over medium heat. Add the onion, garlic, and the bell and jalapeño peppers. Cook for 5 minutes, stirring constantly.

2. Add the rest of the ingredients, one at a time, stirring constantly. Cover and reduce heat to a simmer. Cook for 3 hours, stirring occasionally. Do not let boil.

3. If the liquid cooks down, add water or more broth to keep level consistent.

Lemon and Lime Juice

Even in a jam, do not use the reconstituted or concentrated juice that comes in the little plastic lemons and limes. Buy several lemons and/or limes and squeeze them, straining the juice into plastic bags. Seal and label the bags, and freeze them.

Quick Italian Sausage for Soups, Meatballs, and Sauces

This is a basic recipe with Italian flavorings. You can make it much, much hotter, or eliminate some of the red pepper flakes for a milder sausage.

✺

1. Thoroughly combine all ingredients in a bowl. Form into patties and sauté in a nonstick pan with nonstick spray. Brown for 4 minues per side over medium heat.

2. For sausage meatballs variation: Form the meat into small balls. Roll in bread crumbs.

3. Heat the oil to 350°F in a large frying pan and fry the sausage balls until brown. Drain on paper towels to eliminate as much oil as possible.

4. As an alternative, cook the sausage balls in boiling soup or tomato sauce. Add a few at a time so the liquid doesn't cool down; otherwise, sausage balls will fall apart.

Yields 10 servings; serving size 2 sausages

Calories: 104.32 (with meatballs: 181.2)
Protein: 9.57 grams (with meatballs: 10.97 grams)
Carbohydrates: 1.49 grams (with meatballs: 0.57 grams)
Sugar: 0.57 grams (with meatballs: 0.08 grams)
Fat: 6.66 grams (with meatballs: 12.76 grams

Basic recipe:
2 cloves garlic, minced
½ cup onion, minced
1½ teaspoons fennel seeds
1 teaspoon dried oregano
1 egg lightly beaten
1 teaspoon dried sage
1 pound ground pork
1 pound ground sirloin
Salt and freshly ground black to taste
1 teaspoon hot red pepper flakes, or to taste
2 teaspoons soy sauce
½ cup finely grated Parmesan or Romano cheese

Additional ingredients for meatball variation:
½ cup fresh sugar-free bread crumbs
½ cup canola oil for frying

Zucchini and Sausage Soup

This recipe may seem like it is made with a lot of liquid, but the pasta absorbs an enormous amount.

✺

Yields 6 servings; serving size 8 ounces

Calories: 134.6
Protein: 4.94 grams
Carbohydrates: 14.08 grams
Sugar: 3.89 grams
Fat: 6.75 grams

2 tablespoons olive oil
2 yellow onions, chopped
4 garlic cloves, minced
2 medium zucchini, sliced
2 fresh plum tomatoes, diced
1 teaspoon Splenda
1 teaspoon salt
2 tablespoons white wine vinegar
2 cups water
3 cups chicken broth
½ pound Quick Italian Sausage (page 49), sausage ball variation
1 cup orzo or orchetta, cooked and drained
½ cup fresh basil leaves, trimmed
1 teaspoon dried oregano leaves
1 teaspoon dried red pepper flakes
Freshly ground black pepper to taste
1 teaspoon freshly grated Parmesan cheese per bowl for garnish

1. Heat the olive oil in a large soup kettle over medium heat. Sauté the onion, garlic, and zucchini for 5 minutes, stirring constantly. Add the tomatoes, Splenda, salt, vinegar, water, and broth. Let come to a boil.

2. Add the meatballs to the boiling soup a few at a time. Add the pasta, basil, oregano, and pepper flakes. Let cook for 15 minutes.

3. Garnish with cheese.

There's Something About Meatballs

Whether they are big and beefy, small and Swedish, or slathered in tomato sauce, people love meatballs. Put out some meatballs for your next party and watch them disappear. Sausage meat is excellent for meatballs, as is a combination of beef, pork, and veal.

Italian Escarole, Sausage, and Bean Soup

Escarole is wonderful in soups and salads.
It is slightly bitter and very good for you!

~

1. Heat the oil in a large soup pot over medium heat. Add the sausage, breaking up with a wooden spoon. When it starts to brown, add the onion, garlic, and fennel.

2. Continue to cook and stir until the vegetables soften, but do not brown. Add the rest of the ingredients, with the exception of the garnish.

3. Cover and reduce heat to a slow simmer. Cook for 60 minutes. Ladle into bowls. Sprinkle each bowl with Parmesan cheese.

Yields 12 servings;
serving size 9 ounces

Calories: 167.54
Protein: 9.48 grams
Carbohydrates: 18.14 grams
Sugar: 1.91 grams
Fat: 6.57 grams

2 tablespoons olive oil
½ pounds of Quick Italian
*   Sausage (page 49)*
1 whole red onion, chopped
8 cloves garlic, slivered
1 fennel bulb, slivered
Juice of 1 lemon
1 head escarole, cored and
*   chopped*
2 teaspoons dried rosemary
1 teaspoon dried oregano
2 cups water
2 quarts chicken broth
Salt and freshly ground
*   pepper to taste*
2 13-ounce cans white kidney
*   beans, drained and rinsed*
1 teaspoon grated Parmesan
*   cheese per bowl of soup*
*   for garnish*

Spanish Garlic and Sausage Soup

*As with so many classic rustic dishes, each Spanish village
adds a distinctive touch to this classic soup, and each
cook adds his or her own favorite seasonings.*

**Yields 8 servings;
serving size 8 ounces**

Calories: 199.13
Protein: 8.62 grams
Carbohydrates: 7.2 grams
Sugar: 3.03 grams
Fat: 14.96 grams

*2 tablespoons olive oil
1 head roasted garlic
½ cup red onion
½ pound sugarless chorizo
    sausage, thinly sliced
6 cups chicken broth
1 cup fresh or canned diced
    tomatoes
1 teaspoon dried oregano
1 teaspoon Splenda
1 bunch Italian flat-leaf
    parsley
Salt or pepper to taste*

1. Heat the olive oil in a large soup kettle. Add the garlic and onions and cook, stirring over medium heat until the garlic has become a paste and the onions are translucent.

2. Stir in the rest of the ingredients. Taste before adding the salt and pepper; since the sausage contains sodium, you may not need any. Cover and simmer over low heat for 60 minutes. Serve hot.

Creamy Fish Soup

This is a truly New England recipe. It's hearty and satisfying, just like what you'd have by the cupful on the wharf in Gloucester, Massachusetts, or Cape Cod. The clam broth adds sufficient sodium to the recipe, so no additional salt is needed.

✣

1. Bring the water and clam juice to a boil in a large soup kettle. Add the potatoes. Reduce heat to a simmer. Cover and cook until the potatoes are tender.

2. Add the onions, fish, bay leaf, thyme, Splenda, flour, and soy sauce. Return to a boil and reduce heat to very low. The soup should be very thick.

3. Slowly stir in the milk and cream. Do not boil or your soup may curdle. Remove the bay leaf. Ladle into bowls and garnish with parsley and bacon.

Remove That Bay Leaf!

Bay leaves stay tough even after long cooking, and they have sharp edges. They can stick in the throat, cut the tongue, and be about as destructive as a razor in your food.

Yields 6 servings; serving size 8 ounces

Calories: 366.89
Protein: 25.70 grams
Carbohydrates: 27.37 grams
Sugar: 9.62 grams
Fat: 16.75 grams

1 cup water
1½ cups clam broth
1 pound Idaho potatoes, peeled and sliced
1 pound whole pearl onions
1 pound lean cod or other white fish fillet, skinned and cut into bite-sized pieces
1 bay leaf
½ teaspoon dried thyme or 1½ teaspoons fresh thyme
1 teaspoon Splenda
2 tablespoons whole-wheat flour blended with ¼ cup cold water
Freshly ground black pepper to taste
2 teaspoons soy sauce
3 cups 1% low-fat milk
½ cup heavy cream
½ cup fresh parsley, coarsely chopped
3 slices sugar-free cooked bacon, crumbled, or 2 thick slices boiled ham, crisped

Sicilian Mussel Soup

Yields 6 servings; serving size 7 ounces

Calories: 236.04
Protein: 24 grams
Carbohydrates: 14.13 grams
Sugar: 3.87 grams
Fat: 9.21 grams

2 tablespoons olive oil
4 cloves garlic, chopped
2 shallots, chopped
1 cup water
2½ pounds mussels, scrubbed
1 28-ounce can crushed tomatoes
Zest and juice of ½ lemon
1 teaspoon red pepper flakes, or to taste
1 teaspoon Splenda
Salt and pepper to taste
1 teaspoon dried oregano
½ cup fresh Italian flat-leaf parsley, chopped

Select mussels that are completely closed. They will open when you cook them. Discard any mussels that do not open. Remove the top half of the shell from each mussel to make them prettier to serve and easier to eat.

1. Heat the oil over medium high heat in a four-quart soup pot. Sauté the garlic and shallots. Do not brown. Add the water and mussels. Bring to a boil and cook, stirring.

2. Using a slotted spoon, remove each mussel as it opens and place in a bowl on the side. Let the mussels cool. Add the rest of the ingredients to the pan and reduce the heat to a simmer.

3. When the mussels are cool enough to handle, twist off the top shell from each and add them back into the soup. Cook briefly, until mussels are hot again, and serve.

Lobster-and-Corn Chowder

If you are going to prepare the lobster yourself, you will need two 1¼-pound lobsters, cooked and picked. Most fishmongers and fish departments in supermarkets have fresh lobster meat. The added salt may be omitted from this recipe because the soy sauce provides enough sodium.

1. Melt the butter over medium heat in a large soup pot. Stir in the onion. Cook and stir for 4 minutes or until onion is translucent. Blend in the corn flour and Splenda. Cook for another 3 minutes.

2. Add the tomato paste, clam broth, potato, and soy sauce. Reduce heat to low and cover. Cook until the potato is soft.

3. Stir in the corn and pepper. Let cook for another 3 minutes. Slowly stir in the lobster, milk, and half-and-half. Cook over low heat.

4. Add salt to taste and garnish with parsley. Serve hot with Spicy Cheese Twists (page 62).

Lobster Meat

Cooking and extracting the meat from a lobster is labor-intensive, except for the claws and the tail. You can sometimes find frozen lobster meat, frozen tail, or good fresh lobster meat at an upscale fish market. If you cook the beast yourself, save some of the broth for your chowder.

Yields 8 servings; serving size 8 ounces

Calories: 174.21
Protein: 5.94 grams
Carbohydrates: 15.85 grams
Sugar: 6.23 grams
Fat: 8.98 grams

1 tablespoon butter
½ cup sweet onion, chopped
2 tablespoons corn flour blended with ¼ cup cold water
1 teaspoon Splenda
1 tablespoon tomato paste
1½ cups clam broth
1 large Yukon Gold potato, peeled and chopped
1 tablespoon soy sauce
1 cup corn kernels
Freshly ground black pepper to taste
⅔ pound fresh or canned lobster meat
2 cups 1% low-fat milk
2 cups half-and-half
Salt (optional)
2 tablespoons fresh parsley for garnish

Creamed Broccoli and Cheddar Soup

The broccoli-and-cheddar combination is totally classic and very tasty.
You can purée the soup or leave it chunky; it's great either way.

Yields 4 servings;
serving size 8 ounces

Calories: 241.09
Protein: 12.97 grams
Carbohydrates: 9.68 grams
Sugar: 3.31 grams
Fat: 17.12 grams

1 broccoli crown
1 tablespoon whole-wheat
  flour
2 tablespoons cold water
3½ cups chicken both
1 teaspoon Basic Mustard
  (page 241)
1 teaspoon Splenda
Salt and freshly ground black
  pepper to taste
1 teaspoon fresh lemon zest
½ cup half-and-half
4 tablespoons grated sharp
  Vermont or Wisconsin
  Cheddar cheese
⅛ teaspoon ground nutmeg
¼ cup toasted pine nuts for
  garnish

1. Blanch the broccoli in boiling water for 3 minutes. Drain and cool under cold running water to set the color. When cool, chop and set aside.

2. Stir flour into water and combine to make a smooth paste.

3. In a soup pot, whisk together the broth, the flour paste, mustard, Splenda, salt, pepper, and lemon zest. Return the broccoli to the pot and heat, stirring. Add the half-and-half. Divide between 4 bowls.

4. Float the cheese and nutmeg on top and sprinkle with pine nuts.

Creamy Puréed Mushroom Soup

*Pears contribute a lot of flavor to meat, vegetable,
and fruit dishes, as well as salads.*

❧

1. Mix water with flour and combine to make a smooth paste. Set aside.

2. Heat the olive oil in a soup pot over medium heat. Add the shallots and mushrooms. Cook for 5 minutes, stirring constantly.

3. Carefully mix in the next 6 ingredients one at a time, stirring constantly. Bring to a boil and reduce heat. Cook for 30 minutes. Working in batches, purée soup in blender.

4. Return to the soup pot. Add the half-and-half. Reduce heat to very low and sprinkle the pears around the soup. When hot, ladle into bowls.

5. Float spoonfuls of whipped cream on top of each bowl. Sprinkle with extra black pepper.

Cleaning Mushrooms

Do not wash or peel mushrooms. They are like sponges when it comes to water. Any bits of dirt that cling to their surface is harmless; the soil that mushrooms are grown in has been treated with thermophillic bacteria, which kills all of the "bad" germs. Just use a brush or a damp towel to brush the mushrooms off, cut off the stems, and slice them lengthwise.

**Yields 8 servings;
serving size 8 ounces**

Calories: 177.19
Protein: 8.83 grams
Carbohydrates: 14.14 grams
Sugar: 6.93 grams
Fat: 10 grams

*3 tablespoons whole-wheat
    flour
4 tablespoons cold water
2 tablespoons olive oil
6 shallots, chopped
1 pound of mushrooms,
    stemmed and sliced
1 teaspoon dried savory
1 teaspoon cayenne pepper,
    or to taste
1 teaspoon Splenda
Salt and pepper to taste
Juice of 1 lemon
6 cups beef broth
½ cup half-and-half
2 large pears, peeled, cored,
    and diced
½ cup whipping cream,
    whipped*

Irish Leek-and-Potato Soup

Leeks add a natural sweetness to this dish. Cut them in half and wash them thoroughly to remove any dirt before slicing them.

∼∽∼

Yields 6 servings; serving size 8 ounces

Calories: 263.52
Protein: 8 grams
Carbohydrates: 29.21 grams
Sugar: 8.97 grams
Fat: 12.15 grams

2 tablespoons butter or tub margarine
4 leeks, white part only, thinly sliced
1 large Vidalia or other white sweet onion
2 tablespoon potato flour
2 large Idaho or Yukon Gold potatoes, peeled and diced
3 cups chicken broth
1 teaspoon salt, or to taste
1 teaspoon Splenda
Freshly ground black pepper to taste
1 teaspoon curry powder, or to taste
1 cup 1% low-fat milk
1½ cup half-and-half
½ bunch fresh parsley, chopped
2 slices bacon, diced and boiled in ¼ cup water

1. Melt the butter in a large heavy-bottomed soup kettle over medium heat. Add the leeks and onion. Cook and stir for 3–4 minutes.

2. Stir in the flour to blend well with butter. Add the potatoes, broth, salt, and Splenda. Reduce the heat and cover the pot. Cook over very low heat until the potatoes are tender.

3. Add the milk and cream and stir to blend. Keep warm over low heat until ready to serve, add black pepper and curry powder to taste, then garnish with parsley and bacon.

White Bean and Tomato Soup

*The fresh vegetables and herbs give this soup a
very fresh taste, and the lemon juice adds kick.*

✂

1. Heat the oil in a large soup kettle over medium heat. Sauté the onion and garlic. Stir in the Splenda and add the rest of the ingredients.

2. Bring to a boil. Reduce heat and cover. Simmer for 15 minutes and serve.

Eat Beans!

Beans are a great source of fiber and protein. They are versatile. You can use beans in savory dishes and to complement onions and garlic. They also work well with sweet/hot concoctions such as this recipe. The best thing about beans is they are cheap. If you are on a tight budget, buy dry beans and soak them overnight before cooking.

**Yields 12 servings;
serving size 8 ounces**

Calories: 138.97
Protein: 8.16 grams
Carbohydrates: 20.57 grams
Sugar: 3.17 grams
Fat: 3.62 grams

*2 tablespoons olive oil
1 large Vidalia or other sweet
     white onion, chopped
2 cloves garlic, chopped
1 teaspoon Splenda
1 bunch fresh basil, torn in
     small pieces
½ bunch Italian flat-leaf
     parsley, chopped
Salt and freshly ground
     pepper to taste
1 28-ounce can crushed
     tomatoes
Juice of 1 lemon
2 18-ounce cans beef broth
2 13-ounce cans white beans,
     drained and rinsed*

Tomato Bisque with Sour Cream

*Your dinner companions will think you've worked
all day on this fresh and delightful soup.*

**Yields 6 servings;
serving size 5 ounces**

Calories: 58.59
Protein: 1.67 grams
Carbohydrates: 8.74 grams
Sugar: 1.93 grams
Fat: 2.33 grams

*1 teaspoon butter or tub
   margarine, melted*
1½ tablespoons potato flour
2 shallots, peeled
1 13-ounce can chicken broth
1 teaspoon Splenda
*1 pint cherry tomatoes, stems
   removed*
Salt and pepper to taste
1 teaspoon dried oregano
½ cup low-fat sour cream
*Fresh chives, chopped for
   garnish*

1. Put everything but the sour cream and garnish into your blender and purée. Place in a pot and bring to a boil.

2. Reduce heat and simmer for 10 minutes. Ladle into bowls and float sour cream on top. Sprinkle with chives and serve.

Loaded Crackers

Yummy little garnishes and snacks are often loaded with sugar and trans-fat. For instance, Campbell's cream soups are made with considerable amounts of sugar. Who knew? That's why label-reading is so important. Take your reading glasses with you to the supermarket, and find brands you can trust.

Herb Crackers

These delicious crackers are totally free of sugar and have no trans-fats, unlike many commercially manufactured crackers. They are very easy to make and delicious!

∽

1. Preheat the oven to 425°F. In a large bowl, thoroughly combine the flour, salt, rosemary, and garlic powder. Stir in 4 tablespoons of olive oil.

2. Work the dough with your fingers or a food processor until it is the consistency of oatmeal. Stir milk in gradually, adding enough to make the dough hold together firmly.

3. Line a cookie sheet with parchment paper. Roll out the dough into a 12" x 16" rectangle.

4. Roll onto a rolling pin and place on the parchment paper. Cut into 1" strips. Cut across strips to make 1" squares.

5. Brush the tops of dough squares with remaining tablespoon of olive oil. Sprinkle with oregano and sea salt. Bake for 15 minutes, until lightly browned. Cool. Store in an airtight container. Crackers will last a week.

Yields 48 crackers; serving size 4 crackers

Calories: 130.83
Protein: 2.58 grams
Carbohydrates: 16.25 grams
Sugar: 0.62 grams
Fat: 6.16 grams

1½ cups all-purpose flour
½ cup whole-wheat flour
½ teaspoon salt
2 teaspoons fresh rosemary, finely chopped
1 teaspoon garlic powder
5 tablespoons extra-virgin olive oil, divided
¼ cup low-fat milk (more if needed to moisten dough)
1 tablespoon dried oregano leaves
1 tablespoon coarse sea salt

Spicy Cheese Twists

*These twists are rich and crisp, the perfect companion to
a bowl of soup. If you make extra dough and freeze it,
you can always roll some twists out at the last minute.*

**Yields 32 twists;
serving size 2 twists**

Calories: 198.17
Protein: 4.88 grams
Carbohydrates: 11.93 grams
Sugar: 0.41 grams
Fat: 15.1 grams

*6 ounces unsalted butter
6 ounces cream cheese,
    cubed
2 ounces sharp Cheddar
    cheese, grated
2 ounces Parmesan cheese,
    finely grated
1 teaspoon sea salt
1 teaspoon Splenda
1 teaspoon dried basil leaves
1 teaspoon onion powder
1 tablespoon red hot pepper
    flakes, or to taste
1½ cups corn flour
½ cup whole-wheat flour*

1. Place all ingredients but the flour in a food processor and pulse. Slowly add the flour, a half-cup at a time, and pulse until dough is just mixed and holding together. Divide dough in half. Shape into two oblong loaves and wrap tightly in plastic.

2. Refrigerate loaves for 60 minutes. Line a cookie sheet with parchment paper. Preheat oven to 400°F. Roll one loaf of dough to 12" x 16" and ⅛" thickness.

3. Cut into 16 strips. Gently twist them and place them on the parchment paper. Bake for 12 minutes.

4. Reduce heat to 350°F and bake for another 6 minutes, or until crisp and golden. Let cool. Twists should be very dry and crunchy. Repeat for the second loaf.

Chapter 5
Light and Satisfying Summer Soups

Avocado Soup 64

Chilled Spanish Vegetable Soup 65

Greek Lemon Soup 66

Herb Mélange 67

Iced Celery and Celeriac Soup 68

Cucumber and Skimmed Buttermilk Summer Soup . . . 69

Spinach Soup 70

Jellied Madrilène with Lemon, Herbs, and Shrimp 71

Shrimp Bisque. 72

Iced Tomato-Basil Bisque 73

Coconut-Shrimp Soup 74

Asian Crab Soup with Cabbage and Sprouts 75

Corn-and-Pepper Soup 76

Avocado Soup

Well-ripened avocados are the key to this easy-to-make dish.

1. Purée all ingredients in a blender. Chill and serve, floating the chives on top.

Cilantro

There is very little neutral ground when it comes to cilantro. People either love the way it tastes, or they hate it. On the other hand, most people do like the seeds of the cilantro plant, which have a different name: coriander. You can buy coriander whole or ground.

Yields 4 servings; serving size 7 ounces

Calories: 196.28
Protein: 6.60 grams
Carbohydrates: 16.45 grams
Sugar: 6.77 grams
Fat: 13.65 grams

½ cup Vidalia or other sweet onion, chopped
2 avocados, peeled, pitted, and cut in chunks
Juice of 1 lime
1 cup skimmed buttermilk
½ cup sugar-free low-fat yogurt
1 cup chicken or vegetable broth
1 teaspoon Splenda
1 teaspoon Chili Sauce (page 240)
½ teaspoon ground coriander
Salt and freshly ground black pepper to taste
1 tablespoon cilantro (optional)
1 bunch chives, finely snipped for garnish

Chilled Spanish Vegetable Soup

*In Spain, this soup is served in generous bowls. You choose
the vegetables you'd like to have in your soup from a platter of
vegetables that is passed around the table. The vegetables bring a
fresh crunchiness that contrasts with the sweet, salty, spicy soup.*

1. Heat the oil in a large soup kettle over medium heat. Add the onions and garlic. Sauté until softened, about 5 minutes. Add next 8 ingredients.

2. Reduce the heat to a simmer and cover. Cook the soup for 30 minutes. Chill thoroughly.

3. Place the raw vegetables in mounds on a platter.

4. Ladle the soup into chilled bowls and pass the platter of veggies so that people can help themselves.

**Yields 6 servings;
serving size 5 ounces**

Calories: 131
Protein: 3.8 grams
Carbohydrates: 20.38
   grams
Sugar: 4.4 grams
Fat: 5.34 grams

*2 tablespoons extra-virgin
   olive oil*
*1 whole white onion,
   chopped*
4 cloves garlic, chopped
*1 28-ounce can plum
   tomatoes, crushed*
2 ounces red-wine vinegar
Juice of 1 large lemon
1 teaspoon salt
*1 teaspoon freshly ground
   black pepper, or to taste*
*⅛ teaspoon ground coriander
   seeds*
2 teaspoons Splenda
*1 bunch Italian flat-leaf
   parsley*
*½ cup green bell pepper,
   seeded, stemmed, and
   chopped*
8 radishes, thinly sliced
*2 carrots, peeled and
   julienned*
1 bunch green onions
*1 cup fresh string beans,
   blanched and cut in 1"
   pieces*
*Other fresh raw vegetables,
   according to taste, diced*

Greek Lemon Soup

This is a classic Greek soup with the added flavor of garlic.

**Yields 4 servings;
serving size 8 ounces**

Calories: 83.98
Protein: 4 grams
Carbohydrates: 5.49 grams
Sugar: 1.97 grams
Fat: 5.08 grams

*2 teaspoons olive oil
2 cloves garlic, chopped
1 teaspoon Splenda
1 quart chicken broth
Salt and pepper to taste
2 eggs
Juice of 1 fresh lemon
4 tablespoons fresh parsley
    for garnish
4 lemon wedges for garnish*

1. Heat the oil in a large soup kettle over medium heat. Sauté the garlic. Add the Splenda, broth, salt, and pepper.

2. In a large bowl, whisk the eggs and lemon juice until well blended and light in color. Remove the soup from the stove to let it cool slightly.

3. Whisking the egg mixture constantly, slowly pour 1 cup of the egg into the soup. Whisk until very smooth. Add the rest of the egg, slow, mixing constantly.

4. Serve immediately and garnish with parsley and lemon wedges.

Canned Soups

Read every label! Make sure your canned chicken broth does not have any sugar in it. Look for 100-percent chicken, beef, or vegetable broth. Sugar often sneaks into broths and soups, so be alert.

Herb Mélange

You can use some dried herbs in this recipe, but make sure you opt for fresh basil and parsley. Also use medium or whipping cream, not heavy cream. You can add more if you want a white soup, but it's not necessary.

∾

1. Combine flour and water, stirring to make a smooth paste.

2. Heat the oil in a large pot. Sauté the garlic and onion. When they are soft, blend in the flour, herbs, red pepper, salt, and pepper. Whisk in the chicken broth and soy sauce.

3. Blend the soup in the blender in batches. When puréed, add the cream and serve hot or chilled.

Yields 8 servings; serving size 6 ounces

Calories: 96.66
Protein: 1.76 grams
Carbohydrates: 5.09 grams
Sugar: 1.33 grams
Fat: 7.62 grams

1 tablespoon rice flour
2 tablespoons cold water
2 tablespoons olive oil
4 cloves garlic, chopped
1 small onion, peeled and chopped
2 tablespoons fresh rosemary or 1 tablespoon dried rosemary
2 tablespoons fresh thyme or 1 teaspoon dried thyme
½ cup fresh basil leaves, stemmed and torn
½ cup fresh Italian flat-leaf parsley, chopped
Red pepper flakes to taste
Freshly ground black pepper to taste
6 cups chicken broth
1 teaspoon soy sauce
½ cup medium or whipping cream
Salt and freshly ground black pepper to taste
3 tablespoons freshly snipped chives for garnish

Iced Celery and Celeriac Soup

The celeriac gives this soup its hallmark spicy flavor.

cVo

**Yields 6 servings;
serving size 6 ounces**

Calories: 36.54
Protein: 1.95 grams
Carbohydrates: 6.66 grams
Sugar: 1.54 grams
Fat: 0.41 grams

4 cups chicken broth
*6 stalks celery with leaves,
    chopped*
½ cup baby peas
1 teaspoon Splenda
Salt and pepper to taste
1 tablespoon lemon juice
*¼ cup celeriac, peeled and
    julienned*
*Fresh parsley and chives,
    chopped, for garnish*

1. Place all ingredients except celeriac and the garnish in a blender. Purée until smooth. Serve in chilled cups with celeriac, parsley, and chives floated on top.

Celeriac

Celeriac, also known as celery root, is very popular in Europe and becoming more available in the United States. It is spicy and can be cooked or eaten raw. Diced or julienned raw celeriac may be moistened with homemade sugar-free mayonnaise, simply use enough to coat the vegetable. Pile on thin-sliced rounds of bread. Toast or cups of lettuce, celeriac makes an easy and great-tasting appetizer.

Cucumber and Skimmed Buttermilk Summer Soup

The wonderful thing about cool summer soups is that you don't need to hover over a hot stove to make them. This quick and easy soup is no exception.

◊

1. Purée all ingredients in a blender. Chill and serve.

Sugar-Free and Gluten-Free

This rare soup is a nice treat for people on gluten-free diets. They usually need to stay away from creamy soups, which are thickened with flour, but the yogurt in this cold soup gives it all the body and texture it needs.

Yields 4 servings; serving size 8 ounces

Calories: 123.86
Protein: 9.49 grams
Carbohydrates: 16.71 grams
Sugar: 14.64 grams
Fat: 2.47 grams

1 English cucumber, ends trimmed, left unpeeled and cut in chunks
1 cup skimmed buttermilk
2 cups plain nonfat sugar-free yogurt
Juice of 1 lemon
½ cup sweet white or yellow onion, chopped
1 teaspoon lemon zest
1 teaspoon Splenda
1 teaspoon salt, or to taste
½ teaspoon freshly ground black pepper, or to taste

Spinach Soup

This is a nice soup whether hot or chilled. If you decide to serve it hot, the cheese will melt and meld nicely with the flavors of the soup. Fontina cheese is slightly softer than Parmesan and has an excellent flavor. You can also substitute Provolone cheese.

Yields 8 servings; serving size 5 ounces

Calories: 77.76
Protein: 3.54 grams
Carbohydrates: 5.76 grams
Sugar: 3.24 grams
Fat: 4.69 grams

2 tablespoons olive oil
2 cloves garlic, finely chopped
½ cup onion, finely chopped
1 10-ounce package frozen chopped spinach or 1 8-ounce bag of fresh baby spinach
1 teaspoon Splenda
⅛ teaspoon nutmeg
Salt and freshly ground black pepper to taste
3½ cups sugar-free chicken broth
1 cup low-fat yogurt
1 teaspoon lemon zest
4 teaspoons Fontina cheese, grated
2 teaspoons freshly grated Parmesan cheese or 2 slices low-fat bologna, minced for garnish

1. Heat the olive oil in a large kettle over medium heat. Sauté the garlic and onion until soft, about 5 minutes.

2. If you are using frozen spinach, thaw and squeeze the moisture out of it. If you are using fresh baby spinach, remove the stems and chop it coarsely. Add the spinach and the remaining ingredients to the pot.

3. Bring to a boil. Garnish and serve.

Yogurt Instead of Cream

There are times when only cream will do, but as you change your eating habits you'll find that yogurt supplies a nice creamy consistency and flavor. A bit of sugar substitute added to all-natural sugar-free yogurt will produce a nice creamy taste. Try substituting yogurt for cream in recipes for dressings and dips.

Jellied Madrilène with Lemon, Herbs, and Shrimp

Canned madrilène is available and it can be quite good—but it doesn't compare to making your own. The texture should be semi jelled.

༤

1. Combine water and gelatin in food processor. Let sit for a few minutes, until gelatin has softened.

2. Heat tomato juice to a boil. With the food processor running, add the boiling tomato juice and blend until the gelatin is completely dissolved.

3. Add another cup of tomato juice and blend for a few seconds. Pour into a bowl and whisk in all remaining ingredients but the shrimp and chives.

4. Let the madrilène chill for about 2 hours. When ready to serve, stir gently, ladle into bowls, and add the shrimp and chives.

Yields 6 servings; serving size 5½ ounces

Calories: 49.70
Protein: 3.95 grams
Carbohydrates: 8.90 grams
Sugar: 5.56 grams
Fat: 0.12 grams

¼ cup cold water
2 packages unflavored gelatin
1 cup sugar-free all-natural tomato juice
3 cups cold tomato juice
1 teaspoon Splenda
Juice of 1 lemon
1 tablespoon fresh thyme or 1 teaspoon dried thyme
Salt and pepper to taste
6 shrimp, halved lengthwise
4 teaspoons freshly snipped chives for garnish

Shrimp Bisque

*This soup makes a fantastic starter for a fancy meal or make
it the main course and serve with crackers and a salad.*

**Yields 8 servings;
serving size 5 ounces**

Calories: 79.78
Protein: 7.40 grams
Carbohydrates: 5.39 grams
Sugar: 3.33 grams
Fat: 3.34 grams

*1 tablespoon corn flour
2 tablespoons cold water
½ pound raw shrimp, with
    shells
2 cups water
Juice of 1 large lemon
1 bay leaf
1 tablespoon olive oil
½ cup sweet white onion,
    chopped
1 cup clam broth
1 teaspoon Splenda
1 teaspoon soy sauce
1 cup sugar-free all natural
    tomato juice
Freshly ground black pepper
½ teaspoon hot sauce
2 cups whole milk or half-
    and-half*

1. Combine flour and water and blend to form a smooth paste. Set aside.

2. Peel and devein the shrimp. Reserve the shells from the shrimp.

3. In a 2-quart saucepan, bring the shrimp shells, water, lemon juice, and bay leaf to a boil. Reduce heat to very low and cover. Simmer for 20 minutes. Strain and set aside.

4. Heat the oil in a large soup pot over medium heat. Sauté the onion until soft. Blend in the flour paste. Add the shrimp broth, clam broth, Splenda, pepper, hot sauce, shrimp, and soy sauce. Stir and cook for 6–8 minutes.

5. Let cool. Purée in the blender until very smooth and thick. Return to the pot and stir in the tomato juice. Bring back to a boil. Add the milk or half-and-half. Heat but do not boil. Serve hot or refrigerate to serve cold.

Precooking Soup

Most soups can be made in advance and then reheated or served chilled. If you want to make a hot soup ahead of time, add the milk, cream, sour cream, or yogurt at the last minute. Otherwise you may find that the sour cream or milk will separate when reheated.

Iced Tomato-Basil Bisque

This is an elegant soup, light and lovely as a lunch or as a first course for a fine dinner. It can be made in advance and then served whenever you are ready.

❧

1. Combine flour and water to form a smooth paste.

2. Heat the olive oil in a large soup kettle. Stir in the garlic and onions and sauté until soft. Using a wooden spoon, stir in the flour paste, tomatoes, broth, tomato juice, Splenda, lime juice, and basil.

3. Stir in the salt and pepper. Reduce heat to a simmer. Cover and cook for 40 minutes.

4. Cool slightly and purée in a blender. Reheat and stir in the sour cream immediately before serving.

Yields 8 servings; serving size 5 ounces

Calories: 51.54
Protein: 1.40 grams
Carbohydrates: 7.63 grams
Sugar: 4.13 grams
Fat: 2.01 grams

2 tablespoons corn flour
¼ cup cold water
1 tablespoon olive oil
1 clove garlic, chopped
1 cup Vidalia or other sweet
    onion, chopped
4 ripe tomatoes, cored and
    quartered
1 cup vegetable broth
2 cups all natural sugar-free
    tomato juice
1 teaspoon Splenda
Juice of ½ lime
1 large bunch fresh basil,
    stems removed and torn
    in small pieces
Salt and pepper to taste
½ cup sugar-free yogurt

Coconut-Shrimp Soup

*If you have a lot of crabs or lobsters crawling around,
use either of them instead of shrimp!*

**Yields 10 servings;
serving size 6 ounces**

Calories: 108
Protein: 10.5 grams
Carbohydrates: 3.78 grams
Sugar: 1.23 grams
Fat: 5.49 grams

1 tablespoon rice flour
2 tablespoons cold water
3 tablespoons olive oil
3 garlic cloves, minced
1 teaspoon Splenda
*1 teaspoon curry powder, or
to taste*
Salt and pepper to taste
1 teaspoon lemon zest
*½ teaspoon hot sauce, or to
taste*
1 cup low-fat milk
*2 cups unsweetened coconut
milk*
*1 cup clam juice or shrimp
shell broth (see recipe for
Shrimp Bisque, page 72)*
*1 pound raw shrimp,
deveined, shelled, and
chopped*
*4 tablespoons chopped
parsley or cilantro for
garnish*

1. Combine flour and water to form a smooth paste.

2. Heat oil over medium heat in a large soup kettle. Sauté the garlic for a few minutes, until just softened.

3. Stir in the flour paste, Splenda, curry powder, salt, pepper, and lemon zest. Whisk in the hot pepper sauce. Bring to a boil. Add the milk, coconut milk, and clam juice. Boil for 4–5 minutes.

4. Add the shrimp and cook until the shrimp turns pink. Garnish with parsley or cilantro and serve.

Making Soup

Everyone loves soup, but few know how to make a great batch of it. Now that there is good chicken, vegetable, and beef broth available, you don't really have any excuse to not make your own soup. Shrimp shell broth is the base of many a fine seafood soup or sauce, and you aren't stuck with getting table sugar hidden in your lunch.

Asian Crab Soup with Cabbage and Sprouts

This soup features a nice contrast of sweet crabmeat, spicy chilies, crunchy cabbage, and other subtle flavors. Be sure to keep the cabbage crunchy and not let it get overcooked.

1. Heat the oil in a large soup kettle over medium heat. Sauté the garlic and chilis for five minutes. Add the rest of the ingredients, reserving the sprouts.

2. Bring to a boil. Reduce heat and simmer for 2 minutes. Sprinkle the bowls with sprouts. Serve hot.

Cooling Techniques

Throwing leftovers of hot soup straight into the refrigerator is a recipe for disaster. Soups with meats or meat stock can sour if they're cooled too quickly. Instead, place the leftovers in small individual containers. They'll cool to room temperature more quickly and you can safely store them in the fridge.

Yields 10 servings; serving size 6 ounces

Calories: 72.85 grams
Protein: 9.43 grams
Carbohydrates: 4.40 grams
Sugar: 1.66 grams
Fat: 2.18 grams

1 tablespoon peanut oil
2 cloves garlic, minced
2 green or red hot chili peppers, stemmed, seeded, and minced
1 bunch green onions, chopped
4 cups chicken broth
1 teaspoon Splenda
2 tablespoons sherry-flavored vinegar
1 cup water
1 tablespoon soy sauce
1 tablespoon sesame seeds
½ Napa cabbage, shredded
1 pound cooked lump crabmeat, fresh or frozen
2 cups fresh bean sprouts, rinsed and dried, for garnish

Corn-and-Pepper Soup

This is truly a harvest soup and best made when the corn and peppers are local. Serve it with corn bread or muffins.

Yields 8 servings; serving size 6 ounces

Calories: 131.73 grams
Protein: 3.46 grams
Carbohydrates: 15.66 grams
Sugar: 5 grams
Fat: 7.35 grams

¼ cup cold water
1 tablespoon cornstarch
1 tablespoon olive oil
½ red onion, chopped
1 sweet red bell pepper, stemmed, seeded, and chopped
1 sweet green bell pepper, stemmed, seeded, and chopped
1 hot pepper, stemmed, seeded, and minced
2 cups vegetable broth
2 cups chicken broth
1 teaspoon dried thyme
Salt and freshly ground pepper to taste
4 ears corn, husked and kernels removed from the cob
1 tablespoon Splenda
½ cup half-and-half or heavy cream
2 slices cooked sugar-free bacon, crumbled for garnish (optional)

1. Combine water and cornstarch and mix to form a slurry.

2. Heat the oil in a large heavy-bottomed soup kettle. Add the onion and all the peppers. Sauté over medium heat for 5 minutes, stirring.

3. Add the broth, cornstarch slurry, thyme, salt, and pepper. Bring to a boil, stirring. Boil for about 2 minutes or until the mixture thickens.

4. Add the corn, Splenda, and cream. Reduce heat to very low and cover. Let cook for 3–4 minutes. Serve immediately.

Adding Body to Soups

You can add body to a soup by thickening it with rice, corn, or chestnut flour combined with water to form a loose paste. You can also add diced raw potatoes, puréed red or white beans, lentils, or a slurry of cornstarch and water.

Chapter 6
Poultry

Roast Whole Chicken with Apples and Celery 78

Baked Chicken with Root Vegetables 79

Braised Chicken Thighs with Bacon and Onions 80

Baked Nut-Crusted Chicken Breasts 81

Chicken with Egg and Lemon over Baby Spinach. 81

Chicken Breasts with Fennel and Orange Slices 82

Chicken Breasts in Sicilian Olive Sauce 83

Chicken Breasts with Capers. 84

Braised Chicken with Green Olives and Artichokes . . . 85

Grilled Turkey Thighs with Thyme, Basil, and Butter . . 86

Sliced Turkey Breast with Mushroom Sauce 87

Turkey Chili 88

Cornish Game Hens in Red Wine Mushroom Sauce. . . . 89

Duck Breasts Sautéed with Fresh Cranberries 90

Duck Breasts with Cherry Glaze and Black Cherries . . 91

Grilled Quail with Olive Condiment 92

Pheasant with Fresh Pears. 93

Pheasant with Asian Marinade. 94

Roast Whole Chicken with Apples and Celery

**Yields 8 servings;
serving size 4 ounces**

Calories: 188.83
Protein: 18.86 grams
Carbohydrates: 3.12 grams
Sugar: 1.71 grams
Fat: 10.03 grams

1 tablespoon corn flour
3 tablespoons cold water
5-pound roasting chicken
1 teaspoon salt
Freshly ground black pepper
    to taste
1 teaspoon Splenda
1 teaspoon dried thyme
2 teaspoons olive oil
1 lemon, thinly sliced and
    seeded
6 celery stalks, coarsely
    chopped, leaves reserved
    and separated
3 tart apples, cored, peeled,
    and quartered
1 6-inch stalk fresh rosemary
    or 2 tablespoons dried
    rosemary
1 teaspoon tamari soy sauce
1 cup chicken broth

*This is a great, old-fashioned Sunday dinner entrée that
will keep a family happy and well fed. It's good with rice,
mashed potatoes, and/or biscuits to sop up the lovely sauce.*

1. Combine flour and water to form a smooth paste.

2. Rinse the chicken in cold water and pat it dry with paper towels. Rub it with salt, pepper, Splenda, and thyme, inside and out. Rub the skin with olive oil. Tease 4 lemon slices under the skin.

3. Preheat the oven to 400°F. Prepare the roasting pan with nonstick spray. Place the celery pieces in the bottom of the roasting pan.

4. Place the celery leaves, 2 apple quarters, and half of the rosemary inside the cavity of the chicken. Place the chicken in the pan and roast it for 20 minutes.

5. Add the rest of the apples and the tamari to the pan with the chicken. Return chicken to oven. Baste the chicken with broth every 15 minutes for 90 minutes or until a meat thermometer inserted into a meaty part of the thigh registers 155°F.

6. Remove the chicken, apples, and celery to a serving platter. Pour juices from roasting pan into small saucepan and bring to a boil. Whisk in the flour paste and cook until thickened. Place in the freezer for a few minutes and skim off the fat. Pour into a gravy boat and serve.

Baked Chicken with Root Vegetables

*You do not have to purée the roasted vegetables in this recipe.
If you prefer, leave them in big chunks, place them in a bowl,
and let people serve themselves.*

1. Preheat oven to 400°F. Rub the chicken with oil and sprinkle with salt, pepper, nutmeg, and Splenda. Place chicken, bone-side up, skin down, in a large baking dish with the vegetables. Combine tamari and broth and baste chicken with the mixture.

2. Bake for 15 minutes. Turn the chicken and reduce heat to 350°F. Return chicken to oven and bake, basting frequently until the chicken is browned and the vegetables are fork-tender.

3. Place the chicken on a platter. Place the vegetables on a separate platter. Drain the pan juices into a sauceboat. Put the pan juices in the freezer to de-fat them if you are watching your fat intake.

4. Remove the onions from the vegetable mixture. Add the butter to the remaining vegetables, and put them through a ricer or a food processor.

5. Mound the puréed veggies in a bowl. Snip the chives over the chicken and the vegetables and serve.

Root Vegetables

These are available year-round. They tend to keep for many months. Before the advent of modern-day transportation systems, root vegetables were widely used during the winter when fresh produce was scarce.

Yields 6 servings; serving size 4 ounces of meat and 1 cup vegetables

Calories: 557.10
Protein: 19.43 grams
Carbohydrates: 33.10 grams
Sugar: 9.24 grams
Fat: 39.07 grams

*3½ pound chicken cut into six
    serving pieces*
2 teaspoons olive oil
*Salt and freshly ground
    pepper to taste*
*½ teaspoon freshly grated
    nutmeg*
1 teaspoon Splenda
*2 whole sweet onions, peeled
    and quartered*
*4 carrots, peeled and cut into
    3" lengths*
*4 parsnips, peeled, halved,
    and cut into 3" lengths*
*1 celery root, peeled,
    quartered, thinly sliced*
*3 large Idaho potatoes,
    peeled and quartered*
*½ fennel bulb, cleaned and
    cut into chunks*
1 teaspoon tamari soy sauce
1 cup chicken broth
1 tablespoon unsalted butter
*½ bunch of chives, finely
    snipped for garnish*

Braised Chicken Thighs with Bacon and Onions

Yields 4 servings;
serving size 4 ounces

Calories: 208.34
Protein: 25.05 grams
Carbohydrates: 4.72 grams
Sugar: 1.17 grams
Fat: 9.44 grams

2 slices sugar-free bacon
*4 4-ounce boneless, skinless
     chicken thighs*
*1 small yellow onion, peeled
     and chopped*
*4 sage leaves, torn in small
     pieces*
Freshly ground black pepper
1 teaspoon Splenda
*1½ cup low-sodium chicken
     broth*
2 teaspoons corn or rice flour
*4 tablespoons chopped
     parsley*

*This dish is a bundle of great flavors. It makes a delicious sauce
that is the perfect complement for pasta, rice, or potatoes.*

და

1. Sauté the bacon in a large nonstick pan over medium heat. Place on a paper towel to drain. Leave ½ teaspoon of fat in the pan, and sauté the chicken and onion.

2. Add the sage leaves, pepper, Splenda, and broth to the pan. Cover and reduce heat to a simmer. Simmer for 35–40 minutes. Crumble the bacon and add it to the pot. Cook for another 5 minutes.

3. Spoon the chicken and onions onto a serving patter. Reduce broth to 1 cup. Whisk in flour and cook, whisking constantly for 3–4 minutes or until thickened to make gravy. Add the parsley and pour over the chicken.

Food Safety

Poultry is one of the most finicky foods. Refrigerate poultry in the coldest part of the refrigerator, and use it within two days. Freeze poultry if you do not plan to cook it within two days. Turkey pieces stay good for as long as six months; freeze chicken pieces for up to nine months.

Baked Nut-Crusted Chicken Breasts

If you bake the chicken on parchment paper, you won't have to clean the pan.

1. Preheat the oven to 350°F. Rinse and dry the chicken. Place on paper towels.

2. Combine the oil, tamari, lemon juice, salt, cayenne pepper, and Splenda to make a paste. Spread a piece of parchment paper on a baking sheet. Rub each piece of chicken with the paste. Press the nuts into the chicken.

3. Bake for 35 minutes or until the chicken and the nuts are brown. Serve hot, cold, or at room temperature.

Yields 4 servings; serving size 4 ounces

Calories: 292.57
Protein: 29.78 grams
Carbohydrates: 3.99 grams
Sugar: 0.72 grams
Fat: 18.03 grams

4 4-ounce boneless, skinless chicken breasts
1 tablespoon olive oil
1 tablespoon tamari soy sauce
Juice of ½ lemon
Salt to taste
1 teaspoon cayenne pepper
1 teaspoon Splenda
½ cup ground walnuts or pecans

Chicken with Egg and Lemon over Baby Spinach

This simple recipe, also called Chicken Francaise, is popular in many French and Italian restaurants. You can easily substitute veal scallops for the chicken.

1. Sprinkle the chicken with salt, pepper, and flour. Place the beaten egg in a shallow bowl. Dip the chicken in the egg. Heat 1 tablespoon of the oil in a large frying pan over medium-high heat.

2. Sauté the chicken for about 4 minutes per side or until lightly browned. Add the lemon juice to the pan.

3. Heat the rest of the oil in another sauté pan, and quickly sauté the spinach. Place the spinach on warm plates, arrange the chicken on top, and pour the pan juices over the dish. Sprinkle nutmeg over the dish.

Yields 4 servings; serving size 4 ounces

Calories: 350
Protein: 30.89 grams
Carbohydrates: 15.3 grams
Sugar: 1.47 grams
Fat: 8.75 grams

4 4-ounce boneless, skinless chicken breasts, thinly pounded
Salt and pepper to taste
Pinch of flour
1 egg, beaten
2 tablespoons olive oil, divided
Juice of ½ lemon
2 6-ounce packages fresh, baby spinach
⅛ teaspoon freshly grated nutmeg

Chicken Breasts with Fennel and Orange Slices

Yields 4 servings;
serving size 4 ounces

Calories: 257.92
Protein: 27.93 grams
Carbohydrates: 13.72 grams
Sugar: 4.54 grams
Fat: 8.64 grams

¼ cup flour
Salt and freshly ground black
    pepper to taste
½ teaspoon dried tarragon
1 teaspoon Splenda
4 4-ounce boneless, skinless
    chicken breasts, pounded
    flat
2 tablespoons olive oil
½ cup red onion, peeled,
    sliced, and chopped
1 cup fennel, cleaned and
    thinly sliced
1 orange, thinly sliced
¼ cup dry white wine
¼ cup chicken broth
1 teaspoon dark soy sauce

This elegant recipe is very delicious served with rice to sop up the sauce.
Throw a few raisins and some nuts into the rice for more flavor.

❧

1. On a large piece of waxed paper, mix the flour, salt, pepper, tarragon, and Splenda. Dredge the chicken breasts in the mixture and set aside.

2. Heat the oil over medium heat in a large, nonstick pan. Brown the chicken on both sides. Add the vegetables to the pan.

3. Reduce heat and cook for another 10 minutes, stirring every 2–3 minutes. Remove the chicken and add the orange slices, wine, broth and soy sauce. Cover and simmer for another 10 minutes.

4. Return the chicken to the pan to warm it. Serve with the orange sauce and vegetables.

To Pound or Not to Pound?

Three things happen when you pound a chicken breast or thigh. The pounding tenderizes the meat, and the thinness allows the chicken to cook more quickly and evenly. Do you need any other reason to take a mallet, a meat pounder, or a five-pound barbell and take out your aggressions on a piece of chicken?

Chicken Breasts in Sicilian Olive Sauce

This dish has more flavor than one might expect. The bite of the olives, the sweetness of the sauce, and the richness of the salami provides a true flavor-burst. This dish is excellent with orzo.

✳

1. Sprinkle the chicken with salt, pepper, and flour. Heat the oil over medium heat in a large pan. Brown the chicken, skin side down. Turn and add the garlic and shallots. Cook for 5 minutes.

2. Turn the chicken. Add the mint, oregano, Splenda, olives, and broth. Cover the pan and reduce heat to a simmer. Cook for 40 minutes, checking to make sure the pan doesn't dry out. Add a bit of water if the sauce gets too low.

3. Remove chicken from heat and sprinkle with salami.

Yields 4 servings; serving size 4 ounces

Calories: 240.25
Protein: 17 grams
Carbohydrates: 7.67 grams
Sugar: 1.69 grams
Fat: 15.31 grams

4 chicken breast halves, bone in and skin on
Salt and pepper to taste
4 teaspoons Wondra quick-blending flour
1 tablespoon olive oil
4 cloves garlic, peeled and chopped
4 shallots
1 tablespoon fresh mint leaves, torn in small pieces
1 teaspoon dried oregano
1 teaspoon Splenda
16 Sicilian olives
1 cup chicken broth
1 slice hard salami, minced

Chicken Breasts with Capers

The tartness of the capers contrasts nicely with the aromatic herbs and the sweetness of the chicken and Splenda.

☙

**Yields 4 servings;
serving size 4 ounces**

Calories: 255.97
Protein: 28.55
Carbohydrates: 14.17 grams
Sugar: 1.4 grams
Fat: 9 grams

¼ cup cornmeal
2 tablespoons flour
1 teaspoon cayenne pepper
1 teaspoon salt
1 teaspoon Splenda
¼ cup skim milk
*4 boneless, skinless chicken
    breasts, thinly pounded*
2 tablespoons olive oil
1 tablespoon capers
Juice of ½ lemon
½ cup chicken broth
*½ cup Italian flat-leaf parsley,
    rinsed and chopped*

1. Mix the cornmeal, flour, cayenne pepper, salt, and Splenda on a large piece of waxed paper. Place the milk in a bowl. Dip the chicken in the milk and then dredge it in the cornmeal mixture, pressing the dry ingredients into the chicken.

2. Heat the oil in a large nonstick pan over medium heat. Brown the chicken. Add the rest of the ingredients. Cover, reduce heat, and simmer for 15 minutes.

3. Serve the chicken hot with caper sauce spooned over top.

Capers

Capers grow profusely in Sicily and other areas of the Mediterranean. The finest are the smallest, packed in brine, not salt. They add a very special flavor to soups, stews, salads, and sauces.

Braised Chicken
with Green Olives and Artichokes

This is a dish with a distinctly Mediterranean heritage.

ॐ

1. Combine flour and water to form a smooth paste. Set aside.

2. Heat the olive oil in a large frying pan over medium-high heat. Sprinkle the chicken with salt and pepper. Brown it on both sides. Turn the heat to low and add the garlic, shallots, and rosemary.

3. Add the broth, olives, and artichokes. Simmer for 30–40 minutes. Stir the flour-water mixture into the liquid for a thicker sauce. Garnish with capers.

Braising

Braising is the process of cooking tough cuts of meat in liquid. This technique tenderizes the meat and infuses it with flavor. It is similar to stewing, which also uses liquid to cook meat over an extended period of time.

**Yields 8 servings;
serving size 4 ounces**

Calories: 186.58
Protein: 22.17 grams
Carbohydrates: 8.34 grams
Sugar: 1.2 grams
Fat: 7.04 grams

1 tablespoon corn flour
2 tablespoons cold water to thicken
2 tablespoons olive oil
8 small chicken drumsticks, thighs, or breast halves, skin on, bone in
Salt and pepper to taste
4 cloves garlic, chopped
4 shallots, chopped
1 tablespoon fresh rosemary or 1 teaspoon dried rosemary
¾ cup chicken broth
¼ cup vegetable broth
½ cup green pimento-stuffed olives
1 10-ounce package frozen artichokes, thawed and sliced lengthwise
2 tablespoons capers, optional

Grilled Turkey Thighs
with Thyme, Basil, and Butter

If you add mesquite chips to your fire, this will be even tastier. The mesquite smoke adds a lot of flavor to grilled steaks, burgers, and chicken.

Calories: 312.55
Protein: 26.83 grams
Carbohydrates: 1.62 grams
Sugar: 0.35 grams
Fat: 21.5 grams

¼ cup olive oil
*¼ cup freshly squeezed lemon
juice*
*1 tablespoon fresh thyme, or
1 teaspoon dried thyme*
*1 tablespoon fresh basil, or 1
teaspoon dried basil*
1 teaspoon cayenne pepper
1 teaspoon onion powder
½ teaspoon garlic powder
*2 to 2½ pounds turkey thigh,
bone in, skin on*

1. Fire up the grill. Whisk the olive oil, lemon juice, thyme, basil, cayenne pepper, onion powder, and garlic powder together in a small bowl.

2. Brush both sides of the turkey with the sauce and grill over a medium fire, brushing with sauce every few minutes. Grill until a meat thermometer inserted into the thickest part of the turkey registers 155°F.

3. Slice and serve.

A Skinny Story

Poultry skin is fattening, but studies have shown that leaving the skin on during cooking and removing it before eating doesn't result in any more fat intake than cooking skinless poultry. Leaving the skin on during cooking keeps the meat's juices in, resulting in a more flavorful meal.

Sliced Turkey Breast with Mushroom Sauce

This is pure comfort food, quietly yummy with little pretension and less fuss. If you are preparing it for a party, you can make it a day in advance and simply reheat it very gently just before serving.

1. Combine flour and water to form smooth paste.

2. Preheat the oven to 325°F.

3. Over medium heat, melt the butter in a large ovenproof casserole dish. Dust the turkey with flour, salt, and pepper.

4. Sauté the turkey on each side. Add the shallots, garlic, and mushrooms to the casserole dish. Sauté, stirring constantly.

5. Add the grape juice, Splenda, orange rind, nutmeg, chicken broth, and milk. Cover the turkey with sauce and remove from the stove. Cover the casserole dish and bake in the oven for 35–40 minutes.

6. Arrange the turkey pieces on a serving platter and cut into serving pieces.

7. Over medium heat, whisk the flour and water mixture into the sauce to thicken it. Pour it over the turkey and sprinkle with parsley.

Boneless, Skinless Turkey Breasts

Turkey breasts can masquerade as veal in a parmigiana, and they work well as a substitute for pork. Versatile and delicious, turkey breasts taste wonderful in braised, poached, and sautéed dishes.

Yields 6 servings; serving size 4 ounces

Calories: 200.39
Protein: 30.32 grams
Carbohydrates: 9.71 grams
Sugar: 3.85 grams
Fat: 3.57 grams

1 tablespoon corn flour
2 tablespoons cold water
1 tablespoon unsalted butter
2 teaspoons corn or chestnut flour
Salt and freshly ground black pepper to taste
1½ pounds boneless, skinless turkey breast
4 shallots, chopped
1 clove garlic, minced
½ pound shitake mushrooms, stemmed and brushed clean
½ cup white grape juice
1 teaspoon Splenda
1 teaspoon grated orange rind
⅛ teaspoon ground nutmeg
¾ cup chicken broth
½ cup milk
½ cup fresh parsley, finely chopped

Turkey Chili

Yields 12 servings; serving size 6 ounces

Calories: 355.70
Protein: 25.4 grams
Carbohydrates: 36 grams
Sugar: 6 grams
Fat: 13.87 grams

¼ cup cooking oil
2½ pounds lean ground turkey meat
4 sweet red onions, chopped
6 cloves garlic, chopped
4 Italian green frying peppers, stemmed, seeded, and chopped
2 large sweet red bell peppers, roasted
2 sweet yellow peppers, stemmed, seeded, and chopped
4 jalapeño peppers, stemmed, seeded, and chopped
2 tablespoons chili powder, or to taste
1 tablespoon dry English-style mustard
1 teaspoon cinnamon
1 teaspoon Dutch-process cocoa powder
½ cup strong cold coffee
2 tablespoons Splenda
3 14-ounce cans red kidney beans, drained and rinsed
2 28-ounce cans sugar-free Italian plum tomatoes
Salt and pepper to taste
1 teaspoon liquid smoke, or to taste

This recipe has a few nice Texas-style bells and whistles. You can cook this classic for just a few hours or overnight—the longer the better. Your friends will be shocked when you tell them that turkey is the meat in this fine tasty chili.

⤳

1. Heat the oil over medium heat in a large pot that has a cover. Sauté the turkey, breaking it up with a wooden spoon. Add the onions, garlic, and peppers to the pot. Stir, sautéing until softened, about 12 minutes.

2. Add the chili powder to the meat mixture and stir to combine. In a separate bowl, blend the dry mustard, cinnamon, and cocoa powder with the coffee. Whisk with a fork until smooth. Add to the meat mixture.

3. Stir in remaining ingredients and cover. Reduce the heat to a bare simmer. Cook for a minimum of 3 hours.

Cornish Game Hens in
Red Wine Mushroom Sauce

This is an easy and delicious version of a far more complicated recipe.

∽

1. Preheat oven broiler to 450°F. Prepare a large roasting pan with non-stick spray. Rub each hen with olive oil on both sides.

2. Sprinkle the hens with salt, pepper, and thyme. Place them in the pan, skin side down. Place them under the broiler for 8–10 minutes or until brown. Turn the hens. Add the onions, carrots, red wine, and Splenda to the pan and cover. Turn off broiler and reduce oven heat to 350°F.

3. Roast for another 25 minutes. Add the mushrooms and stir the flour into the liquid. Stir to thicken. Serve the hens with vegetables. Drizzle with the sauce.

Red vs. White Wine

Red and white wines impart distinct flavors when they are used for cooking. You can make this exact recipe with white wine and produce a completely different result. Red wine gives a rich, deep, and subtly spicy flavor. White wine gives the dish a lighter, fruity flavor.

**Yields 4 servings;
serving size ½ hen**

Calories: 397.95
Protein: 26.66 grams
Carbohydrates: 15.52 grams
Sugar: 6.91 grams
Fat: 22.54 grams

2 10-ounce Cornish game
    hens, split
2 teaspoons olive oil
1 teaspoon salt
Pepper to taste
1 teaspoon dried thyme
12 white pearl onions, left
    whole
4 carrots, peeled, halved
    lengthwise, and cut into
    short sticks
⅔ cup dry red wine
1 teaspoon Splenda
1 cup sliced button
    mushrooms
1 tablespoon Wondra quick
    blending flour

Duck Breasts Sautéed with Fresh Cranberries

**Yields 6 servings;
serving size 4 ounces**

Calories: 288.42
Protein: 24.09 grams
Carbohydrates: 13.99 grams
Sugar: 6.07 grams
Fat: 16.9 grams

*8 ounces fresh cranberries
½ cup Splenda
1 cup orange juice
1½ pounds boneless, skinless
    duck breasts
Salt and pepper to taste
¾ cup corn flour
2 tablespoons olive oil
⅔ cup chicken broth
1 teaspoon dried oregano
    leaves
1 teaspoon finely grated fresh
    lemon zest
½ cup chopped, toasted
    pecans for garnish*

*Duck tastes absolutely wonderful with many kinds of fruit. This recipe calls
for cranberries, but you can substitute cherries, berries, pears, or apples.*

⌇

1. In a saucepan over medium heat, bring the cranberries, Splenda, and orange juice to a boil. As soon as the berries pop open, reduce heat to a simmer and cook for 20 minutes. Taste for sweetness and add more Splenda if necessary.

2. Slice each duck breast into three pieces and pound to flatten. Sprinkle with salt, pepper, and corn flour. Heat the olive oil in a large sauté pan over medium heat. Brown the duck.

3. Reduce the heat to a simmer and add the cranberries and all of the other ingredients except the pecans. Cover the pan and simmer for 20 minutes.

4. Remove the duck pieces to a warm platter. Reduce the sauce to just under 1 cup and pour it over the duck. Garnish with pecans.

Fruit Sauces

If you are giving a dinner party, make your fruit sauce in advance. These sauces keep well in the refrigerator for at least a week, and they freeze beautifully. This will shorten your prep time prior to the party.

Duck Breasts with Cherry Glaze and Black Cherries

This is the kind of elegant dish you'd serve on New Year's Eve or any really special occasion.

∽

1. Combine cornstarch and water to form slurry.

2. Mix the cherries, Splenda, apple juice, lemon juice, ½ teaspoon salt, and pepper in a saucepan. Bring to a boil over high heat. Add the cornstarch mixture. Reduce heat, cover, and simmer for 10 minutes.

3. Cut each duck breast into three pieces and set them on a piece of waxed paper. Sprinkle with salt, pepper, and extra cornstarch. Heat the oil in a large frying pan. Quickly brown the duck. Add the broth and rosemary. Cover and simmer for 20 minutes.

4. Arrange the duck on a heated serving platter or warm plates. Add the cherries, and spoon the sugar-free cherry jam on top.

Yields 6 servings; serving size 4 ounces

Calories: 241.50
Protein: 23.35 grams
Carbohydrates: 52.11 grams
Sugar: 11.18 grams
Fat: 3.75 grams

1 teaspoon cornstarch
¼ cup cold water
10 ounces pitted black cherries
4 ounces Splenda, or to taste
½ cup unsweetened apple juice
Juice of ½ lemon
½ teaspoon salt, plus extra for coating the duck
Freshly ground black pepper to taste, plus extra for coating the duck
1½ pounds duck breast, pounded thin
2 tablespoons canola oil
¾ cup vegetable broth
2 tablespoons fresh rosemary or 2 teaspoons dried rosemary
4 teaspoons sugar-free cherry jam

Grilled Quail with Olive Condiment

Champagne makes a fantastic accompaniment to this romantic dish.

Calories: 389.41
Protein: 27.88 grams
Carbohydrates: 2.57 grams
Sugar: 0.01 gram
Fat: 29.43 grams

8 large pitted black olives, chopped
4 pitted green olives, chopped
1 teaspoon lemon zest
2 teaspoons parsley
3 teaspoons olive oil, divided
4 4-ounce quails, cleaned and split open
Salt and freshly ground black pepper to taste

᠁

1. Start your grill. If you are cooking over coals, make sure they have burned down to an ashy gray before cooking. If you are using gas, set your grill at medium high.

2. Mix the first 4 ingredients together in a small bowl with 1 teaspoon olive oil and set aside. Rub the quail with the remaining olive oil and sprinkle with salt and pepper.

3. Grill the quail for about 4 minutes per side or until nicely browned.

4. Serve with the olive mixture as a condiment.

Quail

These tiny birds are not too easy to find in local stores, but the Internet is an excellent source for foods that aren't that easy to come by. Quail is definitely a delicacy and makes a lovely special-occasion dish.

Pheasant with Fresh Pears

Pheasant is a very lean meat that can be very dry. It does require some added fat. Bacon imparts a lot of flavor, but you can substitute low-fat spread or olive oil.

❧

1. Preheat the oven to 375°F. Rinse and pat the pheasant pieces dry. Sprinkle them with salt, pepper, and Splenda. Arrange them in a baking pan and cover with equal amounts of bacon strips.

2. Add the liquids to the pan and sprinkle with sage. Grind extra pepper over the top. Roast the pheasant pieces for 35 minutes, basting every 2–3 minutes.

3. Place on a warm serving platter or plates. Arrange the pears around the pheasant and pour the juice into a sauce boat. You can thicken the juices with Wondra flour if you want a thick sauce.

**Yields 4 servings;
serving size 5 ounces**

Calories: 290.29
Protein: 34.86 grams
Carbohydrates: 7.20 grams
Sugar: 4.44 grams
Fat: 11.91 grams

*1 2- to 2 ½-pounds pheasant,
    cut in serving pieces
Salt and freshly ground
    pepper
1 teaspoon Splenda
2 slices sugar-free bacon, cut
    in strips crosswise
½ cup chicken broth
¼ cup dry white wine
4 sage leaves, minced
2 pears, peeled, cored, and
    quartered*

Pheasant with Asian Marinade

Serve pheasant for a special occasion, a quiet anniversary celebration, a small family birthday, or an empty-nest holiday.

∽

**Yields 4 servings;
serving size 5 ounces**

Calories: 243.51
Protein: 33.74 grams
Carbohydrates: 5.97 grams
Sugar: 4.3 grams
Fat: 8.81 grams

Juice of 1 lime
1 tablespoon olive oil
1 teaspoon tamari sauce
1 teaspoon fresh ginger, minced
1 teaspoon cayenne pepper powder, mixed with 2 teaspoon water
1 teaspoon Splenda
2 ounces unsweetened apple juice
1 pheasant, cut in 4 serving pieces
4 teaspoons sugar-free apricot jam

1. Mix the first 7 ingredients together in a small bowl to create marinade. Place the pheasant pieces in a baking dish that you have prepared with nonstick spray. Pour the marinade over top.

2. Cover the dish with plastic wrap and refrigerate for at least 60 minutes, turning after 30 minutes. Do not marinate more than 90 minutes or the meat will cook in the acid.

3. When ready to cook, preheat the oven to 350°F. Remove plastic wrap and place the dish in the oven. Roast for 35–40 minutes, basting frequently with the pan juices.

4. Spoon apricot jam atop of each piece of pheasant and return to oven. Continue roasting until jam melts and bubbles, about 5 minutes.

Pheasant

This delicious bird is a wonderful special-occasion dinner, but it needs to be handled delicately. Having almost no subcutaneous fat, it easily toughens and dries out completely. For this reason, it does not broil well, but you can roast a whole pheasant if you baste it or cover it with bacon or butter.

Chapter 7
Beef and Veal

Filet Mignon Stuffed with Gorgonzola Cheese 96

Filet Mignon Stuffed with Jack Cheese and Salsa 97

Filet Mignon Grilled with Bacon 98

Beef Sirloin Bites with Asian Spices 99

Beef Pot Roast with Winter Vegetables 100

Pumpkin Beef Harvest Stew 101

Marinated London Broil 102

Barbecue-Spice Rubbed Steak 103

New Orleans Black-and-Red Burgers 104

Texas Burgers 105

Asian-Flavored Burgers. 105

Mushroom Meatballs in Homemade Tomato Sauce . . . 106

Veal Stewed in Tomato Sauce with Garlic 107

Veal Scallops with Prosciutto and Cheese 108

Veal Scallops in Lemon Sauce 108

Veal Shanks Braised with Green Olives 109

Veal Stew with Roasted Vegetables 110

Filet Mignon Stuffed with Gorgonzola Cheese

**Yields 2 servings;
serving size 4 ounces**

Calories: 420.68
Protein: 21.14 grams
Carbohydrates: 3.18 grams
Sugar: 0.38 grams
Fat: 33.2 grams

*2 4-ounce medallions of filet
   mignon*
*2 teaspoons Gorgonzola
   cheese*
Salt and pepper to taste
1 teaspoon olive oil
1 shallot, minced
1 clove garlic, minced
1 ounce red wine
2 ounces beef broth
1 teaspoon tamari soy sauce
1 teaspoon capers
*2 tablespoons chopped
   chives*

*This elegant, old-fashioned recipe boasts lots of flavor. It's perfect
for a special occasion, anniversary, or other romantic occasion.
You can use Roquefort cheese rather than Gorgonzola if you desire.*

1. Use a sharp knife to make a horizontal 1" slit in each filet. Tease in the cheese and close with a toothpick. Sprinkle with salt and pepper.

2. Heat the oil over high heat. Sauté the medallions for 3 minutes per side for rare, 4 minutes for medium, and 5 for well done. Remove to warm plates.

3. Add the shallot and garlic to the pan and sauté for 2 minutes. Stir in the wine, broth, and tamari sauce, and scrape the brown bits off the bottom of the pan.

4. Spoon the sauce over the filets and sprinkle with capers and chives.

Filet Mignon Stuffed with Jack Cheese and Salsa

A tasty beef dish has lots of added flavor. Use sugar-free ingredients and garnishes to make your burgers really healthy and yummy.

✧

1. Heat the grill or frying pan to medium high. Add oil or spray.

2. Sprinkle the filets with salt and pepper. Use a sharp knife to make a horizontal 1" slit in each filet. Stuff the filets with cheese and secure with toothpick. Grill 3 minutes per side for very rare, 4 minutes per side for medium, and 6 minutes per side for well done.

3. Spoon salsa over the meat and serve immediately.

Jack Cheese

Jack cheese adds the final touch to many a burger. This recipe offers a unique twist on the combination of beef and cheese. The cut of beef is different, and the cheese awaits you inside the beef, instead of being spread thinly over the top.

Yields 4 servings; serving size 4 ounces meat, ½ ounce cheese, and ½ ounce salsa

Calories: 275.19
Protein: 27.04 grams
Carbohydrates: 1.6 grams
Sugar: 1.1 grams
Fat: 17.13 grams

1 tablespoon peanut oil or nonstick spray
4 4-ounce filets, well trimmed
Salt and pepper to taste
2 ounces sliced Monterey Jack cheese, with or without peppers
4 ounces Tomato Salsa (page 250)

Filet Mignon Grilled with Bacon

This classic can be greatly improved with the addition of sugar-free, homemade Chili Sauce. Turn these into mini-hero sandwiches for game afternoons in front of the television.

Yields 4 servings;
serving size 4 ounces
of filet, ½ strip bacon

Calories: 305.57
Protein: 25.72 grams
Carbohydrates: 0.6 grams
Sugar: 0.04 grams
Fat: 21.46 grams

1 pound filet mignon, trimmed and quartered
Pepper to taste
4 teaspoons Chili Sauce (page 240)
4 slices smoked sugar-free bacon

1. Sprinkle the filets with pepper. Paint them on both sides with a thin coating of Chili Sauce. Wrap with bacon and secure with metal toothpicks or wooden ones that have soaked in water for 30 minutes.

2. Grill over high heat for abut 4 minutes per side or broil on medium high until the filets reach the desired level of doneness.

3. Slice in thin strips and serve as sandwiches on sugar-free hero rolls, or eat them with a salad on the side.

Nitrate-Free Bacon

Look for nitrate-free bacon when you go grocery shopping. Nitrates are used as curing agents, but when they're exposed to high heats they turn into nitrites, which are suspected carcinogens. Nitrate-free bacon has a browner hue when compared to pinker nitrate-cured bacon.

Beef Sirloin Bites with Asian Spices

*You can string these chunks on skewers or make individual
servings on toothpicks for game days. They are also the perfect
complement for a salad of mixed baby greens.*

1. Whisk all ingredients except the beef in a bowl. When the sauce is well blended, add the sirloin chunks. Marinate for 60 minutes.

2. Heat your grill or broiler to medium high. String the beef on skewers and place on the grill for 8–12 minutes, turning frequently, or run the beef under the broiler for four minutes per side.

Parsley

Not only is parsley good for you, it can also be used for medicinal purposes. The Greeks and Indians discovered parsley's soothing effects on gastrointestinal discomfort and cultivated the plant. The leaves are also a natural sugar-free breath freshener.

**Yields 4 servings;
serving size 4 ounces**

Calories: 181.92
Protein: 20.96 grams
Carbohydrates: 1.40 grams
Sugar: 0.04 grams
Fat: 10.01 grams

*2 tablespoons Toasted
    Sesame Seed Oil (page
    238)*
2 tablespoons soy sauce
*1 teaspoon fresh ginger,
    peeled and grated*
1 clove garlic, minced
1 teaspoon wasabi powder
2 teaspoons lemon juice
*1 tablespoon freshly grated
    orange rind*
1 teaspoon Splenda
*1 tablespoon fresh cilantro or
    parsley, minced*
Salt and pepper to taste
*1 pound lean sirloin, cut in 1"
    chunks*

Beef Pot Roast with Winter Vegetables

Use a slow cooker for most of the cooking in this recipe. Set it up in the morning, let it run all day, and when you get home, wow!

༄

**Yields 6 servings;
serving size 6 ounces**

Calories: 181.86
Protein: 12.77 grams
Carbohydrates: 12.68 grams
Sugar: 3.19 grams
Fat: 8.92 grams

2½ pound bottom round roast, well trimmed
Salt and freshly ground pepper to taste
1 tablespoon unsalted butter
1 whole onion, cut in chunks
2 cloves garlic
2 large carrots, peeled and chopped
4 parsnips, peeled and chopped
4 baby blue-nose turnips, peeled and chopped
1 cup celery tops, chopped
3 Yukon Gold potatoes, peeled and quartered
4 teaspoons Chili Sauce (page 240)
2 13-ounce cans unsalted all-natural beef broth
1 teaspoon Splenda
1 tablespoon Tamari

1. Sprinkle the beef with salt and pepper. Melt the butter in a frying pan or Dutch oven over high heat. Brown the beef. Keep the beef in the Dutch oven or transfer it to a slow cooker. Scrape up the brown bits on the pan with a bit of water and add to the slow cooker.

2. Add remaining ingredients to the pot. Set your slow cooker or oven to very low and let cook for 7–8 hours.

3. Slice the meat and divide dish into serving bowls. This dish makes its own gravy.

Pot Roast Trivia

New Englanders supposedly came up with the dish we know as pot roast. They cooked tough cuts of meat in water or broth to tenderize them and make them suitable for the dinner table. Winter vegetables were readily available and added extra flavor.

Pumpkin Beef Harvest Stew

This is a great Halloween dish! For a stunning presentation, keep the pumpkin shell whole and pour the stew into it instead of serving it from a boring old pot.

∿

1. Melt butter in a large Dutch oven or stew pot. Combine the flour, salt, and pepper on a large piece of waxed paper.

2. Roll the beef in the flour mixture and brown it over medium-high heat.

3. Stir in remaining ingredients. Cover and reduce heat to a simmer. Stir occasionally. Braise for 2 hours.

Dutch Ovens

Make cooking a family affair with a Dutch oven. Recipes that call for Dutch ovens generally do not require heavy amounts of preparation. With supervision, children can participate in making meals in a Dutch oven. Plan activities for your family to do while you wait for the meal to finish cooking.

Yields 8 servings; serving size 6 ounces

Calories: 242.21
Protein: 25.17 grams
Carbohydrates: 13.37 grams
Sugar: 5.21 grams
Fat: 10.01 grams

1 tablespoon unsalted butter
½ cup whole-wheat flour
1 teaspoon salt
Freshly ground black pepper to taste
2 pounds beef stew meat
1 cup red onion, coarsely chopped
1½ pounds fresh pumpkin, rind removed and cut in large chunks
1 tablespoon soy sauce
1 teaspoon Splenda
1 teaspoon dried thyme leaves
1 13-ounce can all-natural beef broth, no sugar added
1 cup fresh apple cider, no sugar added

Marinated London Broil

Most London broil is made from round steak, which can be quite tough and not very flavorful. This makes it a perfect foil for great flavors.

ᐱᐱ

Yields 4 servings; serving size 4 ounces

Calories: 147.82
Protein: 24.89 grams
Carbohydrates: 8.8 grams
Sugar: 2.34 grams
Fat: 3.7 grams

1 cup sugar-free tangerine juice
1 tablespoon fresh gingerroot
2 cloves garlic, chopped
1 bunch green onions, chopped
2 tablespoons soy sauce
Salt and freshly ground black pepper to taste
1 pound round steak, trimmed

1. Mix together all ingredients except for the steak. Put the sauce and steak in a resealable plastic bag. Seal and shake to cover.

2. Marinate the steak for 1–2 hours. Discard the marinade.

3. Grill the steak over medium high heat for 5 minutes per side for medium-rare meat.

4. When done, let steak rest for 8–10 minutes to keep it juicy. Slice on the diagonal.

The Perfect London Broil

London Broil should never be cooked beyond medium-rare. Doing so risks toughening an already tough cut of meat. With a London Broil you should have the best of both worlds: a juicy center with a deliciously flavored outside.

Barbecue-Spice Rubbed Steak

*Rubs are quite variable. Try creating some of your
own combinations and have fun with them!*

❧

1. Place the meat in a glass baking dish. Mix the rest of the ingredients
   into a paste. Spread them over the steak on both sides. Cover and refrigerate overnight, turning occasionally.

2. Set grill at medium. Grill steak to desired level of doneness and let rest
   to finish cooking and keep the juices inside.

Well-Rested Meat

*If you cut or slice a roast, chop, or steak immediately after cooking, all of
the juices run out. If you wait, the meat sucks the liquids in so that your
food stays juicy. Resting also gives the meat time to finish cooking. Cover
the meat with aluminum foil or a kitchen towel while you let it rest.*

**Yields 6 servings;
serving size 4 ounces**

Calories: 221.97
Protein: 30.55 grams
Carbohydrates: 6.69 grams
Sugar: 0.19 grams
Fat: 8.38 grams

1½ pounds bone in sirloin
   steak, well trimmed
1 teaspoon ground turmeric
1 tablespoon garlic powder
1 tablespoon onion powder
1 tablespoon cayenne
   pepper, or to taste
1–2 tablespoons freshly
   ground black pepper, or
   to taste
2 tablespoons tomato paste
1 tablespoon Basic Mustard
   (page 241)
1 teaspoon plain,
   unsweetened cocoa
   powder
2 tablespoons Splenda Brown
   Sugar Blend
1 teaspoon salt, or to taste

New Orleans Black-and-Red Burgers

The different peppers evoke distinct flavors in this red-and-black specialty dish. Add more pepper if you dare!

చ్యు

Yields 4 servings; serving size 4 ounces

Calories: 204.5
Protein: 24.79 grams
Carbohydrates: 0.89 grams
Sugar: 0
Fat: 10.77 grams

½ teaspoon salt
1 teaspoon freshly ground black pepper
1 teaspoon cayenne pepper
½ teaspoon red pepper flakes
1 teaspoon Splenda
2 teaspoons soy sauce
1 tablespoon red-wine vinegar
16 ounces ground round or sirloin beef
4 sugar-free hamburger buns

1. Mix all ingredients but the beef together and combine well to make a slurry. Add beef and mix thoroughly.

2. Form patties. Heat a grill to medium heat and grill the burgers. Serve on sugar-free buns.

New Orleans Cuisine

Influenced by generations of Creole, French, and Cajun residents, New Orleans boasts one of the most distinct cuisines in the country. The flavors and cooking techniques blend together in some dishes and retain their unique tastes in others. Visiting the city is the only sure way to sample the cuisine for yourself—and even then you might need a local guide!

Texas Burgers

*You can make these burgers as spicy or as mild as you like.
Just make sure you use sugar-free homemade Chili Sauce
or you'll sweeten them up much too much.*

1. Mix all of the ingredients together. Form into patties.

2. Grill over medium-high flame or under the broiler to desired state of doneness.

3. Serve each burger on a grilled corn tortilla.

**Yields 4 servings;
serving size 4 ounces**

Calories: 149.53
Protein: 22.76 grams
Carbohydrates: 1.03 grams
Sugar: 1.27 grams
Fat: 5.38 grams

*1 pound ground sirloin
Salt and pepper to taste
1 teaspoon garlic powder
1 tablespoon chili powder
½ cup red onion, minced
2 tablespoons Chili Sauce
    (page 240)
4 corn tortillas*

Asian-Flavored Burgers

Miniaturize these tasty snacks to make bite-sized sliders.

1. Combine all ingredients. Divide and form into patties.

2. Prepare your grill or fry pan with nonstick spray. Set on medium high heat. Grill the burgers to desired level of doneness. Serve hot on Portuguese rolls or with tortilla wraps.

**Yields 4 servings;
serving size 4 ounces**

Calories: 139.3
Protein: 22.9 grams
Carbohydrates: 1.11 grams
Sugar: 0.26 grams
Fat: 5.03 grams

*1 pound freshly ground chuck
    or sirloin beef
¼ cup green onions, minced
2 tablespoons Asian Ginger
    Dipping Sauce (page 242)
Salt and pepper to taste*

Mushroom Meatballs in Homemade Tomato Sauce

Make the meatballs in advance, and refrigerate or freeze them until you're ready to use.

❧

Yields 16 meatballs; serving size 1 ounce

Calories: 147.37
Protein: 6.83 grams
Carbohydrates: 3.99 grams
Sugar: 0.19 grams
Fat: 11.67 grams

1 tablespoon unsalted butter
½ cup canola or peanut oil
1 pound ground beef
4 ounces brown mushrooms, Italian baby bells or porcini, minced
1 teaspoon salt
Freshly ground black pepper to taste
1 whole egg
1 teaspoon dried oregano
¼ cup sugar-free bread crumbs
2 cups Fresh Tomato Sauce with Mushrooms and Herbs (page 247)

1. Heat the butter and oil in a large pot. Meanwhile, mix the beef, mushrooms, salt, pepper, egg, oregano, and bread crumbs in a bowl. Form into balls.

2. Sauté the meatballs in the butter/oil mixture until lightly browned. Drain on a paper towel. Pour off any grease from the pan.

3. Add the tomato sauce to the pan and scrape up all of the brown bits to add flavor. Gently stir in the meatballs. Cover and cook for 45 minutes over low heat.

Beef: A Versatile Companion

When you cook beef with apples, pumpkin, or other vegetables, pay attention to how the meat's flavor changes. Whether hot and savory or very rich and mild, you can make a thousand dinners with beef. By using a good sugar substitute, you'll get a wonderful rich flavor.

Veal Stewed in Tomato Sauce with Garlic

This is a traditional Italian stew. You can trick it up with lots of different ingredients, but the purity of these flavors is quite perfect. Serve over rice or pasta.

✤

1. Heat the olive oil in a large pot over medium-high heat. Combine the salt, pepper, and flour on a piece of waxed paper.

2. Roll the veal in the flour mixture. Sauté it quickly to brown. Add garlic, oregano, lemon juice, Splenda, and tomatoes. Cover and simmer over very low heat for 2 hours.

Cooking with Veal

Veal is classified as a red meat, but its color is naturally a pinkish-gray. Raw veal should always be frozen or refrigerated. Use frozen veal meat within three or four months and refrigerated veal within one or two days.

Yields 6 servings; serving size 4 ounces

Calories: 223.05
Protein: 23.22 grams
Carbohydrates: 15.1 grams
Sugar: 0.37 grams
Fat: 8.24 grams

1 tablespoon olive oil
Salt and freshly ground pepper to taste
¼ cup whole-wheat flour
2 pounds veal stew meat, cut in chunks
3 cloves garlic, chopped
1 teaspoon dried oregano leaves
Juice of 1 lemon
1 teaspoon Splenda
1 28-ounce can sugar-free plum tomatoes, drained

Veal Scallops with Prosciutto and Cheese

This simple and elegant dish is almost too good for every day.

**Yields 4 servings;
serving size 4 ounces**

Calories: 226.09
Protein: 21.62 grams
Carbohydrates: 8.62 grams
Sugar: 1.02 grams
Fat: 11.05 grams

*4 3-ounce veal slices, thinly cut
4 slices Land O' Lakes white
    American cheese
4 paper-thin slices prosciutto
1 egg, well beaten
¼ cup corn flour
Freshly ground black pepper
2 tablespoons olive oil
Fresh lemon wedges for
    garnish*

1. Lay the slices of veal on your workspace. Place a slice of cheese and then a slice of ham over each slice of veal.

2. Roll the veal and fasten with toothpicks. Dip the veal in the egg and sprinkle with flour and pepper.

3. Heat oil in a nonstick pan over medium-high heat. Sauté the veal, turning to brown all over. Reduce heat to low for 3–4 minutes to cook through and let cheese melt.

4. Serve with lemon.

Veal Scallops in Lemon Sauce

*Add some steamed broccoli or broccoli rabe to this sugar-free dish,
and you have a very high level of nutrition.*

**Yields 4 servings;
serving size 4 ounces**

Calories: 173.26
Protein: 23.14 grams
Carbohydrates: 1.99 grams
Sugar: 0.23 grams
Fat: 7.42 grams

*4 4-ounce slices veal,
    pounded very thin
1 tablespoon whole-wheat
    flour
Salt and pepper to taste
1 tablespoon olive oil
1 teaspoon butter
Juice of ½ lemon*

1. Sprinkle the veal with flour, salt, and pepper. Heat the olive oil in a sauté pan over medium high heat and sauté the cutlets, about 2 minutes per side. Place on a warm platter.

2. Add the butter and lemon juice to the pan and heat until the butter melts. Spoon over the veal.

Veal Scallops
The best veal scallops are cut from the leg. They should be pale pink; if they are red, you are eating beef. Veal is versatile, rather like chicken.

Veal Shanks Braised with Green Olives

This delicious dish requires only a little effort from you. Whip all the ingredients together, throw a lid on, put your feet up, and enjoy the scents! It's perfect for cool days.

༂

1. Heat the olive oil in a large heavy-bottomed pot over medium-high heat. Sprinkle the veal with flour, salt, and pepper. Brown the veal on both sides, and reduce heat to a simmer.

2. Add the rest of the ingredients and cover. Simmer for 2 hours, turning once.

Cooking with Olives

Olives change the flavor of sauces dramatically. They soften, and their flavor becomes almost nutty. They are also excellent in salads, risotto, and stews. Olives are a sugar-free source of great flavor.

Yields 4 servings; serving size 4 ounces

Calories: 314.14
Protein: 38.63 grams
Carbohydrates: 5.46 grams
Sugar: 1.15 grams
Fat: 14.56 grams

1 tablespoon olive oil
4 7-ounce veal shanks, bone in
2 teaspoons whole-wheat flour
Salt and freshly ground pepper to taste
Cayenne pepper to taste
½ cup sugar-free tomato juice
1½ cups chicken broth
16 green olives
1 teaspoon Splenda
1 teaspoon dried oregano leaves

Veal Stew with Roasted Vegetables

*This is the very latest method of roasting veggies,
which go perfectly with the veal.*

⟳

**Yields 6 servings;
serving size 4 ounces**

Calories: 256.68
Protein: 23.59 grams
Carbohydrates: 20.41 grams
Sugar: 10.20 grams
Fat: 9.69 grams

*4 carrots, peeled and cut in
large chunks*
*1 bulb fennel, cored and cut
in chunks*
*2 celery stalks with leaves, cut
in chunks*
*4 small blue-nose turnips,
peeled and quartered*
2 Vidalia onions, quartered
2 tablespoons olive oil
*1½ pounds boneless veal stew
meat, cut in chunks*
1 cup water
*1 cup sugar-free tomato
sauce*
1 teaspoon Splenda

1. Preheat oven to 350°F. Place first 5 ingredients in a roasting pan and spray or drizzle them with oil. Roast for 45 minutes.

2. Add the veal, water, tomato sauce, and Splenda. Mix well. Cover the pan and roast for 1–2 hours more or until the veal is tender. Add more liquid to the pan if the meat starts to dry out.

Tomatoes and Sugar

Many recipes with large quantities of tomato sauce or canned tomatoes also call for a teaspoon or two of sugar. Tomatoes are very acidic fruits, and the addition of sugar helps neutralize the acid and strengthen the flavor. The Splenda in this recipe works the same way.

Chapter 8
Lamb

Very Hot Lamb Kabobs 112

Lamb Kabobs with Indian Spices 113

Lamb Chops with Lavender Buds 114

Baby Rack of Lamb with Zest Crust 115

Rosemary-Crusted Lamb Chops 115

Lamb Braised in Tomato Sauce 116

Braised Lamb Shoulder with Lemon and Onions 117

French-Style Braised Lamb Shanks 118

Marinated Roast Leg of Lamb 119

Curried Lamb Stew 120

Irish Stew 121

Basque-Style Lamb Stew 122

Greek Lamb and Eggplant Casserole 123

Greek Lamb-and-Pasta Casserole 124

Very Hot Lamb Kabobs

Yields 4 servings; serving size 4 ounces

Calories: 210.92
Protein: 26.14 grams
Carbohydrates: 13.02 grams
Sugar: 3.66 grams
Fat: 6.71 grams

¼ cup lemon juice
2 tablespoons tomato paste
½ cup sugar-free tomato juice
2 tablespoons Splenda
2 teaspoons ground cayenne pepper
1 teaspoon celery salt
1 tablespoon soy sauce
½ teaspoon freshly ground black pepper
1 pound lean lamb, cut in 1" chunks
8 cherry tomatoes
8 large white mushrooms
8 pearl onions

This dish is very hot and spicy. Adjust the heat according to your own taste preferences. The touch of sweetness from the Splenda enhances the flavors of the pepper.

ᛣ

1. Soak 8 wooden skewers in warm water for at least 30 minutes. Preheat broiler or grill to 400°F.

2. Combine the first 8 ingredients. Place meat and marinade in a resealable plastic bag and mix well. Refrigerate and let marinate for 60 minutes.

3. String the lamb, tomatoes, mushrooms, and onions on the skewers. Broil or grill until well browned on all sides, about 10 minutes, turning constantly.

Finding Great Lamb

Look for very young lamb, pink and small. Sometimes Australian and/or New Zealand lamb can be over-aged. American lamb can be huge but is generally okay. If you can't find any young lamb locally, you can get it on the Internet from Lobel's of New York (online at www.lobels.com*).*

Lamb Kabobs with Indian Spices

At its best, this marinated lamb is silky, juicy, and delicious.

✑

1. Combine all ingredients to create marinade, then add lamb. Marinate for 4–8 hours.

2. Set grill to high heat. Dry lamb on paper towels, then string on skewers. Broil for about 2 minutes per side for medium doneness.

Madras Curry Powder

Madras curry powder is a particular blend of spices. It originated in India and usually contains curry powder, tumeric, coriander, chili pepper, and a dozen other spices. It has a rich flavor without an overpowering spiciness. In this recipe it contributes to the unique marinade, but you can experiment with it in sauces for meats and vegetables as well.

Yields 4 servings; serving size 4 ounces

Calories: 243.18
Protein: 32.43 grams
Carbohydrates: 8.06 grams
Sugar: 4.54 grams
Fat: 8.9 grams

1 cup plain sugar-free yogurt
Juice of ½ lime
2 cloves garlic, mashed
2 tablespoons Madras curry powder
1 teaspoon freshly grated gingerroot
1 tablespoon Splenda
Salt and freshly ground black pepper to taste
1 teaspoon dried mint leaves or 1 tablespoon fresh mint, minced
1 pound lean lamb, well trimmed, cut in 1" pieces

Lamb Chops with Lavender Buds

*This is an easy way to fix a delicious entrée. It tastes
very good with a vegetable risotto and side salad.*

**Yields 4 servings;
serving size 4 ounces**

Calories: 234.23
Protein: 31.5 grams
Carbohydrates: 0.91 grams
Sugar: 0.26 grams
Fat: 10.87 grams

2 teaspoons lavender buds
*1⅓ tablespoons unsalted
    butter, melted*
1 teaspoon Splenda
Juice of ½ lemon
*Salt and freshly ground black
    pepper to taste*
*4 ⅓-pound thick rib lamb
    chops, bone in*

1. Heat grill or broiler to 400°F. Combine all ingredients but lamb. Trim the lamb chops of all fat and paint with lavender mixture.

2. Grill for 3 minutes. Brush additional lavender mixture on the chops, turn, and cook for another 3 minutes. Brush again with lavender mixture and serve.

Lamb and Herbs

Lamb absolutely loves herbs. Rosemary is a natural, and so is parsley. You can also use chives and oregano. Aromatic vegetables also go well with lamb; onions, garlic, carrots, and parsnips all complement its delicate flavor. Herbs are a good, flavor-added addition to a sugar-free diet.

Baby Rack of Lamb with Zest Crust

This elegant and expensive entrée is for very special occasions, romantic dinners, and anniversaries. Although it's expensive, it's worth every penny if you do it well. This sugar-free coating is delectable.

◦◦◦

1. Preheat the broiler to 450°F. Blend the first 7 ingredients together to form a nice moist paste.

2. Make sure that all fat is trimmed from the lamb. Sprinkle with salt and pepper and place in a roasting pan, bone side up.

3. Broil for 4–5 minutes. Turn and broil, meat side up, for another 4–5 minutes.

4. Remove the lamb from the oven and press the paste into the meat side. Turn off broiler and reduce oven temperature to 400°F. Bake for 10–12 minutes. Remove from oven and let rest for 10 minutes. Carve and serve.

Yields 2 servings; serving size 3½ ounces

Calories: 325.35
Protein: 27.76 grams
Carbohydrates: 7.91 grams
Sugar: 0.2 grams
Fat: 19.80 grams

1 teaspoon lemon zest
2 tablespoons orange zest
2 tablespoons dry bread crumbs
1 teaspoon Splenda
1 tablespoon olive oil
1 teaspoon dried mint leaves
1 clove garlic, chopped
1 rack of lamb (with 6 ribs, the smallest you can find)
Salt and pepper to taste

Rosemary-Crusted Lamb Chops

This is as classic a recipe as you can find. It's just as good now as when the Romans grilled it more than 1,000 years ago.

◦◦◦

1. Heat your grill or broiler to 450°F. Make a paste of the first 4 ingredients. Trim the lamb chops of all fat. Sprinkle the chops with salt and pepper. Brush the paste on both sides.

2. Grill the chops for 5 minutes per side or to desired doneness. Let the chops rest for a few minutes before serving.

Yields 4 servings; serving size 4 ounces

Calories: 281.33
Protein: 31.24 grams
Carbohydrates: 1.41 grams
Sugar: 0.28 grams
Fat: 15.9 grams

2 tablespoons olive oil
2 tablespoons fresh rosemary, finely minced
2 cloves garlic, chopped
Juice and zest of ½ lemon
Salt and pepper to taste
4 ⅓-pound thick loin lamb chops, bone in

Calories: 292.44
Protein: 34.14 grams
Carbohydrates: 13.06 grams
Sugar: 6.88 grams
Fat: 10.82 grams

1 tablespoon olive oil
4 thick round-bone shoulder
    lamb chops or 2 pounds
    lamb stew meat
2 large white onions,
    chopped
4 cloves garlic, chopped
2 cups Parmelat brand sugar-
    free Italian tomatoes,
    crushed
1 teaspoon Splenda
¼ cup red wine vinegar
2 bay leaves
1 teaspoon dried oregano
    leaves
1 teaspoon dried rosemary
    leaves
Salt and freshly ground black
    pepper to taste

Lamb Braised in Tomato Sauce

*You can make this dish a day ahead, refrigerate it, and
skim the fat off the top just before you reheat it. Double the
recipe and freeze the leftovers for an easily prepared meal later.*

∽

1. Heat the olive oil in a large, heavy-bottomed soup kettle over medium-high heat. Sprinkle the lamb with salt and pepper. Brown and add the vegetables.

2. Reduce heat to low. Sauté the vegetables until soft. Add the rest of the ingredients. Cover and simmer for 2 hours. Taste to adjust salt and pepper. Cool and remove any fat that collects on top.

3. Fish out the bones or leave them in if you desire; some children (and adults) love to eat the meat off the bones with their fingers.

A House Is Not a Home Without Onions

The onion family is very diverse, ranging from sweet Vidalia onions to green onions, leeks, and garlic. Use onions liberally. They are good for you and add a lot of flavor.

Braised Lamb Shoulder with Lemon and Onions

Shoulder lamb is usually very inexpensive. The cut makes a nice alternative to the more expensive and more popular lamb loin chops.

❧

1. Heat the oil in a large nonstick pan over medium heat. Trim all fat from the lamb and sprinkle it with salt and pepper. Brown and set aside.

2. Stir in the onions and cook until softened. Add the rest of the ingredients.

3. Reduce heat to simmer. Cover and simmer for 60 minutes.

Lamb Fat

Lamb meat is sweet, but the fat is strong. When the fat is removed, the meat tastes much, much better. When you make braised lamb, you can get even more fat off it by refrigerating it until broth has cooled and fat has risen to the top. Skim the fat before reheating.

**Yields 4 servings;
serving size 4 ounces**

Calories: 257.15
Protein: 19.92 grams
Carbohydrates: 6.74 grams
Sugar: 3.47 grams
Fat: 16.54 grams

1 teaspoon olive oil
*4 4½-ounce round-bone
  shoulder lamb chops*
Salt and pepper to taste
1 large red onion, chopped
*1 teaspoon dried mint leaves,
  or 1 tablespoon fresh,
  chopped*
1 teaspoon Splenda
½ cup chicken broth
⅓ cup vegetable broth
Juice of ½ lemon
*½ lemon, thinly sliced, seeds
  removed*

French-Style Braised Lamb Shanks

2 pounds lamb shanks
¼ cup whole-wheat flour
*Salt and freshly ground black
    pepper to taste*
1 tablespoon olive oil
*1 large red Spanish onion,
    chopped*
4 cloves garlic, chopped
4 carrots, chopped
*4 fresh sage leaves, chopped
    or 1 teaspoon dried sage*
1 teaspoon soy sauce
1 teaspoon Splenda
*1 cup fresh plum tomatoes,
    chopped*
1 cup rich chicken stock
*2 cans cannellini beans,
    drained and rinsed*
*2 slices sugar-free smoked
    bacon*
*2 cups sliced white
    mushrooms*

*This is a great dish for a weekend warrior—someone who loves
to cook but has little time during the week. It's great to share
with another couple with a roaring fire in the fireplace.*

1. Trim the lamb shanks of all fat. Dredge in flour, salt, and pepper. Heat olive oil in nonstick pan over medium heat. Add lamb shanks and brown on all sides.

2. Remove the shanks from the pan. Stir in onion and garlic, cooking until softened.

3. Add the next six ingredients. Cover and reduce heat to a simmer. Cook for 2 hours. Stir in the beans.

4. Sauté the bacon in a separate nonstick pan. Drain it on paper towels. Reserve 1 teaspoon of fat and discard the rest. Sauté the mushrooms in reserved bacon fat for 5 minutes, stirring. Add the mushrooms and bacon to the stewed shanks and serve.

Shanks and Beans

Lamb shanks are mostly bone, but they still have luscious meat from the bottom of the leg. Cannellini beans are classically French and a wonderful complement to the meat and sauce. They are a staple in the Mediterranean, and they are among the most versatile of beans.

Marinated Roast Leg of Lamb

This marinade tenderizes the lamb and gives it a delicious flavor and texture. Try to find a piece of really young lamb.

1. Mix the first 7 ingredients in a large glass baking dish or enamel-coated roasting pan. Trim every bit of fat from the lamb. Make slits along the leg of lamb and insert sliced garlic cloves.

2. Sprinkle the lamb with salt and pepper. Turn it in the marinade to coat. Place the anchovy filets on top. Add the parsley and lemon.

3. Cover and refrigerate overnight, turning after 8 hours.

4. Preheat oven to 350°F. Roast the lamb for 20 minutes per pound, basting with the marinade every few minutes. Let rest for 15 minutes before carving.

Yields 10 servings; serving size 4 ounces

Calories: 364.7
Protein: 22.85 grams
Carbohydrates: 8.24 grams
Sugar: 4.33 grams
Fat: 26.46 grams

½ cup olive oil
¼ cup red wine vinegar
4 carrots, peeled and cut in 3" lengths
2 large onions, sliced
4 fresh bay leaves
10 capers
2 tablespoons rosemary leaves
2½-pound boneless leg of lamb
4 garlic cloves, slivered
Kosher salt and freshly ground black pepper to taste
4 anchovy filets
1 bunch Italian flat-leaf parsley, chopped
1 lemon, thinly sliced

Curried Lamb Stew

**Yields 6 servings;
serving size 4 ounces**

Calories: 308.15 grams
Protein: 39.25 grams
Carbohydrates: 7.91 grams
Sugar: 2.95 grams
Fat: 12.63 grams

1 tablespoon peanut or
    canola oil
Salt and pepper to taste
2 pounds lean boneless lamb
    stew meat
2 onions, chopped
3 cloves garlic, chopped
2 teaspoons whole-wheat
    flour
1 tablespoon Madras curry
    powder, or to taste
1 teaspoon Splenda
1 teaspoon cayenne pepper
1 tablespoon tamarind paste
    mixed with ¼ cup water
1 cup vegetable broth
Juice of ½ lime
½ cup water (in case sauce
    gets too thick)

This is a stew that improves with age. Make it the day before you plan to serve it.

∾

1. Heat the oil in a large heavy-bottomed stew pot or soup kettle over medium-high heat. Sprinkle the lamb with salt and pepper.

2. Brown the lamb. Reduce heat to medium and add the onions and garlic. Sauté until softened, about 4 minutes.

3. Moving the meat and vegetables over to the side of the pan, add the flour, curry, Splenda, and cayenne, stirring constantly.

4. Stir in the rest of the ingredients. Cover, reduce heat, and simmer slowly for 3 hours.

Indian Spices

Indian cuisine can be hotter than the hottest Tex-Mex dishes. However, the cuisine can also be delicately subtle or bold and exotically delicious. The use of spices and the diversity of Indian dishes make this culture a rich resource for a sugar-free diet.

Irish Stew

This is a very satisfying old-fashioned family dinner. You can increase the mashed potatoes, add carrots to the stew, or leave them out all together.

ↄᴠↄ

1. Heat the oil in a large heavy-bottomed soup kettle or stew pot over medium heat. Salt and pepper the lamb and brown it.

2. Reduce heat to low. Stir in the onions, garlic, celery, and carrots. Add everything but the potatoes. Cover the pot and simmer over very low heat for 2 hours.

3. When the stew is done, place in a 2-quart soufflé dish. Cover with the mashed potatoes and run under the broiler until lightly browned.

Irish Stew Trivia

Irish stew is a traditional Irish dish that takes advantage of readily available ingredients. In the dish's early days, mutton or older lamb was used; these tough cuts needed to be stewed to make the meat more tender. Some of the ingredients in this recipe, like carrots, are modern additions. Others, like potatoes, have always been used.

Yields 6 servings; serving size 4 ounces

Calories: 426.74
Protein: 33.52 grams
Carbohydrates: 28.12 grams
Sugar: 10.4 grams
Fat: 15.80 grams

1 tablespoon canola oil
Salt and pepper to taste
2 pounds boneless lamb stew, all fat removed
4 onions, chopped
2 cloves garlic, chopped
2 celery stalks with leaves, chopped
4 carrots, peeled and cut in 2" lengths
¼ cup white wine vinegar
1 cup beef broth
1 bay leaf
1 tablespoon dried rosemary
1 teaspoon dried sage
½ cup curly parsley, chopped
2 teaspoons chervil
1 teaspoon horseradish
2 cups mashed potatoes

Basque-Style Lamb Stew

Basque food is somewhat French, somewhat Spanish, and very much its own style. Basque people tend to eat a lot but lead a very active life. In the United States, many sheep farmers are of Basque origin, having brought their native occupation to the Northwestern states.

Yields 6 servings; serving size 4 ounces

Calories: 259.8
Protein: 23.97 grams
Carbohydrates: 4.12 grams
Sugar: 1.65 grams
Fat: 16 grams

3 slices smoked bacon, cooked and drained
4 cloves garlic, minced
1 sprig fresh rosemary
¼ cup red-wine vinegar
1½ pounds shoulder lamb cut in chunks
Salt and pepper to taste
2 teaspoons olive oil
2 yellow onions, chopped
1 tablespoon sweet paprika
2 bottled sweet red roasted peppers, packed in oil
2 bay leaves
½ bunch Italian flat-leaf parsley leaves, minced
1 cup chicken stock

1. Fry the bacon and reserve on paper towels. Mix 1 clove of garlic with the rosemary, vinegar, and lamb in a resealable plastic bag. Marinate overnight in the refrigerator, turning occasionally.

2. Discard the marinade, dry the lamb, and sprinkle it with salt and pepper. Heat the olive oil in a heavy nonstick pan over medium heat. Brown the meat and remove from the pan.

3. Sauté the rest of the garlic and the onions. Return the lamb to the pan and stir in the rest of the ingredients.

4. Reduce heat to a simmer and cover. Cook for 2 hours or until the lamb is falling off the bone. Cool, remove bones, and reheat, adding the crumbled bacon.

Basque Style

This dish draws its inspiration from Basque flavors, but it blends in traditional American flavors for a more familiar taste. The Basque region, located in Spain's northeast region, borders France, and its cuisine has long influenced European palates.

Greek Lamb and Eggplant Casserole

This is a simple, light version of a classic Greek recipe.

✌

1. Heat the olive oil in a frying pan over medium heat. Add the onion and garlic. Cook until soft. Place the cooked vegetables in a large bowl.

2. Preheat the oven to 350°F. Add the salt, pepper, cinnamon, basil, and marjoram, tomato sauce, and lamb to the onion and garlic, mixing thoroughly.

3. Prepare a 2-quart oven-proof casserole dish with nonstick spray. Cover the bottom with eggplant slices. Add the lamb mixture. Cover with more eggplant. Sprinkle with Parmesan cheese. Cover with aluminum foil.

4. Bake for 60 minutes, covered. Remove aluminum foil and bake for 60 minutes more. Serve with rice.

Moussaka

Moussaka, the traditional Greek dish, commonly uses eggplant as one of its layers, but you can substitute zucchini or even potatoes if you prefer. Regardless of your choice of vegetable, the lengthy baking time allows the flavors to blend together nicely. Depending on how your oven cooks, put the aluminum foil back on to prevent the top from over-browning or turn on the broiler to make the top crispy.

Yields 6 servings; serving size 4 ounces

Calories: 296.11
Protein: 15.98 grams
Carbohydrates: 12.16 grams
Sugar: 7.45 grams
Fat: 20.84 grams

2 teaspoons olive oil
2 small yellow onions, chopped
2 cloves garlic
Salt and pepper to taste
½ teaspoon cinnamon
1 teaspoon dried basil
1 teaspoon dried marjoram
1 cup sugar-free tomato sauce
1 pound ground lamb
1 medium eggplant, thinly sliced
¼ cup grated Parmesan cheese

Greek Lamb-and-Pasta Casserole

This dish has a delightful tang and richness. You can make it in advance to serve the next day or freeze and serve the next week.

**Yields 6 servings;
serving size 4 ounces**

Calories: 413.21
Protein: 25.28 grams
Carbohydrates: 25.38 grams
Sugar: 3.41 grams
Fat: 23.44 grams

*1 tablespoon olive oil
1 pound lean ground lamb
1 large sweet onion, chopped
4 cloves garlic, minced
½ cup currants
Salt and freshly ground
    pepper to taste
1 teaspoon Splenda
½ teaspoon cinnamon
1 teaspoon dried mint or 1
    tablespoon fresh mint,
    chopped
3 cups parboiled orzo
½ cup chicken stock or broth
½ cup toasted pine nuts*

1. Preheat the oven to 350°F. Prepare a casserole dish with nonstick cooking spray. Heat the olive oil in a large pan over medium heat. Sauté the meat, onion, and garlic, stirring constantly.

2. Add the currants, spices, Splenda, and mint.

3. Mix with the orzo and pour into the casserole dish. Stir in the broth. Sprinkle with pine nuts. Bake for 30 minutes.

Greek Cooking Trivia

Ancient Greeks didn't have sugar. They used honey to sweeten food, and they also added ingredients like figs and sweet grapes to import sweetness. This recipe takes advantage of the natural sweetness in onions, but it also uses Splenda, which the ancient Greeks definitely didn't have in their kitchens.

Chapter 9
Pork

Pork Chops Sautéed with Grapefruit 126

Pork Chops Sautéed with Artichokes 127

Pork Chops in Homemade Barbecue Sauce 127

Pork Tenderloin with Asian Spices 128

Roasted Citrus Pork Tenderloin 129

Marinated Pork Tenderloin on Skewers 130

Cranberry-Stuffed Pork Tenderloin 131

Crown Roast of Pork with Wild Rice 132

Oven-Braised Country-Style Spare Ribs 133

Asian-Style Baby Back Ribs 134

Barbecued Baby Back Ribs 135

Pork Burgers with Asian Spices 136

Pork Burgers with Apples 136

Pork Chili 137

Italian-Style Baby Pork Balls 138

Pork Chops Sautéed with Grapefruit

This is a nice twist for pork chops. It's quick and very simple to make.
Serve with carrots or another brightly colored vegetable.

❧

Yields 2 servings;
serving size 4 ounces

Calories: 289.73
Protein: 26.19 grams
Carbohydrates: 7.46 grams
Sugar: 3.88 grams
Fat: 16.85 grams

1 teaspoon peanut oil
Salt and pepper
2 4-ounce boneless pork
  chops
1 tablespoon dried rosemary
  leaves
1 teaspoon Splenda
½ cup grapefruit sections
½ cup chicken broth

1. Heat the oil in a nonstick pan over medium-high heat. Sprinkle the pork chops with salt, pepper, rosemary, and Splenda.

2. Sear the chops, browning quickly on each side. Add the grapefruit sections and broth. Reduce heat to very low.

3. Cover and cook for about 4 minutes. Turn and cook for another 4 minutes.

Pork and Fruit

Pork and fruit make a happy combination. The flavors, whether spicy and full of citrus or soft and peachy, are excellent together. On the citrus side, try some lime juice. On the sweet side, try using a mango along with the chops or roast.

Pork Chops Sautéed with Artichokes

*The lovely combination of flavors and the easy preparation
make this an ideal dish for a weeknight meal.*

❧

1. Heat the oil in a large nonstick pan over medium flame. Sprinkle salt, pepper, and Splenda on the chops. Brown them quickly in the oil. Add the artichokes and toss to coat with oil.

2. Reduce heat, add the broth, cover, and cook for 5 minutes at a simmer. Turn and cook for another 5 minutes. Garnish with lemon slices.

**Yields 2 servings;
serving size 4 ounces**

Calories: 455.02
Protein: 35.49 grams
Carbohydrates: 18.10 grams
Sugar: 2.06 grams
Fat: 25.74 grams

*1 teaspoon olive oil
Salt and pepper to taste
1 teaspoon Splenda
2 rib or loin pork chops
1 10-ounce package frozen
    artichoke hearts, thawed
½ cup chicken broth
2 thick slices fresh lemon*

Pork Chops in Homemade Barbecue Sauce

*Since practically all commercial barbecue sauces contain molasses,
brown sugar, and/or white sugar, it's best to make your own.
There are many ways to vary the spices, aromatic vegetables, and
herbs in your sauce, so you can customize it to your taste.*

❧

1. Heat the oil in a nonstick pan over medium heat. Sprinkle the chops with salt, pepper, and cloves. Brown the pork.

2. When the chops are browned on both sides, reduce heat and add the sauce. Cover and simmer for 20 minutes.

**Yields 4 servings;
serving size 4 ounces**

Calories: 320.29
Protein: 37.63 grams
Carbohydrates: 8.07 grams
Sugar: 0 grams
Fat: 14.13 grams

*1 teaspoon olive oil
Salt and pepper to taste
¼ teaspoon ground cloves
4 bone in loin pork chops
1 cup Barbecue Sauce (page
    243)*

Pork Tenderloin with Asian Spices

Stir-frying pork and various vegetables is a very quick way to get lots of flavor in a very short time. Vary this recipe with other sugar-free fruit jams, such as plum or blueberry.

Yields 4 servings; serving size 4 ounces

Calories: 418.13
Protein: 29.40 grams
Carbohydrates: 14.60 grams
Sugar: 7.09 grams
Fat: 25.57 grams

1 tablespoon gingerroot, peeled and grated
1 tablespoon wasabi mustard powder
1 tablespoon soy sauce
2 tablespoons Toasted Sesame-Seed Oil (page 238)
2 tablespoons lime juice
1 teaspoon lemon zest
¼ cup sugar-free apricot jam
1 pound pork tenderloin
Salt and freshly ground black pepper to taste
1 tablespoon peanut oil
1 Napa cabbage, rinsed and shredded
½ cup roasted peanuts

1. Combine the first 7 ingredients into a paste. Spread on the pork tenderloin. Cover and refrigerate. Let marinate for 4 hours. Sprinkle with salt and pepper and slice thinly.

2. Preheat a wok or frying pan over medium-high flame. Add oil. Quickly stir-fry the pork and cabbage, stirring constantly for about 5 minutes.

3. Stir in extra soy sauce and/or oil if the pan gets dry. Sprinkle with peanuts and serve over rice.

Pork Tenderloin

Tenderloin is a lean and forgiving meat. You can cook it medium rare and be perfectly safe from microbes. You can mix it with lots of different vegetables, or roast, fry, sauté, broil, or bake it.

Roasted Citrus Pork Tenderloin

This recipe may seem to have a lot of ingredients, but your prep time will reward you with fast cooking. Any sugar-free diet should include plenty of citrus zest and lemons as they add flavor without calories or sugar.

1. Mix the flour, salt, cayenne, and gingerroot on a piece of waxed paper. Roll the pork pieces in the mixture.

2. Heat the oils in a frying pan or wok over medium heat. Sear the pork and add the rest of the ingredients.

3. Reduce heat and simmer for 3–4 minutes per side. Serve over rice or steamed cabbage.

Serves 6; serving size 4 ounces

Calories: 230.53 grams
Protein: 24.17 grams
Carbohydrates: 6.76 grams
Sugar: 2.29 grams
Fat: 11.58 grams

¼ cup whole-wheat flour
Salt to taste
½ teaspoon cayenne pepper
1 tablespoon fresh
 gingerroot, peeled and
 minced
1½ pound tenderloin of pork,
 pounded to ⅔ inch thick
2 tablespoons peanut oil
1 teaspoon Toasted Sesame
 Seed Oil (page 238)
½ cup freshly squeezed
 orange juice
2 teaspoons fresh orange zest
½ lemon, cut in chunks
1 teaspoon Splenda

Marinated Pork Tenderloin on Skewers

Fire up your grill and make a very quick and delicious entrée with a pork tenderloin. Grilled and marinated pork tenderloin will be super tender. Serve it over chilled mixed greens with a light, lemony dressing.

Yields 6 servings; serving size 4 ounces

Calories: 179.41
Protein: 23.99 grams
Carbohydrates: 5.12 grams
Sugar: 2.31 grams
Fat: 6.24 grams

½ cup Chili Sauce (page 240)
Juice of 3 oranges (to yield
    ½ cup)
2 tablespoons soy sauce
1 teaspoon garlic powder
1 teaspoon dried mint
1 teaspoon ground cayenne
    pepper, mixed with 1
    tablespoon cold water
1½ pounds pork tenderloin,
    cut in 1" chunks

1. Mix all ingredients together in a resealable plastic bag and marinate for 4–6 hours.

2. Set your gas grill to medium high or wait until your coals are hot but not flaming. String the chunks of pork onto metal skewers or well-soaked wooden ones.

3. Grill, turning for 6–8 minutes, or until lightly browned on all sides.

Marinated Variations

Try different aromatic vegetables, herbs, and spices to vary your marinades. You can use garlic or no garlic, fruit juice with wine, or no wine at all.

Cranberry-Stuffed Pork Tenderloin

The dark red cranberries stand out on the inside of this festive dish.

∽

1. Preheat the oven at 400°F. Mix the first 5 ingredients in a small bowl. Set aside.

2. Mix the cranberry juice and Splenda in a small saucepan. Bring to a boil and reduce by half. Cool and add ¼ cup to the stuffing mixture.

3. Using a dull knife, cut a tunnel through the center of the pork tenderloin. Stuff the tunnel with the dried cranberry mixture. Sprinkle the loin with salt and pepper.

4. Place the roast in a pan and slide into the oven. Roast for 10 minutes. Drizzle with the reduced cranberry juice. Reduce heat to 350°F. Roast for another 25–30 minutes. Spoon the rest of the sauce over the roast.

5. Let the roast rest for 10 minutes before slicing.

**Yields 4 servings;
serving size 4 ounces**

Calories: 267.38
Protein: 24.07 grams
Carbohydrates: 10.59 grams
Sugar: 7.68 grams
Fat: 9.13 grams

½ cup dried sugar-free cranberries
1 tablespoon sugar-free applesauce
½ teaspoon cayenne pepper, mixed with 1 teaspoon cold water
½ cup sugar-free corn bread crumbs
1 teaspoon unsalted butter, melted
1½ cups cranberry juice with no added sugar
2 teaspoons Splenda
1 pound pork tenderloin
Salt and pepper to taste

Crown Roast of Pork with Wild Rice

Ask your butcher to prepare this roast for you. It should be separated on the bottom with the bones sticking up in the air. It's delicately flavored and makes an impressive presentation. You can get little paper "panties" for the bone ends, or you can make little covers with aluminum foil.

Yields 6 servings; serving size 4 ounces

Calories: 458.08
Protein: 35.95 grams
Carbohydrates: 27.18 grams
Sugar: 6.82 grams
Fat: 23.28 grams

2 tablespoons olive oil
4 shallots, chopped
½ cup walnuts
½ cup dried apricots with no sugar added, quartered
2 teaspoons dried rosemary or 2 tablespoons fresh rosemary
3 cups cooked wild rice
Salt and pepper to taste
Crown rib roast of pork with 12 small chops, at room temperature
1 teaspoon unsalted butter

1. Preheat oven to 350°F. Heat the oil in a large sauté pan over medium heat. Add the shallots and cook, stirring until softened.

2. Stir in the walnuts, apricots, and rosemary and stir to coat with oil. Combine with the cooked wild rice. Sprinkle the roast with salt and pepper.

3. Place the crown roast on a large piece of aluminum foil, then in a roasting pan. Bring the foil 1" up the sides of the roast. Fill the center with the wild rice mixture.

4. Dot the top of the stuffing with butter. Roast the pork for 50 minutes. Let it rest before cutting into chops at the table.

Crown Roasts

Crown roasts can be made up of lamb or pork chops. The butcher takes the ribs and trims them to be of even length. They are elegant and not at all difficult to cook. Stuffing can vary greatly; just make sure it's very moist and cooked before you put it into the "crown." You can substitute other fruits for the dried apricots, as long as there's no added sugar.

Oven-Braised Country-Style Spare Ribs

This is an easy and delicious family dinner, basic and hearty.

ᐁᐂ

1. Preheat broiler to 500°F. Trim the ribs. Sprinkle them with salt, pepper, Splenda Brown, and soy sauce. In a shallow roasting pan, brown the ribs on both sides.

2. Reset the oven to 350°F. Add the rest of the ingredients. Cover with aluminum foil and braise for 2–3 hours, turning once and re-covering with foil.

3. Remove foil. If the sauce is dry, stir in some of the juice reserved from the canned tomatoes.

One-Dish Dinners

Ribs are the perfect option if you're running low on energy or empty space in your dishwasher. Experiment with different sauces to season your ribs. Try Dijon mustard with beef broth for a tangy sweetness.

Yields 8 servings; serving size 4 ounces

Calories: 407.38
Protein: 28.03 grams
Carbohydrates: 15.55 grams
Sugar: 4.67 grams
Fat: 26.40 grams

Salt and pepper to taste
2 tablespoons Splenda Brown Sugar Substitute
8 country-style spare ribs, well trimmed
2 tablespoons soy sauce
4 onions, peeled and chopped
2 cloves garlic, minced
1 28-ounce can sugar-free plum tomatoes, drained, juice reserved

Asian-Style Baby Back Ribs

Pressure-cooking ribs is a fast way to prepare them,
and all of the flavors permeate the meat.

ↇ

Yields 4 servings;
serving size 4 ounces

Calories: 276.08
Protein: 14.90 grams
Carbohydrates: 2.10 grams
Sugar: 1.14 grams
Fat: 22.99 grams

½ cup soy sauce
½ cup cider vinegar
1 tablespoon fresh gingerroot,
* peeled and chopped*
2 tablespoons Toasted Sesame
* Seed Oil (page 238)*
1 tablespoon Splenda
1 teaspoon ground cayenne
* pepper, blended with 1*
* tablespoon cold water*
Salt and pepper to taste
2 pounds baby back ribs

1. Whisk all ingredients but ribs together in a small bowl. Place the ribs in a pressure cooker and pour the sauce over them.

2. Start on medium-high heat. When the pressure cooker comes up to temperature, let it whistle for 10 minutes. Turn it off and let the ribs cool in the pot before serving.

Pressure Cooker Basics

Pressure cookers work by increasing the pressure in the pot. This increases the boiling point of water. The pressure cooker also holds the steam inside the pot instead of letting it escape. The steam combined with the pressure cook the meat more quickly than conventional methods. You wind up with moist meat that's ready to eat in no time.

Barbecued Baby Back Ribs

Using the pressure cooker is the opposite of slow-cooked traditional barbecue.
You'll love it! Try various sugar-free juices in the sauce.

⌒∿⌒

1. Place the ribs in a pressure cooker and pour sauce over them.

2. Place over medium-high heat. When the pressure cooker comes up to temperature, let it whistle for 10 minutes. Turn it off and let the ribs cool in the pot before serving.

3. Serve when cool enough to cut and put on a plate.

Weeknight Dinners

A pressure cooker can make short work of many recipes. Try it with the braised country-style short ribs recipe to save time. Another good way to ease dinner preparation is a slow cooker. Just put all of the ingredients into the pot, set it on low, and go to work.

Yields 4 servings;
serving size 4 ounces

Calories: 502.27
Protein: 27.06 grams
Carbohydrates: 8.49 grams
Sugar: 0 grams
Fat: 39.03 grams

1½ cups Barbecue Sauce
    (page 243)
2 pounds baby back ribs, well
    trimmed

Pork Burgers with Asian Spices

Make sure all the ingredients are mixed well prior to grilling. These burgers are quite spicy, but you can adjust the seasonings to taste.

∿

1. Combine all ingredients but pork. Using a fork, blend into the pork. Gently form into burgers.

2. Set grill on high. Quickly sear burgers on both sides. Reduce heat to low and cook for 5 minutes per side. Serve on buns or over rice.

Yields 4 servings; serving size 4 ounces

Calories: 304.30
Protein: 19.59 grams
Carbohydrates: 1.09 grams
Sugar: 0.22 grams
Fat: 24.08 grams

1 tablespoon soy sauce
1 teaspoon gingerroot, peeled and minced
½ teaspoon ground cayenne pepper, mixed with 1 teaspoon cold water
2 teaspoons fresh green onions, minced
2 cloves garlic, minced
1 pound lean ground pork

Pork Burgers with Apples

You can do these on the grill or on the frying pan with a skim of oil. One apple provides enough natural fructose for four people.

∿

1. Using a fork, lightly blend all ingredients together.

2. Heat grill to high. Form meat and apple mixture into burgers. Sear quickly, turn heat to low, and cook for 5 minutes per side.

Yields 4 servings; serving size 4 ounces

Calories: 322.46
Protein: 19.55 grams
Carbohydrates: 5.81 grams
Sugar: 4.36 grams
Fat: 24.13 grams

1 tart green apple, peeled, cored, and diced
1 tablespoon soy sauce
2 green onions, minced
1 clove garlic, minced
Salt and freshly ground pepper to taste
1 pound lean ground pork

Ground Meat
Ask the butcher for the very leanest pork to grind, or do it yourself in the food processor. It's a great addition to spaghetti sauces, stews, and soups. Start with meatballs and burgers. Your sugar-free sauces, such as chili or barbecue, will be great garnishes.

Pork Chili

This recipe has a few classic Texas-style bells and whistles.
You can cook it for just a few hours or overnight—the longer the better.
Vary the pepper content and the amount of garlic and onion.

Yields 12 servings;
serving size 6 ounces

Calories: 456.51
Protein: 24.67 grams
Carbohydrates: 34.87 grams
Sugar: 5.53 grams
Fat: 26 grams

1. Heat the oil in a large pot over medium heat. Sauté the pork, breaking it up with a wooden spoon. Add all of the vegetables and stir, sautéing until softened, about 12 minutes.

2. Mix the chili powder into the meat mixture. Blend the dry mustard, cinnamon, and cocoa powder with the coffee, whisking with a fork until smooth. Add to the meat mixture.

3. Stir in the rest of the ingredients and cover. Reduce the heat to a bare simmer. Cook for at least 3 hours. The chili is done when the flavors have married and you can't taste any one ingredient.

¼ cup canola oil
2½ pounds lean ground pork
4 sweet red onions, chopped
6 cloves garlic, chopped
4 Italian green frying peppers, stemmed, seeded, and chopped
2 large sweet red bell peppers, roasted
2 sweet yellow peppers, stemmed, seeded, and chopped
4 jalapeño peppers, stemmed, seeded, and chopped
2 tablespoons chili powder, or to taste
1 tablespoon dry English-style mustard
1 teaspoon cinnamon
1 teaspoon Dutch-process cocoa powder
½ cup strong cold coffee
2 tablespoons Splenda
2 tablespoons Splenda brown
3 14-ounce cans red kidney beans, drained and rinsed
2 28-ounce cans Italian plum tomatoes
Salt and pepper to taste
1 teaspoon liquid smoke

Pork: Healthy White Meat

Decades ago, pork was full of fat. Today's pigs are fed healthier food, and they make healthier food for us. Lean ground pork is one of the healthier forms of a modern, healthy meat.

Italian-Style Baby Pork Balls

You can make these for a cocktail party or a snack on game night. They also make a good family meal served with pasta or mashed potatoes.

Yields 32 small meatballs; serving size 3 meatballs

Calories: 331.32
Protein: 11.34 grams
Carbohydrates: 12.28 grams
Sugar: 6.14 grams
Fat: 26.89 grams

½ cup canola oil
1 teaspoon oregano
1 tablespoon freshly minced
   garlic
½ cup dry bread crumbs
½ cup white or black raisins
Salt and freshly ground
   pepper to taste
1 teaspoon red pepper flakes,
   or to taste
½ cup pine nuts
1 pound lean ground pork

1. Heat the oil in a large nonstick frying pan over medium heat. Mix all of the rest of the ingredients together and roll into marble-sized balls, about 1" in diameter.

2. Fry the meatballs, turning constantly to brown evenly, about 5 minutes per side. Drain on paper towels.

Meatballs

Learn to make meatballs, and you have an instant party. Experiment with beef, turkey, pork, and lamb for exciting flavors. Try meatless meatballs with soy products.

Chapter 10
Shrimp and Lobster

Baked Stuffed Shrimp I. 140

Baked Stuffed Shrimp II 141

Barbecued Shrimp 141

Baby Shrimp in Cream 142

Grilled Shrimp with Asian Seasonings 143

Mexican Shrimp with Chipotles 143

Shrimp Butter for Hors d'Oeuvres 144

Shrimp-and-Avocado Salad. 144

Shrimp Crunch Filling for Ravioli 145

Shrimp Scampi 146

Shrimp Salad with Tomatillos, Jicama,

    Grilled Peaches, and Chimichuri 147

Shrimp Stir-Fry with Broccoli and Almonds 148

Boiled Lobster 149

Lobster on the Grill. 150

Baked Stuffed Shrimp I

Yields 4 servings;
serving size 4 ounces

Calories: 125.43 grams
Protein: 10.34 grams
Carbohydrates: 9.42 grams
Sugar: 0.70 grams
Fat: 5.05 grams

1 tablespoon unsalted butter
2 cloves garlic, smashed
2 tablespoons Parmesan
    cheese
6 tablespoons sugar-free
    bread crumbs
Juice of ½ lemon
1 teaspoon dried oregano
Salt to taste
1 teaspoon freshly ground
    black pepper
16 jumbo shrimp, peeled and
    butterflied
Fresh chopped parsley for
    garnish

Serve one or two shrimp for an appetizer, four for lunch.
Make these easy and delicious stuffed shrimp ahead of time.
Make sure the bread crumbs you use are sugar-free.

⌁

1. Preheat the oven to 500°F. Melt the butter in a saucepan over medium heat. Sauté the garlic for about 4 minutes.

2. Stir in the next 6 ingredients and mix well. Place the shrimp on a baking pan. Mound the stuffing on each.

3. Bake for about 6–8 minutes or until the shrimp have turned pink and the stuffing is lightly brown.

Wild vs. Farm-Raised Shrimp

Immediately after Hurricane Katrina destroyed the fishing towns around the Gulf of Mexico, it was harder to get wild Gulf shrimp. However, the fishermen are back, so opt for wild shrimp if you can find them. They are more flavorful than their captivity-raised counterparts.

Baked Stuffed Shrimp II

Avocados taste very sweet but they are actually low in carbs.
They are an excellent source of many vitamins and omega fats.

∽ঔ৴

1. Preheat oven to 450°F. Using a fork, mash the first five ingredients together into a smooth paste.

2. Place a piece of aluminum foil on a baking sheet. Arrange the shrimp on the paper. Divide the avocado stuffing, placing an equal amount on each shrimp.

3. Bake for 8–10 minutes or until the shrimp is pink and the stuffing hot.

Yields 4 servings;
serving size 4 ounces

Calories: 244.14
Protein: 8.35 grams
Carbohydrates: 8.93 grams
Sugar: 0.34 grams
Fat: 21.22 grams

3 tablespoons Basic
Mayonnaise (page 238)
2 medium-sized ripe
avocados
Juice of one lime
Dash cayenne pepper
½ teaspoon salt
12 jumbo shrimp, peeled and
butterflied

Barbecued Shrimp

The jumbo shrimp in this recipe make a wonderful lunch, but you can opt
instead to substitute smaller shrimp by weight if you're making a cocktail
snack. Keep plenty of homemade barbecue sauce and chili sauce on hand.

∽ঔ৴

1. Set your grill or broiler on high. Mix the sauce with lemon juice. Coat the shrimp.

2. String the shrimp on the skewers. Grill or broil for 3 minutes per side.

Yields 4 servings;
serving size 4 ounces

Calories: 95.49
Protein: 9.47 grams
Carbohydrates: 9.53 grams
Sugar: 0.14 grams
Fat: 1.94 grams

1 cup Barbecue Sauce (page
243)
1 tablespoon lemon juice
16 jumbo shrimp, peeled and
cleaned
4 8" wooden skewers, soaked
in water for 30 minutes

Baby Shrimp in Cream

Serve for brunch over rice and a crisp green salad of watercress or arugula.

෴

Yields 4 servings; serving size 4 ounces shrimp

Calories: 300.85
Protein: 26.45 grams
Carbohydrates: 9.22 grams
Sugar: 1.87 grams
Fat: 17.60 grams

1 tablespoon unsalted butter
2 shallots, chopped
1 tablespoon corn or whole-wheat flour
1 teaspoon Splenda
½ cup milk
1 cup light-medium cream
1 teaspoon dill weed
1 teaspoon tomato paste
1 teaspoon cayenne pepper
Salt and freshly ground black pepper to taste
1 teaspoon lemon zest
1 pound frozen baby shrimp, thawed

1. Heat the butter in a heavy-bottomed sauté pan over medium heat.

2. Sauté the shallots until softened. Stir in the flour and Splenda. Add the milk and cream.

3. Stir and cook until thickened. Add the rest of the ingredients. Make sure the shrimp is both thawed and dried on paper towels prior to cooking.

The First 100 Shrimp Recipes

There must be thousands of shrimp recipes, but you'll learn what you really like on the first one hundred you make. Try shrimp salad in an avocado soup or spooned into half a fresh avocado. Try a shrimp sauce over asparagus or broccoli. Stir fry shrimp with Napa cabbage. Experiment with new flavors to discover your tastes.

Grilled Shrimp with Asian Seasonings

*Shrimp is wonderful for a sugar-free diet. It's full of protein,
and you can use a bit of sugar substitute to sweeten it.*

1. Mix the sauce ingredients together and coat the shrimp. Set either your outdoor grill or your broiler on high.

2. Grill the shrimp for 2 minutes per side. Serve with extra lime wedges.

Yields 4 servings; serving size 4 pieces of shrimp

Calories: 96.94
Protein: 9.20 grams
Carbohydrates: 3.84 grams
Sugar: 0.72 grams
Fat: 5.01 grams

2 tablespoons soy sauce
1 tablespoon gingerroot, peeled and grated
1 tablespoon Toasted Sesame Seed Oil (page 238)
1 teaspoon Splenda
Juice of 1 lime
1 tablespoon dry English mustard
16 raw jumbo shrimp, peeled
Extra lime wedges for serving

Mexican Shrimp with Chipotles

Serve the shrimp in toasted sugar-free corn tortillas.

1. Heat the oil in a large sauté pan over medium heat. Sauté the onion and garlic.

2. Stir in the tomatoes, pepper, salt, pepper, pepper flakes, and cilantro. Cook until slightly thickened. Add the shrimp and cook for about 4 minutes, flipping shrimp to cook thoroughly. Serve immediately.

Yields 4 servings; serving size 4 ounces

Calories: 220.70
Protein: 30.28 grams
Carbohydrates: 9.89 grams
Sugar: 4.57 grams
Fat: 6.37 grams

1 tablespoon olive oil
½ cup chopped sweet onion
3 cloves garlic, minced
4 ripe tomatoes, diced
2 chipotle peppers, finely chopped
Salt and freshly ground black pepper to taste
1 teaspoon red pepper flakes
1 tablespoon minced cilantro or parsley
1 pound shrimp

Shrimp Butter for Hors d'Oeuvres

This is a very simple spread for crackers. You can also use it for elegant tea sandwiches. Just make sure that the bread or crackers are sugar-free!

1. Purée all ingredients in a food processor, stopping occasionally to scrape down the sides. When smooth, transfer to a bowl. Cover and refrigerate until ready to use.

Shrimp with Herbs and Aromatic Vegetables
As delicate as shrimp may be, it stands up to oregano and garlic in Italian dishes. It's fine with Creole spicing in gumbo. Onions, celery, Dijon-Style Mustard (page 241), and Basic Mayonnaise (page 238) turn cold shrimp into a wonderful salad. Go ahead and play with the flavors you love.

Shrimp-and-Avocado Salad

Use a melon baller to cut the avocados into little balls to add a pretty touch to this dish.

1. Arrange the shaved fennel, avocado balls, and diced apple on serving plates.

2. Whisk the next 5 ingredients together for a quick dressing. Drizzle half of it over the salads, about a teaspoonful each.

3. Brush the rest of the dressing on the shrimp and set your indoor grill on high. Grill the shrimp for about 1½ minutes per side.

4. Arrange the shrimp on the plates and serve.

Yields 8 ounces; serving size ⅓ ounce

Calories: 26.07
Protein: 1.03 grams
Carbohydrates: 0.31 grams
Sugar: 0.07 grams
Fat: 2.39 grams

4 ounces cooked shrimp
2 ounces unsalted butter at room temperature
2 tablespoons low-fat sugar-free mayonnaise
Juice from 1 lime
½ teaspoon Splenda
½ teaspoon cayenne pepper
½ teaspoon dill weed

Yields 4 servings; serving size ¼ pound shrimp

Calories: 433.21
Protein: 10.46 grams
Carbohydrates: 17.78 grams
Sugar: 5.07 grams
Fat: 37.78 grams

1 fennel bulb, shaved on a mandolin
2 avocados
1 green apple, peeled, cored, and diced
1 tablespoon lemon juice
3 tablespoons olive oil
4 tablespoons Basic Mayonnaise (page 238)
Salt and pepper to taste
1 teaspoon curry powder, or to taste
16 jumbo shrimp

Shrimp Crunch Filling for Ravioli

When you shop, look for noodles or dumpling wrappers that are clearly marked as sugar-free. Double this recipe and freeze enough for another meal. The next time you want ravioli, all you need to do is to put the pasta in a pot of boiling water for a few minutes.

1. Bring water to a boil on the stove. Cook shrimp in water for two minutes. Remove the shrimp and cool. Chop into fine pieces.

2. Place all ingredients but the dumpling wrappers and pasta sauce in your food processor and pulse to blend.

3. Set another pot of water on the stove to boil. Meanwhile, lay out the dumpling wrappers and spoon a bit of filling into the middle of each wrapper.

4. Fill a small bowl with cold water. Dip your finger in the water and dampen the perimeter of each ravioli. Fold each ravioli in half and press lightly to seal.

5. Gently slip the filled ravioli into the boiling water. As soon as they rise to the top, they are done. Serve with warm sauce.

Smashed Garlic

When you take the flat side of a knife and smash a garlic clove, the shell or covering comes right off, making it easier and faster to chop or mince. Garlic is an important aromatic herb that is also sugar-free and good for your arteries.

Yields 4 servings; serving size 4 ounces

Calories: 331.30
Protein: 15.65 grams
Carbohydrates: 37.82 grams
Sugar: 3.19 grams
Fat: 13.31 grams

16 medium shrimp
½ cup toasted walnuts, chopped
2 tablespoons fresh parsley, chopped
2 tablespoons fresh chives, chopped
1 egg, well beaten
Salt and pepper to taste
½ teaspoon Splenda
1 tablespoon Chili Sauce (page 240)
16 sugar-free Asian dumpling wrappers
1½ cups of your favorite sugar-free pasta sauce

Shrimp Scampi

Most Italians do not put Parmesan cheese over shrimp, but Americans do add it. Try a little on the side and see how you feel about it. Grinding your own cheese makes a difference; it tastes better.

༚

Yields 6 servings; serving size 4 ounces

Calories: 287.33
Protein: 27 grams
Carbohydrates: 24.31 grams
Sugar: 1.42 grams
Fat: 8.76 grams

1½ pounds jumbo shrimp in shell
¼ cup lemon juice
¼ cup water
2 teaspoons unsalted butter
2 tablespoons extra-virgin olive oil
4 cloves garlic, smashed
½ cup Italian flat-leaf parsley leaves, chopped
1 pound linguini or sugar-free baguette
Parmesan cheese for garnish (optional)

1. Peel the shrimp. Place the shrimp in the refrigerator. In a large saucepan, bring the shrimp shells, water, and lemon juice to a boil. Reduce heat and simmer for 20 minutes, covered. Strain and reserve broth.

2. Start a big pot of water for the linguini or begin toasting the bread.

3. Heat a large sauté pan and add the butter, oil, shrimp, and garlic. Cook very fast, turning until shrimp are done.

4. Remove the shrimp to a warm platter. Immediately add the parsley and shrimp shell broth to the pan.

5. When the linguini is cooked, drain it and pour into a bowl. Pour the shrimp and broth over the noodles. If serving on baguette, toast bread and pour shrimp over top.

Shrimp Salad with Tomatillos, Jicama, Grilled Peaches, and Chimichuri

With no mayonnaise, this summer lunch is less fattening and wonderful.

❧

1. Thaw the shrimp under cool running water. Drain and dry on paper towels. Mix shrimp with the tomatillos, jicama, green onions, and parsley or cilantro. Keep chilled.

2. Spray the top of the stove grill pan with nonstick spray and place over high heat. Grill the peaches. Turn when they sizzle.

3. Arrange the greens on serving plates. Spoon the shrimp salad over the greens. Tip a peach half against each salad. Spoon Chimichuri sauce over all.

Exciting Entrée Salads with Shrimp

Try making shrimp salad with chunks of fresh pineapple, tangerine, or coconut! Add some fresh ginger to mayonnaise and create a new dressing.

Yields 4 servings; serving size 4 ounces

Calories: 373.61
Protein: 19.23 grams
Carbohydrates: 21.31 grams
Sugar: 8.85 grams
Fat: 24.71 grams

1 pound frozen salad shrimp
4 tomatillos, peeled and chopped
1 cup jicama, peeled and cut in julienne
1 bunch green onions, trimmed and chopped
2 tablespoons cilantro or parsley, minced
2 large ripe peaches, halved
1 cup Chimichuri sauce
4 cups salad greens

Shrimp Stir-Fry with Broccoli and Almonds

*This recipe can be done as quick as a flash. Add different veggies,
such as carrots, cauliflower, or green onions.*

Yields 2 servings;
serving size 4 ounces

Calories: 579.39
Protein: 36.06 grams
Carbohydrates: 53.36 grams
Sugar: 3.09 grams
Fat: 24.16 grams

1 teaspoon olive oil
1 teaspoon Toasted Sesame
    Seed Oil (page 238)
1 clove garlic, minced
1 teaspoon fresh gingerroot,
    peeled and minced
½ cup slivered almonds
1 teaspoon Splenda
1 teaspoon red pepper flakes,
    or to taste
½ pound shrimp
1½ cups broccoli florets,
    blanched and drained
2 tablespoon soy sauce
1 tablespoon lemon juice
1½ cups cooked rice

1. Heat both oils in a wok or large frying pan over medium-high heat. Stir in the garlic, gingerroot, and almonds.

2. Cook and stir for 2–3 minutes. Add the Splenda and pepper flakes. Mix in all but the rice and stir until the shrimp turns pink.

3. Serve over the rice with extra soy sauce on the side.

Almond Trivia

Almonds are actually more closely related to peaches and cherries than they are to pecans and walnuts. They are the fruit of the almond tree; they have a hard coating that forms around the seed instead of the fleshy meat of an apple or apricot.

Boiled Lobster

For a sweet and delicious lobster, you need one that is very much alive prior to cooking. Never buy or cook a dead lobster. To measure its liveliness, take a knife tip and run it gently down the inside of the tail. The tail should flap wildly.

1. Place all ingredients but the lobster in a lobster pot, squeezing the lemon juice into the pot and adding the rinds to the mixture. Turn the burner on high heat and bring to a boil. Snip the bands off the claws of the lobsters. Holding the lid of the lobster pot like a shield, put one lobster in. When it stops flapping, quickly add the second.

2. Return to a boil and reduce heat to medium. Cook the lobsters for 15 minutes. Place on newspapers. Let cool slightly. Make an incision from the head to the end of the tail and remove the vein.

3. Serve with Hollandaise or melted butter.

Yields 2 servings; serving size ⅓ pound lobster

Calories: 399.85
Protein: 30.46 grams
Carbohydrates: 7.57 grams
Sugar: 1.29 grams
Fat: 27.77 grams

4 quarts water
½ cup white-wine vinegar
10 juniper berries
1 lemon, halved
1 tablespoon sea salt
1 teaspoon Splenda
10 black peppercorns, bruised
4 bay leaves
2 1¼-pound lobsters
½ cup Hollandaise sauce or 2 ounces melted butter
Extra lemon wedges for garnish

Lobster on the Grill

This is a lovely way to do lobster on the grill. The sauce is subtle enough but adds a great flavor. Have your fishmonger split the lobster, removing the bitter parts of the head and the intestine.

∽

Yields 2 servings; serving size one ¼ pound lobster

Calories: 197.03
Protein: 23.74 grams
Carbohydrates: 8.31 grams
Sugar: 3.68 grams
Fat: 7.88 grams

½ cup red wine vinegar
1 tablespoon Splenda
¼ cup freshly squeezed orange juice
Juice of ½ lemon
1 tablespoon olive oil
Salt and pepper to taste
1 teaspoon fennel seeds
2 1¼-pound lobsters, split lengthwise in their shell

1. Bring the first 7 ingredients to a boil in a small saucepan. Reduce for 4 minutes. Meanwhile, heat the grill to medium or prepare your coals.

2. Brush sauce on the cut sides of the split lobster and place them on the grill, cut side up. Close lid and let roast for 10 minutes, adding sauce every five minutes.

3. Turn and quickly grill cut side down. Serve immediately or chill and serve at a romantic picnic.

Lobster Is a Treat

Its deliciousness makes lobster a treat, but it's very expensive. Some people love the tails, while others eat nothing but the claws. The claws are very tender and sweet, and the tail meat is easier to get to and eat daintily. Claws are finger-food. When it comes to a sugar-free celebration, lobster cannot be beat!

Chapter 11
Clams, Oysters, and Mussels

Clam-Poached Cod 152

Cockles over Linguini 153

Steamed Clam Bellies with Lemon-Butter Sauce 154

Pan-Roasted Clams 155

Grilled Littleneck Clams

    with Homemade Barbecue Sauce 156

Clam Hash 156

Oysters on the Half-Shell

    with Bacon and Green Onions 157

Clam-Stuffed Tomatoes 157

Fried Oysters 158

Mussels with Tomato Balsamic-Vinegar Sauce 159

Steamed Mussels with Lemon Butter 160

Steamed Mussels with Fresh Tomatoes and Herbs . . . 161

Italian-Style Seafood Salad 162

Clam-Poached Cod

**Yields 2 servings;
serving size 4 ounces**

Calories: 189.39
Protein: 21.43 grams
Carbohydrates: 5.89 grams
Sugar: 1.02 grams
Fat: 9.52 grams

*½ pound codfish steaks, bone
in and skin on
Salt and pepper to taste
⅓ tablespoon unsalted butter
1 teaspoon olive oil
Juice and zest of ½ lemon
2 shallots, chopped
½ cup clam broth from a
bottle or dried packet
1 tablespoon Basic
Mayonnaise (page 238)
2 tablespoon fresh Italian
flat-leaf parsley, chopped*

*Cod is a large and versatile ocean-going lean fish.
It offers big, juicy flakes when properly cooked. Even in its
dried form, baccalà, it's still delicious when reconstituted.*

1. Rinse and dry the cod. Sprinkle with salt and pepper. Heat the butter and oil in a nonstick pan over high heat.

2. Sear the cod on both sides and reduce heat to a simmer. Add remaining ingredients and cover.

3. Simmer very slowly for 6–8 minutes. Serve with rice or pasta.

Poaching Tips

The lemon juice in this recipe does more than add flavor to this dish. The acid in the lemon juice neutralizes a chemical reaction between the fish's flavone pigment and the alkali in your pan. The reaction makes the fish turn an unappetizing yellow, but the addition of lemon juice or another acidic ingredient keeps the fish's flesh white.

Cockles over Linguini

*Cockles are very tiny clams, the size of a thumbnail.
When you can find a source of good fresh cockles, consider yourself
blessed! They are mild, not strong, and absolutely delicious. Serve with
a spoon for the juice and a tiny fork to get the little morsels out of the
shells. Also have a big bowl on the table to hold the empty shells.*

1. Heat the oil and butter in a large sauté pan over medium heat. Stir in the garlic and shallots. Cook until softened.

2. Add the clam broth, bring to a boil, and stir in the oregano and clams. Keep stirring, using a slotted spoon to remove the cockles to a large bowl as they open.

3. When all of the cockles are open, pour the sauce over them. Drain the pasta and serve in bowls. Spoon cockles over the linguini and sprinkle with parsley.

**Yields 2 servings;
serving size 3 ounces**

Calories: 531.24
Protein: 27.13 grams
Carbohydrates: 75.33 grams
Sugar: 3.16 grams
Fat: 15.39 grams

*2 teaspoons olive oil
1 teaspoon unsalted butter
2 cloves garlic, minced
4 shallots, minced
½ cup clam broth
1 teaspoon dried oregano
1½ pounds cockles, rinsed
    and scrubbed
½ pound cooked linguine
½ bunch fresh Italian flat-leaf
    parsley, chopped*

Cockles and Mussels, Alive, Alive–O

Cockles are finally becoming available in supermarket fish departments. You'll find yourself dining pleasurably and slowly when you prepare these tiny treats. All mollusks are an important part of a sugar-free diet. They are satisfying and have a slightly sweet flavor.

Steamed Clam Bellies with Lemon-Butter Sauce

**Yields 2 servings;
serving size 12 clams**

Calories: 337.39
Protein: 30.77 grams
Carbohydrates: 20.57 grams
Sugar: 3.49 grams
Fat: 14.02 grams

*3 quarts plus ½ cup cold
    water*
½ cup cornmeal
24 large soft-shell clams
4 ounces unsalted butter
Juice of ½ lemon

Clams are called bivalves because they have two valves, one to take in nutrients and another to expel them. However, they also take in sand. You can get rid of this by soaking them for about 35 minutes prior to cooking.

❧

1. Wash the clams under cold running water. Soak them in 3 quarts of water for 35 minutes. Make sure that their necks are fully retracted before cooking and that they are not cracked. Mix the cornmeal into the soaking water and add clams.

2. Heat ½ cup of water in a steamer or large pot. Add the clams and cook until they open. Using a slotted spoon, remove clams to a bowl and reserve juices.

3. Make sauce by heating the butter and lemon juice. Serve the clam juices and sauce in separate bowls on the side. Take clams out of their shells one at a time, dip first in clam broth and then in the butter sauce. Slurp! If you want to eat the neck, remove the black sheath and prepare to chew.

When in Doubt, Throw It Out!

If you have the slightest doubt abut the freshness and liveliness of any mollusk, throw it out! If the shell is open and won't close with repeated tapping, throw it out! If it's cracked, throw it out! Don't take a chance on eating something that's going to leave a bad taste in your mouth—or make you sick.

Pan-Roasted Clams

The sweetness for this dish comes from the homemade chili sauce and the cream. You probably can't make this without spending a fortune on calories, but it's a classic and worth it every once in a while!

࿇

1. Heat the clam broth in a large sauté pan over medium heat. Add butter and heat until melted. Add the clams.

2. Cook, stirring and shaking the pan over high heat until the clams just begin to open. Add the Chili Sauce.

3. Remove the opened clams to a bowl. Stir the cream into the pan and warm over very low heat. Do not boil or the cream will curdle.

4. Return the clams to the pan to warm in the sauce. Serve in their shells with the sauce poured over them.

Traditional Food

You may find yourself surrounded by fattening, sugar-rich traditional foods that you just can't help loving. Pick and choose your foods and eat a little bit of the treats you love—but eat them rarely. Experiment with sugar substitutes and try to reduce the sugar in your favorite dishes. Bring a sugar-free dish of your own to holiday gatherings so you're guaranteed to have something delicious to munch on.

Yields 2 servings; serving size 8 clams and ¼ cup sauce

Calories: 288.43
Protein: 20.47 grams
Carbohydrates: 8.04 grams
Sugar: 1.98 grams
Fat: 18.79 grams

¼ cup clam broth
2 tablespoons butter
16 littleneck clams, scrubbed and checked for liveliness
¼ cup Chili Sauce (page 240)
¼ cup light cream or heavy whipping cream, depending on your diet

Grilled Littleneck Clams
with Homemade Barbecue Sauce

**Yields 2 servings;
serving size 6 clams**

Calories: 150.61
Protein: 16.06 grams
Carbohydrates: 14.84 grams
Sugar: 1.71 grams
Fat: 2.61 grams

*12 1" littleneck clams, well
    scrubbed*
*⅔ cup sugar-free Barbecue
    Sauce (page 243)*
2 thick lemon wedges

*The clams should be tightly closed and pop open with the heat of the grill.
Be sure to scrub them thoroughly and test them for life by tapping them
together. If you hear a sharp click, they're alive. If you hear a dull thud, the
clam is probably dead. Discard any that are cracked or that won't close.*

1. Scrub and check clams. Preheat grill to high or wait until coals stop flaming. Place a piece of aluminum foil on the grill and arrange the clams on top. Close the lid.

2. As the clams open, spoon on plenty of barbecue sauce. Serve immediately with lemon wedges on the side.

Clam Hash

**Yields 4 servings;
serving size ⅔ cup**

Calories: 153.69
Protein: 13.36 grams
Carbohydrates: 19.97 grams
Sugar: 3.86 grams
Fat: 2.79 grams

*2 teaspoons unsalted butter
    plus extra*
*2 medium-sized Idaho or
    Yukon Gold potatoes,
    peeled and diced*
*½ cup Vidalia or other white
    onions, diced*
1 cup clam broth
*6 ounces clams, drained and
    minced, juice reserved*
*Freshly ground black pepper
    to taste*
½ cup Chili Sauce (page 240)

*Try this instead of corned beef or roast beef hash for brunch.
Clam lovers will be delighted. The sweetness comes from the potatoes
and homemade chili sauce served on the side.*

1. Heat the butter in a large sauté pan over medium heat. Add the potatoes and onions. Sauté until the onions have softened.

2. Add the broth and reduce heat to a simmer. Cover and cook until the potatoes are soft, about 15 minutes.

3. Using a potato masher or a fork, mash the mixture up a bit, then add the drained clams and plenty of pepper. Serve hot with homemade chili sauce on the side.

Oysters on the Half-Shell with Bacon and Green Onions

This is a luxurious treat. Oysters can be prepared without any sugar at all. They go well with spinach, cream, sugar-free mayonnaise, and good old lemon juice.

∽

1. Preheat the broiler to 425°F. Arrange the oysters on a metal tray.

2. Sprinkle with salt, pepper, lemon juice, green onions, and bread crumbs. Dot with bacon.

3. Run under hot broiler until bacon is crisp. Serve hot.

Yields 2 servings; serving size 4 oysters

Calories: 315.57
Protein: 7.99 grams
Carbohydrates: 8.81 grams
Sugar: 1.69 grams
Fat: 27.51 grams

8 oysters on the half shell, open
Salt and pepper to taste
4 tablespoons freshly squeezed lemon juice
4 green onions, peeled and minced
4 teaspoons sugar-free dry bread crumbs
4 slices smoked bacon, minced

Clam-Stuffed Tomatoes

This is a wonderful light lunch or first course at an elegant dinner party.

∽

1. Preheat the oven to 350°F. Wash the tomatoes and remove the tops. Scoop out the pulp and seeds. Place the tomato shells on a baking dish that you've prepared with nonstick spray.

2. Combine all ingredients except the Parmesan cheese. Stuff the tomatoes. Sprinkle the tops with Parmesan cheese.

3. Bake tomatoes for 30 minutes or until they are hot and the tops are lightly browned.

Yields 4 servings; serving size 2 stuffed tomatoes

Calories: 215.56
Protein: 17.98 grams
Carbohydrates: 27.03 grams
Sugar: 9.04 grams
Fat: 4.37 grams

8 medium-sized tomatoes
6 ounces clams, chopped
⅔ cup bread crumbs made with sugar-free French or Italian bread
1 teaspoon soy sauce
1 egg
½ teaspoon Splenda
1 tablespoon fresh lemon juice
Freshly ground black pepper to taste
4 teaspoons Parmesan cheese, grated

Fried Oysters

These are very crisp and you'll find the oil doesn't stick to the oysters if your oil is at the proper temperature (375°F). If you slow-fry them, they'll be loaded with oil. If you fast fry, they won't. Be sure to drain the oil on paper towels.

Yields 4 servings; serving size 6 oysters

Calories: 410.42
Protein: 8.54 grams
Carbohydrates: 27 grams
Sugar: 0.81 grams
Fat: 30.41 grams

24 freshly shucked oysters in their juice
1 egg, well beaten
2 tablespoons milk
½ cup whole-wheat flour
½ cup cornmeal
1 teaspoon salt
½ teaspoon pepper
1 teaspoon double-acting baking powder
¼ teaspoon nutmeg
½ teaspoon pepper
1 cup canola oil for frying

1. Set the oysters in a colander to drain. Beat the egg and milk together in a shallow bowl.

2. Put all of the dry ingredients in a paper bag and shake until combined. Turn out on a large piece of waxed paper. Dip the oysters in the egg-milk combination and roll them in the dry ingredients.

3. Bring the oil to 375°F in a heavy-bottomed frying pan. Set out plenty of paper towels.

4. Fry the oysters a few at a time until evenly brown.

5. Drain on paper towels and serve immediately with lemon wedges.

Frying Crisp

Whether you are frying oyster, shrimp, clams, or chicken, adding the baking powder to the coating is your secret weapon. It helps give the coating extra crunch. You can also add paprika, mace, or nutmeg to add to the flavor of your coating. To increase the heat, put a few drops of Tabasco sauce in the egg mixture.

Mussels with Tomato Balsamic-Vinegar Sauce

This sauce comes from an old friend who once had a fine Italian restaurant. It's hard to describe the taste of this fabulous concoction, but it's absolutely delicious and very much in order for a sugar-free diet. Serve it with whole-wheat pasta or whole-grain Italian bread.

1. In a large pan, sauté the garlic and onion in the oil until softened. Add the tomatoes and vinegar. Salt and pepper to taste.

2. Bring to a boil and reduce heat to a simmer. Cover partially and cook until you have 2 cups of sauce, stirring occasionally for about 60 minutes.

3. Heat ½ cup of water over high heat in another large pot. Add the mussels. Cook, stirring until they all are open. Remove the mussels to a large bowl as they open.

4. Pour hot sauce over each portion. Serve with hot crusty Italian bread or over pasta.

Yields 6 servings; serving size ½ pound mussels and 2 cups sauce

Calories: 252.14
Protein: 28.18 grams
Carbohydrates: 16.95 grams
Sugar: 8 grams
Fat: 7.54 grams

1 tablespoon olive oil
4 cloves garlic, chopped
½ cup sweet red or white onion, diced
3 cups sugar-free plum tomatoes, drained
Salt and pepper to taste
½ cup balsamic vinegar
3 pounds mussels in their shells, well scrubbed and checked for liveliness

Steamed Mussels with Lemon Butter

*You can eat these mussels with lemon and skip the butter
if you're watching your weight. Just serve them in their own
delicious broth laced with pepper and parsley.*

**Yields 4 servings;
serving size 4 mussels**

Calories: 198.76
Protein: 8.25 grams
Carbohydrates: 4.05 grams
Sugar: 1.62 grams
Fat: 16.95 grams

*2 pounds mussels, well
    scrubbed and checked for
    liveliness
½ cup dry white wine
½ cup unsalted butter
Juice of ½ lemon
½ teaspoon Dijon-Style
    Mustard (page 241)
¼ teaspoon freshly ground
    black pepper
Salt to taste
½ bunch Italian flat-leaf
    parsley, stemmed and
    chopped*

1. Heat a large pot over high heat. Place the mussels and white wine in the pot.

2. In a small bowl on the side, whisk the rest of the ingredients together to make a sauce.

3. Serve the mussels in large bowls with the sauce on the side. Reserve mussel liqueur for soup.

Seafood Broth

Freeze leftover broth and use it as a soup or sauce base for the next seafood dish you plan to make. Mussel broth is wonderfully delicate. Clam broth has a bit more bite. Shrimp-shell broth is another wonderful base for soups, stews, and sauces.

Steamed Mussels
with Fresh Tomatoes and Herbs

*Serve this dish alongside a light salad of mixed greens. Snip a teaspoon
or two of chives over the greens to unify the flavors of salad and entrée.*

⌇

1. Setting a pot over medium heat, combine everything but the mussels in a large stew pot. Cook and stir for 20 minutes until nice and thick.

2. Add the mussels and remove them to a large bowl as they open. Serve with whole-grain Italian bread or over pasta.

Selecting Mussels

If you ever get to go on a rustic beach vacation and can walk out on a breakwater to gather mussels, you can collect enough to eat for days. If you buy them in a fish market or supermarket, they will most likely be farm-raised and free of sand. Farm-raised mussels are ready to cook.

Yields 2 servings; serving size ½ pound mussels

Calories: 263.22
Protein: 29.42 grams
Carbohydrates: 18.54 grams
Sugar: 8.06 grams
Fat: 5.93 grams

4 Roma or plum tomatoes, stemmed and diced
2 cloves garlic
½ bunch Italian flat-leaf parsley, stemmed and chopped
1 tablespoon fresh oregano leaves or 1 teaspoon dried oregano
1 tablespoon fresh chives, snipped
¼ cup dry red wine
½ teaspoon Splenda
½ teaspoon red pepper flakes
Salt to taste
1 pound mussels in their shells, scrubbed and checked for liveliness

Italian-Style Seafood Salad

Cooking the seafood in the dressing is a wonderful technique. You'll double this delicious dish for a group, quadruple the recipe for a party, and love it every time you serve it.

⌇

1. Mix the first 6 ingredients in a blender. Transfer to a heavy nonreactive pot.

2. Bring to a boil. Stir in the mussels and clams. Cook and stir until the shells open. Add the shrimp and remove from the heat. Cool.

3. Sprinkle with salt and pepper. Either chill or serve at room temperature over greens.

Seafood and Citrus

You can substitute lime, grapefruit, or tangerine juice for lemon juice in many seafood recipes. Try variations to see what you like. You can also use various members of the onion family—shallots, leeks, or green onions—for any sweet onion in a seafood recipe.

Yields 4 servings; serving size ½ cup salad

Calories: 190.58
Protein: 9.43 grams
Carbohydrates: 3.95 grams
Sugar: 1.42 grams
Fat: 15.22 grams

¼ cup extra-virgin olive oil
2 tablespoons lemon juice
1 tablespoon Lucini Pinot Grigio vinegar
½ teaspoon Splenda
1 tablespoon fresh oregano leaves or 1 teaspoon dried oregano
1 teaspoon fresh garlic, minced
8 fresh mussels, well scrubbed
6 fresh littleneck clams, well scrubbed
4 raw shrimp, cleaned
Salt and pepper to taste
2 cups fresh baby greens

Chapter 12
Entrée Salads

Green Bean and Tuna Salad with Romaine Lettuce . . 164

Chicken, Apple, Celery, and Nut Salad. 165

Green Bean and Bacon Salad

    with Hot Gorgonzola Dressing 166

Grapefruit-and-Chicken Salad 167

Grilled Vegetable Salad 168

Curried Tart Apple and Rice Salad 169

Wild Rice Salad with Fruit and Nuts. 170

Lobster Salad 171

Greek-Style Mussel Salad. 172

Dilled Shrimp Salad with Cucumbers 173

Bloody Mary Tomato Aspic with Hard-Boiled Eggs. . . 174

Pink Tomato Aspic with Shrimp 175

Salad with Nuts and Cheese Chunks 176

Pasta Salad with Hot Peppers

    and Sweet Red Pepper Dressing 177

Broccoli and Pasta Salad 178

Pasta Salad with Shrimp and Snow Pea Pods 179

Warm Lentil Salad 180

Green Bean and Tuna Salad with Romaine Lettuce

Fresh tuna is best, but you can substitute canned tuna or vacuum bags of tuna.

࿇

**Yields 4 servings;
serving size 3 ounces
tuna, 4 ounces beans,
¼ head lettuce**

Calories: 261.43
Protein: 21.03 grams
Carbohydrates: 9.77 grams
Sugar: 4.23 grams
Fat: 14.99 grams

*¼ cup extra-virgin olive oil
2 tablespoons balsamic
    vinegar
1 tablespoon lemon juice
Salt and pepper to taste
½ teaspoon Splenda
12 ounces fresh tuna steak
1 head romaine lettuce,
    rinsed, trimmed, spun
    dry, and shredded
1 pound fresh green beans,
    trimmed, blanched, and
    chilled*

1. Whisk the olive oil, balsamic vinegar, lemon juice, salt, pepper, and Splenda together to make the dressing.

2. Brush the tuna with 1 teaspoon of the dressing. Grill at medium high heat for 3 minutes per side.

3. Place the lettuce on the serving plates. Add the beans and place the tuna on top. Drizzle with the dressing.

Luncheon Salads

A nice crisp salad with plenty of veggies, some protein, and a tiny bit of oil will carry you from lunchtime until teatime. Make plenty of dressing in advance. Your dressing will always be better than commercial, and you control the sweetness by regulating the amount of Splenda you add.

Chicken, Apple, Celery, and Nut Salad

*This very tasty version of a Waldorf salad tastes
just as good with thinly sliced deli turkey.*

ᴏⱱᴏ

1. Whisk the mayonnaise, lime, Dijon mustard, salt, and pepper together
   in a large bowl. Add the chicken, apple, celery, and walnuts, tossing to
   coat. Serve chilled over baby greens.

**Yields 4 servings;
serving size ½ cup**

Calories: 395.91
Protein: 13.54 grams
Carbohydrates: 9.01 grams
Sugar: 4.21 grams
Fat: 35.25 grams

¾ cup sugar-free Basic
 Mayonnaise (page 238)
Juice of ½ lime
½ teaspoon prepared Dijon
 mustard
Salt and pepper to taste
1 cup cooked chicken breast,
 diced
1 tart green apple, cored and
 chopped
2 stalks celery, chopped
½ cup walnut pieces, toasted
4 cups baby greens, rinsed
 and spun dry

Green Bean and Bacon Salad with Hot Gorgonzola Dressing

Be sure to use fresh—not frozen or canned—green beans.
You want them to be crunchy and crisp.

❧

Yields 4 servings;
serving size ⅔ cup

Calories: 221.23
Protein: 9.33 grams
Carbohydrates: 11.59 grams
Sugar: 5.68 grams
Fat: 15.37 grams

1 small head iceberg lettuce, outer leaves removed, quartered
1 pound green beans, trimmed, rinsed, and blanched
2 slices bacon, cooked
4 ounces Gorgonzola cheese, crumbled
2 tablespoons red wine vinegar
½ teaspoon Splenda

1. Divide the lettuce among the 4 serving plates. Arrange the beans on top. Crumble the bacon over each serving.

2. Mix the Gorgonzola, vinegar, and Splenda in a small bowl. Microwave for 30 seconds or until the cheese is melted. Spoon the melted cheese dressing over each salad.

Melting Cheese

Melting seems to enrich cheese flavor, making it even more delicious than eating it cool or at room temperature, which improves the flavor even more. Try melting it for salads for even more flavor.

Grapefruit-and-Chicken Salad

If you find the grapefruit too tart for your taste, add more Splenda.

∽

1. Whisk the grapefruit juice, olive oil, Splenda, rosemary, salt, and pepper together in a bowl to make dressing. Arrange the greens on serving plates.

2. Drizzle 2 teaspoons of dressing on the chicken. Grill the chicken over medium heat.

3. Slice the chicken and arrange it over the greens. Add the grapefruit sections and drizzle the rest of the dressing over the dish.

Selecting Grapefruit

Don't rely on a grapefruit's color to gauge its ripeness; grapefruit skins can have a greenish tint yet still be perfect on the inside. Pick a grapefruit that feels heavy for its size. The extra weight translates into extra juice. Avoid lumpy fruit; it's usually overripe.

Yields 2 servings; serving size ¾ cup salad greens, ½ grapefruit, and 4 ounces chicken

Calories: 251.46
Protein: 27.85 grams
Carbohydrates: 16.70 grams
Sugar: 13.51 grams
Fat: 8.46 grams

¼ cup fresh grapefruit juice, no sugar added
1 tablespoon olive oil
½ teaspoon Splenda
1 teaspoon fresh rosemary leaves
Salt and pepper to taste
2 cups mixed baby field greens
1 8-ounce boneless, skinless chicken breast, halved lengthwise
1 ruby red grapefruit, cut in sections

Grilled Vegetable Salad

This is a very Mediterranean dish. It's also very good for you and pretty to serve.
You can serve the grilled veggies over pasta instead of lettuce.

❧

Yields 6 servings;
serving size 1 cup

Calories: 163.33
Protein: 4.46 grams
Carbohydrates: 9.36 grams
Sugar: 4.77 grams
Fat: 13.10 grams

Salt and freshly ground
pepper to taste
½ cup olive oil
Juice of ½ lemon
3 Japanese eggplants, halved
4 medium zucchini, trimmed
and quartered lengthwise
2 yellow peppers, quartered
and cored, seeds and
membranes removed
6 plum tomatoes, cored and
halved lengthwise
½ cup freshly grated
Parmesan cheese
3 cups romaine lettuce
½ cup arugula
Lemon-Herb Dressing (page
244), to taste

1. Heat a grill to medium high. Salt and pepper the vegetables on both sides. Whisk the oil and lemon juice together and brush the vegetables on both sides.

2. Grill for about 3 minutes per side, looking for grill marks on the eggplant and zucchini. Sprinkle with cheese.

3. Serve over the greens. Dress the greens in Lemon-Herb Dressing if desired.

Grilling Vegetables

If you make a lot of vegetables, you can always make a great salad or pasta sauce. Try grilling vegetables with sprigs of fresh mint, basil, or oregano. This is ideal for a late summer treat when everything is in season and gardens are bursting.

Curried Tart Apple and Rice Salad

You can make large quantities of brown rice at a time and put aside the leftovers for breakfast with fruit and yogurt, quick lunches, or dinner sides.

⌀

1. Whisk the mayonnaise, curry powder, and lemon juice in a serving bowl. Add the apple, onion, rice, and nuts. Combine well. Serve at room temperature or chill.

Granny Smith

One of the world's most famous apple varieties, Granny Smiths are bright green and shiny. They are very juicy and have a slight tangy flavor. Granny Smiths were first cultivated in Australia in 1865 by Marie Ana Smith. They slowly made their way around the world, reaching the United States more than one hundred years after they were first cultivated.

Yields 4 servings; serving size ⅔ cup

Calories: 354.49
Protein: 5.05 grams
Carbohydrates: 25.90 grams
Sugar: 6.54 grams
Fat: 26.94 grams

⅔ cup sugar-free Basic Mayonnaise (page 238)
1 teaspoon Madras curry powder, or to taste
1 tablespoon lemon juice
2 large Granny Smith or other tart apples, peeled, cored, and chopped
½ cup red onion, finely chopped
2 cups cooked brown rice, chilled and fluffed with a fork
½ cup toasted pine nuts

Wild Rice Salad with Fruit and Nuts

Wild rice is a very healthful, freshwater grain. It's highly nutritious and good plain or hot with butter.

∾

Yields 4 servings; serving size 1 cup

Calories: 377.78
Protein: 7.61 grams
Carbohydrates: 22.59 grams
Sugar: 4.24 grams
Fat: 30.52 grams

½ cup raspberry vinegar
⅔ cup Basic Mayonnaise (page 238)
1 tablespoon fresh rosemary
Salt and pepper to taste
2 cups cooked wild rice, warmed
1 cup fresh raspberries
1 cup fresh or frozen peach slices, thawed if frozen
2 stalks celery, chopped
¾ cup chopped, toasted walnuts
2 cups Napa cabbage, trimmed, cored, and shredded

1. Whisk the vinegar, mayonnaise, rosemary, salt, and pepper together in a large serving bowl. Add the rice and fluff with a fork to coat.

2. Mix in the fruit, nuts, and celery. Mound the cabbage on serving plates and spoon the salad on top.

Wild Rice

Package directions usually underestimate the cooking time for wild rice. You may have to cook it for 60 minutes or more. You will know that it is done when it "blooms" from little spikes to tiny buds.

Lobster Salad

Most fish markets sell cooked lobster meat. It's expensive but not as much work as cooking and shelling your lobsters at home.

1. In a large bowl, whisk the mayonnaise, lime juice, curry powder, Dijon mustard, salt, pepper, and pineapple juice together.

2. Gently fold in the cooked lobster meat. Arrange the greens on serving plates.

3. Spoon the salad over the greens and garnish with peanuts.

Wine Pairings

You can't go wrong with a full-bodied Chardonnay to complement the delicate lobster and tangy greens in this recipe. Chardonnay is a stylish dry white wine. Dry wines generally have low concentrations of sugar—usually a few grams per liter—inevitably left over from the fermentation process.

Yields 4 servings; serving size ⅔ cup salad

Calories: 649.59
Protein: 28.12 grams
Carbohydrates: 10 grams
Sugar: 3.01 grams
Fat: 56.54 grams

1 cup Basic Mayonnaise (page 238)
Juice of ½ lime
1 teaspoon curry powder
1 teaspoon prepared homemade Dijon Mustard (page 241)
Salt and freshly ground pepper to taste
1 tablespoon concentrated unsweetened pineapple juice
1 pound cooked lobster meat
2 cups bitter greens, such as arugula or watercress, rinsed and dried on paper towels
½ cup roasted peanuts for garnish

Greek-Style Mussel Salad

This high-protein salad will provide a luscious dining experience. Serve it on your terrace or patio with a soft breeze cooling your face, and feel like you're in Greece.

Yields 4 servings; serving size 1 cup salad

Calories: 683.14
Protein: 43.97 grams
Carbohydrates: 22.23 grams
Sugar: 9.43 grams
Fat: 46.66 grams

Juice of 1 lemon
Zest of ½ lemon
⅔ cup extra-virgin olive oil
2 tablespoons fresh mint or 1 tablespoon dried mint
1 teaspoon dried oregano
2 cloves garlic, minced
1 teaspoon cracked coriander seeds
Salt and pepper to taste
1 raw egg
2 pounds fresh mussels, steamed, drained, and shelled
2 ripe tomatoes, rinsed, cored, and diced
½ bunch green onions, chopped
2 cups fresh romaine lettuce, rinsed, drained, and shredded
2 tablespoons capers
4 large sprigs Italian flat-leaf parsley for garnish

1. Purée the lemon juice, lemon zest, olive oil, mint, oregano, garlic, coriander, salt, pepper, and eggs in a blender. Pour them into a large bowl.

2. Stir in the mussels, tomatoes, and green onions. Chill or serve at room temperature over the greens with capers sprinkled on top. Decorate each serving with a sprig of parsley.

Mediterranean Food

You may find some of the most delicious dishes in the various coastal countries of this rich and life-filled sea. Use native Mediterranean ingredients that are grown here and enjoy the sunny flavors.

Dilled Shrimp Salad with Cucumbers

Shrimp salad is very versatile and easy to make. Frozen shrimp takes all the work out of making a great shrimp salad.

❧

1. Mix the dill, mayonnaise, yogurt, lemon, spices, and Worcestershire sauce together in a bowl. Add the cucumber and shrimp. Toss gently to coat with dressing.

2. Serve chilled over your favorite greens.

Dill and Seafood

Dill is a common accompaniment to seafood dishes. Serve the dressing for this recipe over baked or poached fish. It stands up to salmon and other flavorful seafood very well. The chilled dressing protects the flavor of the dill and allows it to interact with the seafood.

Yields 4 servings; serving size 1 cup salad

Calories: 329.29
Protein: 25.07 grams
Carbohydrates: 4.11 grams
Sugar: 1.60 grams
Fat: 23.51 grams

1 tablespoon fresh dill or 1 teaspoon dried dill
½ cup sugar-free Basic Mayonnaise (page 238)
¼ cup all-natural, sugar-free, low-fat yogurt
Juice of 1 lemon
Salt and pepper to taste
Red pepper flakes to taste
1 teaspoon sweet Hungarian paprika
1 teaspoon Worcestershire sauce or Asian fish sauce
½ English cucumber, rinsed and diced
1 pound of cooked shrimp, frozen and thawed is fine, fresh is better

Bloody Mary Tomato Aspic with Hard-Boiled Eggs

You can make this a day or two ahead for a very elegant lunch, or serve it as an appetizer or side dish for a larger meal. This is a very low calorie dish, and the only natural sugars are in the tomato juice.

⌇

Yields 8 servings; serving size ½ cup aspic, 2 teaspoons sauce

Calories: 63.18
Protein: 5.22 grams
Carbohydrates: 5.34 grams
Sugar: 3.72 grams
Fat: 2.75 grams

¼ cup cold water
½ ounces unflavored gelatin
1 cup boiling tomato juice with no added sugar
2 cups cold tomato juice with no added sugar
1 teaspoon soy sauce
½ teaspoon cayenne pepper, or to taste
Juice of ½ lime
1 teaspoon Splenda
1 teaspoon prepared horseradish
Salt and pepper to taste
4 hard-boiled eggs, peeled and halved
8 teaspoons low-fat sour cream for garnish

1. Place the cold water and gelatin in the bowl of a blender. Let bloom for 3 minutes. Start the motor and slowly add the hot tomato juice, then the cold tomato juice.

2. With the motor running, pour in the soy sauce, cayenne pepper, lime juice, Splenda, horseradish, salt, and pepper. Pour into a 4-cup mold.

3. Refrigerate for 45 minutes. Add the hard-boiled eggs. When firm, about 3 hours, turn out on a serving plate.

4. Spoon sour cream on each serving of this pretty salad.

Gel Is Great Fun

Aspics made with tomatoes and other veggies, plus eggs, chicken, or seafood, are wonderful! They are easy to make, can be prepared in advance, and make an elegant presentation. Rings can be stuffed with other salads to make a full-course lunch.

Pink Tomato Aspic with Shrimp

The low-fat sour cream gives the aspic a smooth, silky consistency. Using gelatin is a good way to add protein, and the tomato juice is delicious.

1. Place the cold water and gelatin in the bowl of a blender. Let bloom for 3 minutes. Start the motor and slowly add the hot tomato juice, then the cold tomato juice.

2. With the motor running, pour in the soy sauce, lemon juice, Splenda, and dill.

3. Add the sour cream and pulse. Pour into a 4-cup ring mold and add the shrimp, stirring to even the distribution of shrimp.

Yields 8 servings; serving size ½ cup

Calories: 58.70
Protein: 7.09 grams
Carbohydrates: 5.72 grams
Sugar: 3.66 grams
Fat: 1.28 grams

¼ cup cold water
½ ounce unflavored gelatin
½ cup boiling tomato juice with no added sugar
2 cups cold tomato juice with no added sugar
1 teaspoon soy sauce
Juice of ½ lemon
1 teaspoon Splenda
1 tablespoon chopped fresh dill or 1 teaspoon dried dill
½ cup low-fat sour cream
¾ cup cooked shrimp, chopped
Whole cooked shrimp for garnish (optional)

Salad with Nuts and Cheese Chunks

This salad could be considered "architectural" since you build it from the bottom up. When you layer flavors, you get a lot of interesting food.

დო

**Yields 4 servings;
serving size ¾ cup**

Calories: 479.31
Protein: 23.64 grams
Carbohydrates: 17.60 grams
Sugar: 6.94 grams
Fat: 36.72 grams

*2 cups mixed watercress and
    Boston lettuce
8 ounces Jarlsberg or other
    high-quality Swiss-style
    cheese, cubed
1 English cucumber, cut in
    spikes
2 medium carrots, peeled and
    cut in julienne strips
1 cup bean sprouts
1 yellow pepper, cored, seeds
    removed, and cut in
    match-stick size pieces
1 cup toasted walnut pieces
4 ounces of Lemon-Herb
    Dressing (page 244)*

1. On chilled individual serving plates, stack the ingredients in the order listed. Drizzle with dressing and serve.

Color Your Salads

The more colors you have in your salad, the healthier! Intensely colored fruits and vegetables are loaded with antioxidants. These will counteract anything that's unhealthy in your body and fight infection.

Pasta Salad with Hot Peppers and Sweet Red Pepper Dressing

Watercress and arugula are delicious bitter greens.

1. Heat the olive oil in a large sauté pan. Add the garlic, onion, and peppers. Cook until just slightly softened.

2. Stir in the vinegar, mayonnaise, salt, and pepper.

3. Add the whole wheat pasta and mix well. Place the greens on a serving platter and put the pasta salad on top.

Picking Peppers

Jalapeno and chipotle peppers are in the same genus as sweet bell peppers, despite the differences in taste and temperament! Look for peppers that are smooth, dry, and firm. If they feel light, leave them; they're probably dried out. Store fresh peppers loose in the refrigerator. Use them within a week.

**Yields 4 servings;
serving size ⅔ cup**

Calories: 316.76
Protein: 8.07 grams
Carbohydrates: 39.72 grams
Sugar: 3 grams
Fat: 15.81 grams

¼ cup olive oil
4 cloves garlic
1 red onion, finely chopped
4 jalapeño peppers, minced
2 chipotle peppers, minced
½ cup red wine vinegar
¼ cup Basic Mayonnaise
　　(page 238)
Salt and freshly ground
　　pepper to taste
⅔ pound small whole wheat
　　pasta, cooked
4 cups of your favorite bitter
　　greens

Broccoli and Pasta Salad

*If you dress the pasta and broccoli while still hot or warm,
they will take on a great deal of flavor from the dressing. Whole
grain pasta is better than regular because it's a complex carb.*

๛

**Yields 4 servings;
serving size ⅔ cup**

Calories: 338.48
Protein: 7.12 grams
Carbohydrates: 33.41 grams
Sugar: 2.17 grams
Fat: 21.06 grams

*Juice and zest of 1 lemon
2 tablespoons Pinot Grigio
    vinegar
½ cup olive oil
1 teaspoon Toasted Sesame
    Seed Oil (page 238)
1 teaspoon soy sauce
Salt and pepper to taste
1 teaspoon red pepper flakes,
    or to taste
1 teaspoon Splenda
⅔ cup Basic Mayonnaise
    (page 238)
1 pound of broccoli florets,
    rinsed and blanched
1 pound small whole wheat
    pasta, cooked*

1. Whisk the lemon juice and zest, vinegar, oils, soy sauce, spices, Splenda, and mayonnaise in a serving bowl. Stir in the broccoli and pasta. Chill and serve.

Blanched Vegetables

Dropping your green veggies in boiling water for a minute or two doesn't overcook them. If you shock them in icy water afterward, they will retain their beautiful color. Blanch 'em and shock 'em for vegetables that look as good as they taste.

Pasta Salad with Shrimp and Snow Pea Pods

This dish can be served hot, warm, or chilled. Shrimp supplies both protein and fat, and pasta provides carbs. The carbs are diluted by the shrimp and veggies.

⌒⌒

1. Heat the oil in a large pot over medium heat. Sauté the garlic for about 3 minutes. Add the shrimp and toss until pink.

2. Stir in the pea pods, pasta, mayonnaise, mustard, salt, pepper, juice, and capers. Serve, sprinkling dill over the top.

Snow Pea Pods

Snow pea pods are commonly used in Asian cooking. Blanch the pea pods briefly in boiling water to help them retain their vivid green color. Don't have snow peas? That's okay. Use green beans instead.

Yields 6 servings; serving size 1 cup

Calories: 454.35
Protein: 17.28 grams
Carbohydrates: 40.38 grams
Sugar: 3.82 grams
Fat: 24.78 grams

½ cup olive oil
4 cloves garlic, chopped
1 pound raw, cleaned shrimp
1 pound snow pea pods, washed and trimmed
1 pound curly pasta, cooked
⅔ cup Basic Mayonnaise, plus more to taste (page 238)
1 teaspoon Basic Mustard (page 241)
Juice of ½ lime
Salt and pepper to taste
2 teaspoons capers
4 springs fresh dill to garnish

Warm Lentil Salad

This is a hearty salad, high in fiber and rich in protein.
Aside from being good for you, it's inexpensive and delicious!

❧

Yields 6 servings;
serving size ¾ cup

Calories: 164.63
Protein: 8.84 grams
Carbohydrates: 22.94
   grams
Sugar: 3.97 grams
Fat: 5.02 grams

1 cup dry green lentils
1 onion, peeled and stuck
   with 3 whole cloves
1 clove garlic, unpeeled
3 cups water
2 tablespoons olive oil
½ cup sweet red onion,
   minced
¼ cup red wine vinegar
Salt and pepper to taste
½ pound grape tomatoes,
   rinsed
3 cups lettuce

1. Bring the lentils, onion, garlic, and water to a boil in a large saucepan. Reduce heat to low and cover. Simmer until tender, about 20–35 minutes.

2. Arrange the lettuce on salad plates. Discard the cooked onion and garlic. Drain the lentils and place in a bowl. Stir in the olive oil, red onion, vinegar, salt, pepper, and grape tomatoes. Serve on beds of lettuce

Various Bean Salads

Just as in the lentil salad, you can use chick peas, red kidney beans, and white beans to make delicious salads. If you cook the beans yourself, you can infuse them with many flavors, including onions, garlic, and spices. These beans, legumes, are excellent sources of protein and slowly digested carbs.

Chapter 13
Side Salads

*Editor's note: a side salad will have 4–5 ounces
of vegetables over about ¾ cup of greens

Tomatillo and Tomato Salad with Salsa Dressing. . . . 182

Avocado, Tomato, and Bacon over Bib Lettuce 183

Spinach, Pear, and Smoked Ham Salad 183

Pears and Walnuts over Mixed Greens. 184

Radicchio, Cucumber, and Gorgonzola Salad 185

Mozzarella, Caper, and Olive Salad 186

Arugula Salad with Asparagus. 186

Grapefruit and Romaine 187

Jicama, Mandarin Orange, and Arugula Salad 188

Red Salad 189

Cabbage Salad with Toasted Sesame Seeds. 190

Marinated Mushroom Salad 190

Tomato and Mozzarella Salad 191

Wild Rice Salad with Fresh Apricots

    and Water Chestnuts 192

Red Cabbage and Apple Salad 193

Tricolored Cole Slaw 193

Celeriac Slaw 194

Tomatillo and Tomato Salad with Salsa Dressing

*The mixture of salsa and mayonnaise makes a terrific dressing!
There are so many sugar-free dressings that you can make yourself.
Try different combinations, such as avocado and lime juice with a
tablespoon of homemade, sugar-free mayonnaise. Just keep playing
with your ingredients and you'll create some you really love.*

❧

1. Arrange the greens on serving plates. Mix the tomatillos, tomatoes, and onion in a bowl. Spoon over the greens.

2. Whisk the rest of the ingredients together and dress the salads.

Creating New Combinations

You can create unexpected combinations of fruits, vegetables, and dressing ingredients to add interest to your meals. Fruit is an excellent addition to many salads. Try using some of the dressings and salads as a base for grilled meat and fish.

**Yields 4 servings;
serving size ⅔ cup**

Calories: 153.32
Protein: 2.35 grams
Carbohydrates: 11.87 grams
Sugar: 5.76 grams
Fat: 11.80 grams

*2 cups fresh baby greens
4 tomatillos, peeled and
    chopped
2 large tomatoes, peeled and
    chopped
4 thin slices sweet red onion
½ cup Tomato Salsa (page
    250)
¼ cup Basic Mayonnaise
    (page 238)
Pepper to taste*

Avocado, Tomato, and Bacon over Bib Lettuce

*The sweetness is naturally in the vegetables and added to the dressing.
The capers add a nice Mediterranean touch.*

1. Arrange the lettuce on four plates. Stack the rest of the ingredients or arrange them artfully.

2. Dress and sprinkle with capers.

**Yields 4 small salads;
serving size about 5 ounces**

Calories: 219.25
Protein: 5.61 grams
Carbohydrates: 14.45 grams
Sugar: 4.21 grams
Fat: 18.25 grams

*2 strips crisp bacon, drained
2 small heads of bibb lettuce,
   cored, leaves separated,
   rinsed, and spun dry
2 avocados, halved, pits and
   skins removed, thinly
   sliced
2 medium tomatoes, cored
   and diced
½ cup Lemon-Herb Dressing
   (page 244)
1 tablespoon capers*

Spinach, Pear, and Smoked Ham Salad

*This salad is naturally just a bit sweet but not overpowering,
and the mayonnaise-lemon juice combo is delicious.*

1. Arrange the spinach on four plates. Sprinkle the diced pears over the spinach and add the ham.

2. Mix the mayonnaise and lemon juice together and drizzle over the salad. Garnish with toasted pecan pieces.

**Yields 4 servings;
serving size 1 cup**

Calories: 305.67
Protein: 7.09 grams
Carbohydrates: 18.10 grams
Sugar: 11.74 grams
Fat: 23.94 grams

*2 cups baby spinach
2 pears, unpeeled, cored, and
   diced
¼ pound smoked ham,
   shredded
½ cup Basic Mayonnaise
   (page 238)
2 tablespoons lemon juice
½ cup toasted pecan pieces
   for garnish (optional)*

Pears and Walnuts over Mixed Greens

*This classic side dish is perfect for a brunch, lunch, or a dinner side dish.
It's quite good with steak, chicken, or pork. Make sure the pears are
good and ripe, not hard, and the nuts are just crisply brown, not burned.
Nuts add nutrition to any salad and are very delicious.*

**Yields 4 servings;
serving size 5 ounces**

Calories: 436.38
Protein: 5.76 grams
Carbohydrates: 18.03 grams
Sugar: 11.62 grams
Fat: 39.93 grams

*2 ounces Roquefort or
    Gorgonzola cheese,
    crumbled
1 tablespoon red wine
    vinegar
½ cup olive oil
Freshly ground black pepper
2 large ripe Anjou pears,
    quartered, peeled, and
    cored
2 cups watercress
½ cup walnuts, toasted*

1. Whisk together the first 4 ingredients in a heavy bottomed saucepan over medium heat. As soon as the cheese melts, remove from the heat.

2. Prepare the pears and arrange the greens. Slice the pears over the greens. Drizzle with warm dressing. Sprinkle with walnuts and serve.

Toasted Nuts

All nuts improve in flavor with a quick run under the broiler or toasted in a nonstick sauté pan. However, you must watch them while cooking or they will burn in a blink of an eye.

Radicchio, Cucumber, and Gorgonzola Salad

*This is a colorful combination. It makes an excellent side with
fish or shellfish. It's is also sugar-free, healthy, and delicious!
You can garnish with nuts or fresh herbs from your garden.*

1. Whisk the first 4 ingredients together. Spoon over the cucumbers. Marinate for 2 hours.

2. Spoon over the shredded radicchio and sprinkle with Gorgonzola cheese.

Cheese Topped Salads

*Adding cheese to a salad is all about contrasting the soft with the sharp.
Add a sharp blue cheese to a soft flavor, such as a pear or peach, or add
a soft cheese flavor, such as Jarlsberg, to a lemony dressing.*

**Yields 4 servings;
serving size 1 cup,
loosely arranged**

Calories: 358.43
Protein: 6.04 grams
Carbohydrates: 7.07 grams
Sugar: 3.27 grams
Fat: 35.78 grams

½ cup cider vinegar
½ cup Basic Mayonnaise
   (page 238)
1 teaspoon Splenda
Salt and pepper to taste
8" English, seedless cucumber,
   thinly sliced
2 heads of radicchio,
   shredded
½ cup Gorgonzola cheese,
   crumbled
1 tablespoon fresh herbs for
   garnish
½ cup toasted walnuts,
   pecans, or pine nuts for
   garnish

Mozzarella, Caper, and Olive Salad

Skip the lettuce and serve this as an antipasto. The natural sugar in the cheese is the only sugar you have to deal with, and that's healthful!

Yields 4 servings;
serving size 4 ounces

Calories: 136.50
Protein: 4.65 grams
Carbohydrates: 3.50 grams
Sugar: 0.17 grams
Fat: 12.19 grams

2 cups lettuce, shredded
4 ounces Sicilian black olives,
   pitted and chopped
2 ounces buffalo mozzarella,
   cut in chunks
¼ cup parsley, chopped
2 teaspoons capers
4 teaspoons olive oil
4 lemon wedges
4 anchovies for garnish
   (optional)

1. Place the lettuce on chilled plates. Divide the rest of the ingredients among the servings.

2. Drizzle with oil and add anchovies if desired.

Arugula Salad with Asparagus

This is a very healthful and delicious side salad.

Yields 4 servings; serving
size ½ cup asparagus
over ½ cup greens

Calories: 135.87
Protein: 3.06 grams
Carbohydrates: 6.72 grams
Sugar: 2.89 grams
Fat: 11.03 grams

1 pound of asparagus, tough
   stems removed, cut in 1"
   pieces
Juice of ½ lemon
2 cups chilled arugula
4 tablespoons Basic
   Mayonnaise (page 238)

1. Bring a saucepan of water to a boil. Boil the asparagus for 2 minutes. Drop the asparagus in a bowl of ice water. Drain.

2. Sprinkle asparagus with lemon juice. Place on the beds of arugula. Spoon the mayonnaise on top of each serving.

Grapefruit and Romaine

This is a very light salad, great when you are serving a rich course for brunch. Try it as a side with grilled salmon for a refreshing sugar-free addition to a menu. You can substitute ugli fruit or kiwifruit for the grapefruit and have a delightful side.

❧

1. Place grapefruit sections in a bowl. Sprinkle with Splenda and mint leaves.

2. Arrange the greens on serving plates. Place the grapefruit sections over the greens.

3. Whisk the grapefruit juice and oil together. Add salt and pepper. Drizzle over salads, sprinkle with nuts, and serve.

Grapefruit Skins

Save your grapefruit skin; it may help you manage your heartburn. Use a vegetable peeler to peel the grapefruit skin. Spread the grapefruit strips on a flat surface to dry. When you feel your heartburn starting to act up, chew on the strips of dried grapefruit skin.

Yields 2 servings; serving size ½ cup grapefruit and ½ cup lettuce

Calories: 284.93
Protein: 5.14 grams
Carbohydrates: 19.44 grams
Sugar: 14.11 grams
Fat: 22.85 grams

1 ruby red grapefruit, peeled and cut in sections
1 teaspoon Splenda
1 tablespoon fresh mint leaves, shredded
¼ cup freshly squeezed grapefruit juice
2 tablespoons olive oil
Salt and pepper to taste
1 cup romaine lettuce, shredded
¼ cup slivered almonds, toasted

Jicama, Mandarin Orange, and Arugula Salad

Yields 4 servings; serving size 6 ounces jicama and oranges plus dressing

Calories: 87.64
Protein: 1.34 grams
Carbohydrates: 13.20 grams
Sugar: 7.82 grams
Fat: 3.52 grams

1 6-ounce jicama tuber, peeled and julienned
Juice of ½ lemon
Salt and freshly ground black pepper to taste
2 teaspoons fresh rosemary, finely chopped
2 teaspoons fresh Italian flat-leaf parsley
1 tablespoon olive oil
1 cup canned mandarin oranges, no sugar added, drained and chilled
2 cups arugula leaves, stemmed and arranged on plates

Jicama is a wonderful tuber, a bit like a potato but of finer, firmer texture and much sweeter. It can be cooked, but it's absolutely lovely raw in salads or as a garnish, shredded over soups. It adds a great deal of crunch to any dish, salad, or soup or as a cocktail snack on toast.

1. Place the jicama in a large bowl. In a small bowl, whisk the lemon juice, salt, pepper, herbs, and olive oil together.

2. Add the oranges to the jicama and pour dressing over them.

3. Arrange the leaves on plates and spoon dressed jicama and orange over the top.

The Fruit Part of a Salad

Add grapes, bananas, avocados, melon balls, pears, and apples in any combination to salads. These additions add fiber, flavor, and natural complex sugars. Try adding carrots, grapes, melon balls, and orange to a green salad.

Red Salad

Expert nutritionists and food scientists say the more color in your food, the better it is for you. This recipe is full of great color and flavor.

1. Whirl the first 6 ingredients in your blender.

2. Arrange the red lettuce on serving plates. Add the dilled beets, radishes, and onions. Spoon the dressing over the salads.

Roasted Beets

It's easy to roast beets without peeling them. Wash them and wrap them in aluminum foil, add a bit of water, close the foil, and roast at 400°F. Baby beets take about 30-40 minutes to roast; larger ones will take 10-15 minutes longer. Let them cool and simply slide off the skins. A small amount of red or golden beets is acceptable for a sugar-free diet.

Yields 6 servings; serving size ⅓ cup vegetables over 1 cup red leaf lettuce

Calories: 196.92
Protein: 1.70 grams
Carbohydrates: 8.24 grams
Sugar: 4.08 grams
Fat: 18.35 grams

¼ cup red wine vinegar
1 teaspoon Splenda
½ cup olive oil
1 teaspoon dried thyme or 1 tablespoon fresh thyme
1 teaspoon horseradish
Salt and freshly ground pepper to taste
12 small red beets, roasted, skins peeled off, sliced
18 radishes, thinly sliced
1 red onion, thinly sliced
6 cups red leaf lettuce, rinsed, drained, and torn in small pieces

Cabbage Salad with Toasted Sesame Seeds

*Try this instead of coleslaw or as a side to any Asian meal.
It tastes great with lobster or shrimp.*

Yields 6 servings; serving size 4–5 ounces

Calories: 323.42
Protein: 2.50 grams
Carbohydrates: 4.90 grams
Sugar: 0.23 grams
Fat: 33.66 grams

*1 cup Basic Mayonnaise
 (page 238)
3 tablespoons toasted
 sesame seeds
1 tablespoon Toasted Sesame
 Seed Oil (page 238)
1 tablespoon soy sauce
1 tablespoon lemon juice
1 head Napa cabbage, cored,
 rinsed, drained, and
 shredded*

1. Whisk the first 5 ingredients together in a small bowl.

2. Fill a big bowl with cabbage, pour dressing over it, toss, and serve.

Marinated Mushroom Salad

*Marinated mushrooms can be made in many forms.
Marinate huge Portobellos for use in sandwiches, over steaks,
or with melted cheese. Mushrooms are an excellent source of
fiber and complex carbs and are absolutely sugar-free!*

Yields 6 servings; serving size ½ cup mushrooms and onions, served over greens

Calories: 30.41
Protein: 1.83 grams
Carbohydrates: 6.25 grams
Sugar: 1.92 grams
Fat: 0.42 grams

*1 cup Lemon-Herb Dressing
 (page 244)
2 cups tiny button
 mushrooms
½ sweet white onion, minced
3 cups chopped romaine
 lettuce
2 teaspoons coriander seeds,
 crushed or ground
1 cup Italian flat-leaf parsley,
 stemmed and chopped*

1. Heat the dressing in a sauté pan over medium heat. Put the mushrooms in a bowl and pour the hot dressing over them. Add the onion and coriander. Marinate for 2 hours.

2. Chill the plates. Add lettuce. Just before serving, sprinkle the mushroom mixture with parsley and spoon over lettuce.

Tomato and Mozzarella Salad

This is a classic Italian dish. It's also good served on sliced sugar-free baguettes as a snack. It's even better with buffalo mozzarella, but the fat content is much higher than regular American mozzarella or low-fat mozzarella.

Yields 2 servings; serving size 3 ounces

Calories: 131.72
Protein: 7.11 grams
Carbohydrates: 7.36 grams
Sugar: 3.59 grams
Fat: 8.91 grams

4 slices ¼ inch thick fresh mozzarella cheese
4 Roma tomatoes, sliced
1 cup fresh basil leaves, rinsed and torn in small pieces
4 teaspoon red wine vinegar
Salt and freshly ground pepper to taste
1 teaspoon olive oil

1. Assemble the ingredients in the order listed, stacking the cheese on top of the tomatoes. Add vinegar, salt, pepper, and basil with a final drizzle of oil.

Shredding Vegetables

There is a food processor attachment that spins on top of the jar, shredding cabbage, carrots, and other raw vegetables. You can shred a whole head of cabbage in seconds. Simply cut it in quarters, remove the outside leaves, and press it down the tube. A densely packed, ¼ pound head of cabbage may give you 2 cups of shredded cabbage.

Wild Rice Salad with Fresh Apricots and Water Chestnuts

Yields 4 servings; serving size 6 ounces

Calories: 231.34
Protein: 4.07 grams
Carbohydrates: 24.44 grams
Sugar: 4.10 grams
Fat: 14.03 grams

2 cups cooked wild rice
4 unskinned apricots, rinsed, pitted, and cut up
½ cup canned water chestnuts, rinsed, dried, and sliced
⅓ cup raspberry vinegar
¼ cup fresh chopped parsley leaves
1 tablespoon fresh rosemary leaves or 1 teaspoon dried rosemary
1 teaspoon Splenda
¼ cup olive oil
Salt and pepper to taste

This is an aromatic salad that works well with turkey, goose, or pork. Look for contrasting textures and add crunchy veggies and nuts whenever possible instead of adding Splenda to sugar-free dishes.

1. Mix the rice, apricots, and water chestnuts in a serving bowl. Whisk the rest of the ingredients together and pour over the rice, apricots, and water chestnuts.

2. Chill or serve at room temperature.

Apricots

Apricots have one seed in a hard shell. The skin is not fuzzy but can be spotty in appearance. The fruit is soft and easy to eat. Apricots can range in size from small golf ball-sized fruits to larger tennis ball-sized ones.

Red Cabbage and Apple Salad

This salad improves with age. Make it the day before so the flavors can mature and "marry."

✧

1. Mix the cabbage, onions, and apple. Whisk the rest of the ingredients together and pour over the cabbage, onions, and apple.

2. Toss and let rest in the refrigerator, covered for at least 60 minutes.

Yields 4 servings; serving size 4 ounces

Calories: 146.60
Protein: 2.12 grams
Carbohydrates: 16.93 grams
Sugar: 11.56 grams
Fat: 9.18 grams

1 head red cabbage, cored and shredded
½ sweet white onion, sliced paper thin
2 crisp unskinned Macintosh apples, cored and diced
1 teaspoon Splenda
½ cup red wine vinegar
¼ cup olive oil
Salt and fresh pepper to taste
1 teaspoon caraway seeds (optional)

Tricolored Cole Slaw

This is a very healthful dish. Cabbages have a great deal of antioxidants in them, which help you to resist cancer. Remember to eat colorful foods for health. And, cabbage is in the cruciferous family, which is full of cancer-preventing antioxidants.

✧

1. In a large bowl, mix the first 4 ingredients evenly. Whisk the mayonnaise and vinegar together and dress the salad. Add pepper to taste.

Yields 6 servings; serving size ⅔ cup

Calories: 286.31
Protein: 1.26 grams
Carbohydrates: 6.14 grams
Sugar: 3.10 grams
Fat: 29.30 grams

1 cup shredded red cabbage
1 cup shredded Napa cabbage
2 large carrots, peeled and shredded
½ cup Vidalia or other sweet white onion
1 cup Basic Mayonnaise (page 238)
2 tablespoons cider vinegar
Freshly ground black pepper to taste

Celeriac Slaw

*The French love celeriac, and it's more and more readily available here.
It's an excellent and very tasty sandwich additive to a slice of ham or turkey.*

ᴏⅡᴏ

**Yields 4 servings;
serving size ¼ cup**

Calories: 248.32
Protein: 1.43 grams
Carbohydrates: 10.58 grams
Sugar: 1.11 grams
Fat: 22.86 grams

*1 celery root, peeled and
    slivered
½ teaspoon salt and freshly
    ground pepper to taste
½ cup Basic Mayonnaise
    (page 238)
2 tablespoons cider vinegar
½ teaspoon Splenda
¼ teaspoon celery seeds
12 thin slices sugar-free
    baguette, toasted*

1. Place the grated celeriac in a bowl and sprinkle with salt and pepper. Whisk the rest of the ingredients together and dress. Serve on toasted baguette, crackers, or over lettuce.

Salads for Weight Control

There is nothing like a big salad to fill you up. The trick is to use little or light dressing. Dressings with lots of oil, cheese, and sour cream will negate the progress you make with fiber and vegetables.

Chapter 14
Vegetables

Tuna-Stuffed Artichokes 196

Artichokes with Lemon Dipping Sauce 197

Asparagus with Chopped-Egg Sauce 197

Broccoli Stir-Fry 198

Eggplant Rolls 199

Eggplant Soufflé 200

Eggplant, Tomatoes, and Peppers 201

Baked Yellow and Green Squash,

   Dressed in Herbs with Crumb Topping 202

Baked Stuffed Mushrooms 203

Baked Stuffed Tomatoes with Herbs and Cashews . . . 204

Spinach-Stuffed Yellow Tomatoes 205

Kohlrabi with Lemon 206

Fennel with Orange Slices 207

Sauerkraut with Apples and Ham 208

Pumpkin Soufflé 208

Tuna-Stuffed Artichokes

Yields 4 servings;
serving size 1½ ounces
tuna and 1 artichoke

Calories: 212.40
Protein: 15.46 grams
Carbohydrates: 14.82 grams
Sugar: 1.53 grams
Fat: 11.58 grams

4 artichokes
4 quarts water
6 ounce can tuna, well
    drained
½ cup fresh Italian flat-leaf
    parsley, chopped
1 tablespoon capers
4 tablespoons Basic
    Mayonnaise (page 238)
1 tablespoon lemon juice
½ teaspoon Splenda
Salt and freshly ground black
    pepper to taste

This makes an excellent lunch for a hot day. Serve with a cold soup and you can include a pasta or rice salad to round out a satisfying and sugar-free meal.

⌒

1. Trim any discolored leaves off the artichokes. Cut off the base of the stem. Cut off the very top of each artichoke. Boil in water for 18–20 minutes.

2. Cut the stem off the artichoke. Spread leaves open and, using a grapefruit spoon or melon baller, remove the choke, leaving leaves attached to the base.

3. Mix the rest of the ingredients together. Work the tuna in between the leaves and in the hole where the choke was.

Italian Flat-Leaf vs. Curly Parsley

Both varieties of parsley are quite good, but the Italian flat-leaf has a sharper flavor. It's more peppery and makes a really great garnish or aromatic herb. Curly parsley has a different texture and a less distinct flavor. Experiment with both and decide for yourself which you prefer.

Artichokes with Lemon Dipping Sauce

This is one of the best dipping sauces you'll ever find. When you are cooking the artichokes, you'll know they are done when an outside leaf pulls off easily.

✒

1. Trim any discolored leaves off the artichokes. Cut off the base of the stem. Cut off the very top of each artichoke. Boil in water with coriander for 18–20 minutes.

2. Whirl the lemon juice and egg in your blender. Slowly pour in the melted butter, olive oil, Splenda, salt, and paprika.

3. Serve the artichokes hot or at room temperature with the sauce on the side.

Yields 4 servings; serving size 1 artichoke

Calories: 310.98
Protein: 5.84 grams
Carbohydrates: 21.31 grams
Sugar: 1.98 grams
Fat: 26.93 grams

4 globe artichokes, trimmed
4 quarts water
1 teaspoon ground coriander seeds
Juice of 1 lemon
1 whole egg
¼ cup unsalted butter, melted
¼ cup extra-virgin olive oil
½ cup Splenda
½ teaspoon salt
½ teaspoon paprika

Asparagus with Chopped-Egg Sauce

This is a very special side that goes extremely well with fish or shellfish. Add an extra egg and serve it on whole-wheat English muffins for lunch.

✒

1. Mix the first 8 ingredients in a small bowl. Steam the asparagus for 5 minutes. Shock it, drain it, and place on a serving plate.

2. Arrange asparagus on a platter and drizzle sauce over it. Serve hot or at room temperature.

Yields 4 servings; serving size ¼ pound of asparagus

Calories: 154.75
Protein: 4.98 grams
Carbohydrates: 6.53 grams
Sugar: 2.94 grams
Fat: 12.16 grams

4 tablespoons Basic Mayonnaise (page 238)
1 tablespoon Pinot Grigio vinegar
¼ cup chopped parsley
1 teaspoon Splenda
1 teaspoon lemon zest
Salt and pepper to taste
1 whole egg and 1 egg white, hard-boiled and chopped
4 green onions, chopped
1 pound asparagus, ends trimmed

Broccoli Stir-Fry

Yields 4 servings; serving size 5 ounces

Calories: 293.19
Protein: 11.81 grams
Carbohydrates: 12.57 grams
Sugar: 3.43 grams
Fat: 21.12 grams

1 pound broccoli florets, stems removed
2 tablespoons olive oil
1 tablespoon Toasted Sesame Seed Oil (page 238)
2 cloves garlic, chopped
2 shallots, chopped
4 ounces of chorizo, chopped
8 ounces shiitake mushrooms, cleaned and stemmed
2 tablespoons lemon juice
2 tablespoons soy sauce
Freshly ground black pepper to taste

Broccoli is an excellent source of fiber and vitamins, which act as protective antioxidants. Every weekly menu should include two or more servings of broccoli, whether you are eating sugar-free or simply want to be healthy.

1. Drop the broccoli into a pot of boiling salted water. Blanch for 3 minutes, shock in cold water, and drain and dry on paper towels.

2. Place a wok over medium high heat. Add both oils, garlic, shallots, chorizo, and mushrooms. Cook, stirring for 5 minutes.

3. Return the broccoli to the pan and continue to stir-fry for another 3–5 minutes. Sprinkle with lemon juice and soy sauce. Serve with plenty of freshly ground black pepper.

Salt vs. Soy

Soy sauce is a fine substitute for salt. You do not need to use any salt when you are using soy. You can also use herbs, such as oregano or borage, as salt substitutes. Soy sauce also has sugar, so whenever possible use tamari or sugar-free soy sauce.

Eggplant Rolls

Eggplant is an excellent vegetable popular around the Mediterranean.
They come in many varieties, from white miniature eggplants
to the traditional purple egg-shaped vegetable. They all contain
complex carbs and are excellent for a sugar-free diet.

1. Preheat the oven to 350°F. In a bowl, whisk together the first 5 ingredients. Set aside.

2. Place the eggplant slices on a piece of parchment paper. Spray both sides with olive oil. Bake for 5–8 minutes.

3. Cool slightly and spread a spoonful of the cheese mixture on each. Roll.

4. Place in a baking dish that you have prepared with nonstick spray. Cover with tomato sauce. Bake for 30 minutes. Serve.

Yields 6 servings;
serving size 2 rolls

Calories: 175.05
Protein: 9.28 grams
Carbohydrates: 13.77 grams
Sugar: 5.48 grams
Fat: 10.07 grams

1 cup low-fat ricotta cheese
1 egg
¼ cup Parmesan cheese
1 teaspoon dried oregano
⅛ teaspoon or a good
grinding of black pepper
2 medium eggplants, thinly
sliced
2 tablespoons olive oil in a
spray container
1 cup sugar-free tomato
sauce

Eggplant Soufflé

If you don't like eggplant, you've never had it prepared like this! The flavor combination is lovely and the texture very much like a soufflé. You can add various cheeses to the recipe in small quantities to give it a spike of protein.

ᴄᴠᴏ

Yields 4 servings; serving size 3 tablespoons

Calories: 133.70
Protein: 7.11 grams
Carbohydrates: 13.99 grams
Sugar: 6.66 grams
Fat: 6.30 grams

1 medium eggplant, peeled
   and cubed
1 teaspoon salt
1 tablespoon olive oil
1 clove garlic
½ cup sweet white onion,
   diced
1 teaspoon dried oregano
1 teaspoon dried basil
Juice of ½ lemon
½ teaspoon salt
Freshly ground black pepper
   to taste
2 egg yolks
4 egg whites, beaten stiff
½ cup sugar-free tomato
   sauce

1. In a large bowl, sprinkle the cubed eggplant with salt. Let rest for 20 minutes and then squeeze out the liquid using paper towels or linen kitchen towels.

2. Preheat oven to 400°F. Prepare a 1 quart soufflé dish with nonstick cooking spray. Heat the olive oil in a nonstick sauté pan over medium flame. Sauté the eggplant, garlic, and onion.

3. Remove from the heat and place in a food processor. Add the oregano, basil, and lemon juice, and pulse. Add the salt, pepper, and egg yolks. Pulse until smooth.

4. Pour into the soufflé dish. Fold in egg whites. Bake for 35–40 minutes or until puffed and golden. Serve with warm tomato sauce.

Eggplant

Soak or salt exceptionally large eggplants to reduce the bitterness. Larger eggplants tend to be more bitter than smaller ones. The tiny white, mauve, and purple ones are always sweet. They are too young to get bitter—just like other babies.

Eggplant, Tomatoes, and Peppers

You can serve this recipe as a side dish, as an hors d'oeuvre, or over salad greens. You can also spoon it onto hot pasta for a nutritious lunch or supper. Mixing the sweet-tasting vegetables with the aromatic ones creates a wonderful balance of flavors.

1. Heat the olive oil in a large sauté or frying pan over medium high heat. Add the eggplant, stirring constantly.

2. Every 2 minutes stir in the next ingredient. Cover, reduce heat to low, and cook for 10 minutes.

All in the Family

Eggplants, tomatoes, and peppers are clearly related to each other. They are all members of the nightshade family. Colonial Americans and Europeans were originally suspicious of tomatoes and believed they were poisonous. Eggplants, also known as aubergines, have a slightly bitter taste that can be countered by sprinkling salt over the meat of the eggplant.

Yields 6 servings; serving size 1 eggplant

Calories: 99.87
Protein: 2.02 grams
Carbohydrates: 13.87 grams
Sugar: 7.45 grams
Fat: 5.09 grams

2 tablespoons olive oil
6 tiny eggplants, stemmed and diced
3 cloves garlic, chopped
1 medium-sized red onion, chopped
1 sweet red bell pepper, stemmed, seeded, and chopped
1 sweet green bell pepper, stemmed, seeded, and chopped
1 tablespoon capers
4 medium-sized plum tomatoes, stemmed and chopped
1 teaspoon Splenda
1 teaspoon salt
20 basil leaves, rinsed and torn
1 teaspoon dried oregano
1 teaspoon red pepper flakes

Baked Yellow and Green Squash, Dressed in Herbs with Crumb Topping

Yields 4 servings;
serving size ⅔ cup

Calories: 278.89
Protein: 5.08 grams
Carbohydrates: 21.38 grams
Sugar: 4.31 grams
Fat: 19.86 grams

*1 teaspoon dried oregano
leaves*
*1 teaspoon dried rosemary
leaves*
½ cup unsalted butter, melted
Juice of ½ lemon
*1 teaspoon salt and freshly
ground black pepper to
taste*
*1 sweet red onion, thinly
sliced*
*1 large zucchini, ends
removed, sliced ¼ inch
thick*
*1 large yellow squash, ends
removed, sliced ¼ inch
thick*
*1 cup sugar-free bread
crumbs*

*This dish is as pretty as it is good for you. You can add to the
protein by putting a layer of white American or grated
Fontina cheese in between the layers of squash.*

⌒〰⌒

1. Preheat the oven to 350°F. Prepare a disposable bread tin with nonstick spray.

2. Whisk the oregano and rosemary into the butter. Add lemon juice, salt, and pepper.

3. Layer the squash and onion in a baking dish. Sprinkle each layer with the melted butter and some bread crumbs.

4. When you get to the top, sprinkle with remaining bread crumbs and add the rest of the melted butter. Bake for 35 minutes.

Mix It Up

You can bake, steam, or sauté many different vegetables. Don't be afraid of adding some colorful peppers, a tomato or two, and some onions to just about any vegetable dish. Use whatever you have fresh and in season.

Baked Stuffed Mushrooms

This makes a delicious side, appetizer, or luncheon entrée. Salt and pepper have been omitted because the pepperoni has plenty of both.

༄

1. Preheat the oven to 350°F. Brush the mushrooms clean and place them on a baking sheet over parchment paper. Reserve the chopped stems.

2. Heat the olive oil in a large sauté pan over medium flame. Stir in the garlic, celery, shallots, parsley, and oregano.

3. Cook, stirring constantly. Add the chopped mushroom stems. Mix in the rest of the ingredients, moistening with the broth.

4. Pile stuffing into the mushroom caps, about 1 heaping tablespoon of filling per mushroom, and bake for 25 minutes. Serve hot or at room temperature.

Yields 12 mushrooms; serving size 3 mushrooms

Calories: 339.54
Protein: 11.08 grams
Carbohydrates: 24.64 grams
Sugar: 2.85 grams
Fat: 21.98 grams

12 white or brown mushrooms, stems trimmed
12 white or brown mushroom stems, chopped
¼ cup olive oil
2 cloves garlic
1 stalk celery, minced
4 shallots, minced
4 sprigs Italian flat-leaf parsley, stemmed and chopped
1 teaspoon oregano
1 cup sugar-free bread crumbs
½ cup freshly grated Parmesan cheese
¼ cup pepperoni sausage, finely chopped
3 tablespoons chicken broth, more if necessary

Baked Stuffed Tomatoes
with Herbs and Cashews

This is a delicious new twist on baked, stuffed tomatoes.
It's easy and a very surprising combination of textures and flavors.

~⌇~

Yields 4 servings;
serving size 1 tomato
plus nuts and herbs

Calories: 245.38
Protein: 6.97 grams
Carbohydrates: 29.48
grams
Sugar: 6.30 grams
Fat: 11.45 grams

4 ripe, medium-sized
tomatoes
4 teaspoons olive oil
1 small red onion, minced
½ cup cashews, toasted and
chopped
1 cup fresh sugar-free bread
crumbs
1 teaspoon dried thyme leave
or 1 tablespoon fresh
thyme
Salt and freshly ground
pepper to taste
2 tablespoons sugar-free
tomato juice or freshly
squeezed lemon juice

1. Preheat oven to 350°F. Prepare a baking pan with parchment paper or nonstick spray. Cut the tops off the tomatoes and remove seeds and pulp with a melon ball maker or grapefruit spoon.

2. Arrange the tomatoes on the baking sheet. Heat the olive oil in a large sauté pan over medium flame.

3. Add the ingredients listed one by one. Cook for 4–5 minutes and then pile into tomato shells.

4. Bake for 40 minutes.

Stuffed Tomatoes

It's amazing the myriad delicious things you can stuff into tomatoes. Various vegetables, nuts, sausages, shrimp, scallops, and different herbs all make intensely flavored fillings. You can also use cooked rice, meats, and shellfish for cold stuffed tomatoes.

Spinach-Stuffed Yellow Tomatoes

Yellow tomatoes are less acidic and milder than red ones. They are easy to grow in your garden but not always to easy to find in the market. Tomatoes do have a certain amount of naturally occurring sugar, but it's complex, with a string of molecules that make a tomato acceptable for a sugar-free diet.

1. Preheat oven to 350°F. Prepare a baking pan with parchment paper or nonstick spray. Cut the tops off the tomatoes and remove seeds and pulp with a melon ball maker or grapefruit spoon.

2. Place the tomatoes in the baking pan. Sprinkle the insides with salt, pepper, and Splenda.

3. Sauté the garlic for 3 minutes in a sauté pan over medium heat. Add the spinach and nutmeg. Sprinkle with lemon juice.

4. Remove the sauté pan from the stove. Stir in the cheese and bread crumbs. Stuff the tomatoes and bake for 30 minutes. Serve hot.

Yields 4 servings; serving size 1 tomato

Calories: 225.01
Protein: 11.47 grams
Carbohydrates: 20.57 grams
Sugar: 1.25 grams
Fat: 12.06 grams

4 ripe medium-sized yellow tomatoes
1 teaspoon salt
½ teaspoon freshly ground black pepper, or to taste
1 teaspoon Splenda
2 tablespoons olive oil
2 cloves garlic, minced
1 10-ounce package of frozen, chopped spinach, thawed, all moisture squeezed out
⅛ teaspoon nutmeg
Juice of ½ lemon
½ cup grated Parmesan cheese
½ cup fresh bread crumbs

Kohlrabi with Lemon

*Kohlrabi is a very sweet and delicious vegetable.
It's available in the fall and winter. It tastes delicious sprinkled
with grated Parmesan cheese and run under the broiler.*

**Yields 4 servings;
serving size ⅔ cup**

Calories: 37.72
Protein: 2.30 grams
Carbohydrates: 8.41 grams
Sugar: 3.42 grams
Fat: 0.24 grams

*1 pound kohlrabi, stems
removed, peeled, and
sliced*
*½ cup sugar-free chicken
broth*
Juice of ½ lemon
Salt and pepper to taste
½ cup fresh parsley, chopped

1. Place the kohlrabi slices in a saucepan. Add the broth, lemon juice, salt, and pepper. Simmer over low heat for 25–30 minutes. Sprinkle with parsley. Serve hot.

Grating Your Own Cheese

A chunk of high-grade imported Parmesan cheese will last for months in the refrigerator when stored in a plastic bag. It only takes seconds to grate cheese and is very well worth the time. Freshly grated cheese has a stronger flavor, and you get exactly the amount you want.

Fennel with Orange Slices

Fennel, also called anise, can be grilled when you've got a charcoal fire going.

୶

1. Preheat oven to 350°F. Place the fennel chunks in a baking pan. Drizzle with oil and orange juice. Cover with aluminum foil.

2. Roast for 35–40 minutes. Remove the foil covering, baste with pan juice, and broil until slightly singed.

Vegetable Options

You can add baby beets to fennel with delicious results or you can make it very savory with herbs and tomatoes. During the summer, put the fronds on the grill when you are grilling fish or chicken. It's also great raw in salads.

Yields 4 servings; serving size ¼ bulb

Calories: 107.86
Protein: 1.30 grams
Carbohydrates: 11.56 grams
Sugar: 6.48 grams
Fat: 6.96 grams

1 large fennel bulb, trimmed and quartered
2 tablespoons olive oil
½ cup freshly squeezed orange juice
1 temple or navel orange, skin on, seeds removed, sliced ½" thick

Sauerkraut with Apples and Ham

This healthy comfort food is tasty and wonderful with another vegetable side, or a thin pork chop.

❧

1. Heat the oil in a large frying pan over medium heat.

2. Stir in the onion and apple and sauté for 4 minutes. Stir in the rest of the ingredients.

3. Cook, stirring for another 5 minutes. Serve hot.

Yields 4 servings; serving size ⅔ cup

Calories: 127.58
Protein: 6.87 grams
Carbohydrates: 14.77 grams
Sugar: 9.17 grams
Fat: 5.32 grams

1 tablespoon canola oil
½ sweet red onion, coarsely chopped
2 tart apples, cored and chopped, skins on
¼ pound smoked ham, diced
2 cups canned or packaged sugar-free sauerkraut
2 teaspoons Splenda
½ teaspoon pepper or to taste
½ teaspoon caraway seeds

Pumpkin Soufflé

This is a very good substitute for potatoes on a festive occasion. It goes well with poultry and game.

❧

1. Preheat the oven to 400°F. Prepare a soufflé dish with nonstick spray.

2. Put all but the egg whites in your electric mixer and beat until smooth.

3. Gently fold in the egg whites. Scrape into the soufflé mold. Bake for 55 minutes.

4. Check for doneness by inserting a knife. If it comes out clean, the soufflé is done. Serve immediately.

Yields 6 servings; serving size 4 tablespoons

Calories: 123.23
Protein: 4.56 grams
Carbohydrates: 8.05 grams
Sugar: 2.41 grams
Fat: 9.92 grams

1 13-ounce can puréed pumpkin, unsweetened
2 egg yolks
½ cup whipping cream or half-and-half
2 tablespoons Splenda
¼ teaspoon cloves
½ teaspoon cinnamon
¼ teaspoon nutmeg
¼ teaspoon allspice
1 teaspoon salt
1 teaspoon orange zest
5 egg whites, beaten stiff

Chapter 15
Rice, Risotto, and Wild Rice

Caribbean Coconut Rice 210

Baked Rice with Vegetables 211

Saffron Rice with Shrimp, Capers, and Pine Nuts . . . 212

Curried Rice with Nuts 213

Rice with Ham, Onions, and Rosemary 214

Brown Rice with Bacon and Apples 215

Fried Rice 215

Rice with Tomatoes and Olives. 216

Risotto with Lemons and Mascarpone Cheese 217

Risotto with Seafood 218

Risotto with Cheese and Baby Spinach 219

Risotto with Chicken Livers 220

Wild Rice with Pears and Pecans 220

Wild Rice, Snow Peas, and Water Chestnuts 221

Wild Rice with Mushrooms and Rosemary 222

Caribbean Coconut Rice

You can make this dish as hot or as mild as you want.

**Yields 6 servings;
serving size 5 ounces**

Calories: 307.96
Protein: 7.88 grams
Carbohydrates: 31.44 grams
Sugar: 5.5 grams
Fat: 17.92 grams

*1 tablespoon canola oil
1 small onion, chopped
1 cup fresh pineapple,
   chopped
1 cup brown or white rice
1 cup unsweetened coconut
   cream
2 cups water
1 teaspoon salt, or to taste
1 tablespoon chili powder, or
   to taste
1 teaspoon Splenda
½ cup sugar-free smoked
   ham*

1. Heat the oil in a large saucepan over medium heat. Sauté the onion. Add the rest of the ingredients.

2. Cover the pan tightly and reduce heat to low. Simmer for 40 minutes, stirring occasionally. Serve hot or at room temperature.

Versatile Rice

Rice is probably the most versatile of starches. It mixes well with vegetables, herbs, fish, shellfish, poultry, and just about any meat. It can magically turn into dessert in a flash. Rice pudding or a rice dessert made with lots of fruit is delicious.

Baked Rice with Vegetables

*You can throw in some sausage, leftover chicken
or whatever you have on hand to add more flavor.*

⌁

1. Preheat oven to 350°F. Heat the olive oil in a 2-quart ovenproof casserole over medium heat. Sauté the onion in the olive oil. After about 4 minutes, add the rice and stir to coat.

2. Add the rest of the ingredients and cover. Bake for 45 minutes, stirring every 10 minutes.

Season First

When you ready vegetables for steaming, add fresh or dried herbs, spices, sliced or diced onions, minced garlic, grated ginger, or just about any other seasoning you'd usually use. The seasonings will cook into the vegetables during steaming.

Yields 4 servings; serving size 8–9 ounces

Calories: 308.95
Protein: 11.44 grams
Carbohydrates: 45.01 grams
Sugar: 5.26 grams
Fat: 8.95 grams

1 tablespoon olive oil
1 medium onion, minced
1 cup long-grain rice
3 cups all natural, sugar-free chicken broth
1 zucchini, grated
6 radishes, trimmed and sliced
1 cup broccoli florets, cut in small pieces
½ cup Parmesan cheese
1 teaspoon dried basil
½ cup Italian flat-leaf parsley, chopped
Salt and pepper to taste

Saffron Rice with Shrimp, Capers, and Pine Nuts

This is a slightly reduced version of paella, the Spanish classic.
Any number of ingredients can be added to rice to make it delicious.

**Yields 4 servings;
serving size 1 cup rice
and ¼ pound shrimp**

Calories: 340.02
Protein: 27.69 grams
Carbohydrates: 42.32 grams
Sugar: 1.72 grams
Fat: 5.60 grams

1 tablespoon unsalted butter
2 cloves garlic, minced
1 small onion, minced
1 cup rice
1 cup clam broth
2 cups chicken broth
1 tablespoon thyme
*1 teaspoon freshly ground
    pepper*
2 teaspoons saffron threads
3 tablespoons capers
1 pound medium shrimp

1. Heat the butter in a large pot over medium heat. Stir in the garlic and onion and stir, cooking until softened. Add the rice and stir to coat.

2. Add the broth, thyme, pepper, and saffron. Cover and reduce heat to low. Stir the rice after 15 minutes.

3. Add the capers and shrimp after 25–30 minutes. Cover and cook for another 10 minutes.

Instant Rice

It's okay to use if you're in a wild rush, but instant rice is highly processed and lacks the basic good flavor of rice. Regular rice absorbs many wonderful flavors and nutrients from the veggies and broth in the cooking liquid.

Curried Rice with Nuts

Serve this with stir-fried vegetables or with seafood, meat, or fish.

❧

1. Heat the oils in a large pot over medium heat. Add the onions, chilies, garlic, and curry powder. Cook for 5 minutes.

2. Add the rice and stir to coat. Add broth, salt, and pepper. Cover. Reduce heat and simmer for 40 minutes.

3. Add the peanuts. Mix well, remove from heat, and serve.

Rice Variations

Mix up your nice dishes by adding different flavors. For more East Asian tastes, add chopped green onions, a dash of soy sauce, and ¼ teaspoon toasted sesame oil to rice. For a touch of spice, add two tablespoons chopped fresh cilantro and ½ teaspoon orange peel.

Yields 6 servings; serving size 5 ounces

Calories: 308.61
Protein: 9.63 grams
Carbohydrates: 36.60 grams
Sugar: 4.83 grams
Fat: 14.69 grams

1 tablespoon cooking oil
1 teaspoon Toasted Sesame Seed Oil (page 238)
2 onions, chopped
2 hot chilies, stemmed, seeded, and minced
3 cloves garlic, minced
1 tablespoon Madras curry powder
1 cup rice
3 cups chicken broth
1 teaspoon salt
Freshly ground black pepper to taste
1 cup roasted unsalted peanuts

Rice with Ham, Onions, and Rosemary

**Yields 6 servings;
serving size 6 ounces**

Calories: 226.15
Protein: 10.25 grams
Carbohydrates: 29.89
    grams
Sugar: 3.12 grams
Fat: 6.93 grams

2 tablespoons cooking oil
1 red onion, minced
1 tablespoon dried rosemary
    or 2 tablespoons fresh
    rosemary
1 teaspoon Splenda
1 cup long-grain rice
1 cup sugar-free smoked ham
3 cups chicken broth
¼ teaspoon freshly ground
    black pepper, or to taste
1 cup sugar snap peas, ends
    trimmed, cut in halves

This is a very easy lunch-sized meal that can double as a dinner side dish.

❧

1. Heat the oil in a large, heavy bottomed pot over medium flame. Add onion and cook, stirring for 4 minutes. Add rosemary and stir thoroughly.

2. Add the Splenda, rice, ham, chicken broth, and pepper. Cover and cook for 40 minutes, stirring once.

3. Add the peas, stirring for five minutes until they are hot.

Adding Meat to a Rice Dish

Since these items generally contain a great deal of sodium, do not use any salt when cooking these dishes. Ham, bacon, and sausage add a great deal of flavor, richness, and zing to the rice dishes in this chapter. You can also use them to turn a side dish into an entrée.

Brown Rice with Bacon and Apples

You can serve this for breakfast, brunch, or as a side dish at dinner.

ᐱ

1. Cook the bacon until crisp, crumble, and set aside on a fresh paper towel. In a large frying pan, heat the oil over medium heat.

2. Sauté the onion for about 5 minutes. Add the apples and jicama and stir. Mix in the rest of the ingredients.

Brown Rice

Brown rice has far more nutrition and flavor than white rice. White rice loses nutrients during processing, so brown rice retains more fiber and has extra vitamin B as well. The fiber makes the rice easier to digest.

Yields 4 servings; serving size 6 ounces

Calories: 234.78
Protein: 3.70 grams
Carbohydrates: 27.82 grams
Sugar: 6.32 grams
Fat: 12.42 grams

4 slices sugar-free bacon
2 tablespoons cooking oil
1 cup sweet white onion, chopped
2 tart apples, peeled, cored, and chopped
½ cup jicama, peeled and diced
1 teaspoon freshly grated nutmeg
1 teaspoon Splenda
3 cups brown rice, cooked

Fried Rice

This is an easy version of fried rice that you can actually use instant rice to make.

ᐱ

1. Heat the oils in a large frying pan over medium heat. Add all of the ingredients at once. Cook for 4–5 minutes, stirring often.

Yields 4 servings; serving size 5 ounces

Calories: 251.98
Protein: 5.13 grams
Carbohydrates: 37.95 grams
Sugar: 2 grams
Fat: 9.16 grams

2 tablespoons peanut oil
1 teaspoon Toasted Sesame Seed Oil (page 238)
¼ cup soy sauce
1 teaspoon Splenda
1 bunch green onions, chopped
1 tablespoon fresh gingerroot, minced
3 cups white or brown rice, cooked

Rice with Tomatoes and Olives

Try this as a side dish for roasted pork filet or pork chops.

Calories: 187.38
Protein: 3.08 grams
Carbohydrates: 28.82 grams
Sugar: 3.22 grams
Fat: 7.17 grams

2 tablespoons cooking oil
1 medium-sized yellow onion,
    chopped
4 Roma tomatoes, stemmed
    and diced
2 tablespoons fresh lemon
    juice
1 teaspoon Splenda
½ cup pitted green olives,
    chopped
Salt and freshly ground
    pepper to taste
1 tablespoon dried basil or
    ¼ cup fresh basil, torn in
    small pieces
3 cups brown rice, cooked

1. Heat oil in a large, heavy-bottomed pot over medium heat. Add the onion and sauté for 4–5 minutes. Stir in the tomatoes and lemon juice.

2. Stir in the Splenda, olives, salt, pepper, basil, and rice. Cover and let sit for 10–15 minutes.

Delicious Substitutions

Substitute marinated mushrooms or artichoke hearts for the olives in the Rice with Tomatoes and Olives recipe.

Risotto with Lemons and Mascarpone Cheese

*Making risotto is a Sunday afternoon operation
unless you are preparing for a dinner party.*

ᐧᏔᐧ

1. Heat the butter in a large heavy-bottomed pot over medium heat. Sauté the lemon pieces quickly and add the rice. Stir to coat.

2. Add the salt, pepper, and parsley. Stir in the broth ½ cup at a time. Add more broth as the rice absorbs the liquid.

3. As soon as the risotto "talks" to you, add another ½ cup of hot broth. When all of the broth is absorbed, stir in the mascarpone cheese and serve hot.

Something to Say

The key to foolproof risotto is listening to what it has to tell you. Stir until you hear a hiss at the bottom of the pot. This means it's time to add more liquid to the rice. The hiss comes from it drying out. When all of the liquid is absorbed, the risotto is done. And remember, although 5 cups of water or broth seems like a great deal, one-third of it evaporates or is absorbed into the rice.

**Yields 6 servings;
serving size 5 ounces**

Calories: 284.40
Protein: 6.2 grams
Carbohydrates: 48.07 grams
Sugar: 1 gram
Fat: 5.76 grams

2 tablespoons unsalted butter
½ Meyer lemon or ¼ regular lemon, peeled, seeded, and chopped
1½ cups Italian short-grain Arborio rice
1 teaspoon salt
1 tablespoon red pepper flakes
½ cup Italian flat-leaf parsley, chopped
5 cups chicken broth
3 tablespoons mascarpone cheese

Risotto with Seafood

The beauty of this dish is its stunning presentation. Oh—it's also delicious!

Yields 8 main course servings, 10 side dish servings; serving size 5 ounces as a side, 9 ounces as a main dish

Calories: 337.17
Protein: 31.98 grams
Carbohydrates: 37.55 grams
Sugar: 0.58 grams
Fat: 5.32 grams

2 cups clam or shrimp-shell broth
3 cups water
2 tablespoons olive oil
4 shallots, chopped
2 cloves garlic, chopped
1½ cups Arborio rice
1 teaspoon Splenda
Salt and pepper to taste
1 cup Italian flat-leaf parsley, chopped
Juice of 1 lemon
1 pound raw shrimp, peeled and cleaned
½ pound bay scallops, rinsed
1 pound Alaskan crabmeat, in shells, cut in 1" lengths

1. Heat the broth and water together in a pot. Place on a back burner over low heat.

2. Heat the oil in a large heavy-bottomed pot over medium-high heat. Sauté the shallots and garlic.

3. Stir in the rice and mix to coat. Add the broth/water combination ½ cup at a time. When half of the liquid has been used up, stir in the Splenda, salt, pepper, parsley, and lemon juice.

4. Mix in the seafood and let cook for 5 minutes or until the shrimp turns pink and the crab pieces are hot.

Risotto with Cheese and Baby Spinach

*Classically, whole milk and plenty of butter would be used
in this recipe. This healthy version is just as delicious.*

1. Heat the broth and milk to a simmer in a saucepan. Place on a back burner over low heat.

2. Heat the oil in a large, heavy-bottomed pot. Sauté the onion and garlic over medium heat. Add the rice and stir to coat.

3. Stir in the salt, pepper, nutmeg, and lemon juice and zest. Start adding the milk/broth combination, ½ cup at a time. When all but ½ cup of the liquid has been incorporated into the rice, stir in the spinach.

4. Cook the spinach, adding the final ½ cup of liquid. Stir in the cheese and serve immediately.

Vegetables and Risotto

You can add cauliflower, broccoli, tomatoes, or zucchini to risotto. Seasonal vegetables lend delicious flavor to risotto dishes, so add whatever you have on hand for more variation.

**Yields 6 servings;
serving size 6 ounces**

Calories: 178.84
Protein: 7.44 grams
Carbohydrates: 26.56
  grams
Sugar: 3.24 grams
Fat: 5.72 grams

*3 cups chicken broth
2 cups skim milk
2 tablespoons olive oil
1 medium yellow onion,
    chopped
4 cloves garlic, chopped
1½ cups Arborio rice
Salt and pepper to taste
¼ teaspoon freshly grated
    nutmeg
Juice and zest of ½ lemon
10 ounces fresh baby spinach,
    stems removed
1 cup freshly grated
    Parmesan cheese*

Risotto with Chicken Livers

This delectable dish is wonderful on a buffet table.

Yields 6 servings; serving size 5 ounces

Calories: 252.50
Protein: 9.49 grams
Carbohydrates: 38.72 grams
Sugar: 0.65 grams
Fat: 5.45 grams

2 cups beef broth
3 cups water
3 tablespoons olive oil, divided
1 small onion, chopped
1¼ cups Arborio rice
1 teaspoon salt
*Freshly ground black pepper
    to taste*
*½ pound chicken livers,
    cleaned and quartered*
1 teaspoon soy sauce

1. Combine the beef broth and water and heat to a simmer. Place on a back burner over low heat.

2. Heat 1 tablespoon oil in a large, heavy-bottomed pot over medium heat. Sauté the onion. Add the rice and stir to coat. Sprinkle with salt and pepper.

3. Add the broth/water combination, ½ cup at a time stirring constantly. Wait for it to hiss before adding more broth.

4. In a separate pan, heat 2 tablespoons oil. Sauté the chicken livers for about 10 minutes over medium heat. Add the soy sauce.

5. Gently mix the livers into the rice and serve.

Wild Rice with Pears and Pecans

This is simple and perfect with game, turkey, game hens, or roast chicken.

Yields 6 servings; serving size 5 ounces

Calories: 337.81
Protein: 6.69 grams
Carbohydrates: 39.52 grams
Sugar: 12.97 grams
Fat: 19.07 grams

1 cup wild rice
3 cups chicken broth
2 tablespoons butter
*4 pears, peeled, cored, and
    quartered*
Salt and pepper to taste
1 cup toasted pecan pieces
*½ cup extra broth, if
    necessary*

1. Preheat the oven to 350°F. Mix all of the ingredients except for the pecan pieces and extra broth in a casserole dish. Cover tightly and bake for 90 minutes.

2. Check the rice. Add more liquid if necessary.

Wild Rice, Snow Peas, and Water Chestnuts

*This dish's wonderful, nutty flavor is the perfect
complement to broiled salmon, cod, or halibut.*

❧

1. Heat olive oil in a large heavy-bottomed pot. Sauté the onion over medium heat. Add the rice, broth, salt, and pepper. Cover tightly and simmer for 90 minutes.

2. Stir in the snow peas, water chestnuts, soy sauce, and sesame seed oil. Add a half-cup more broth or water if the rice is too dry. Cook and stir for 5 minutes and serve hot.

Wild Rice

Wild rice is an indigenous North American grain that grows in water. It grows naturally and can also be cultivated. It is a delicious and healthy alternative to white and brown rice and risotto.

**Yields 6 servings;
serving size 5 ounces**

Calories: 212.10
Protein: 6.91 grams
Carbohydrates: 30.48 grams
Sugar: 4.22 grams
Fat: 7.49 grams

2 tablespoons olive oil
1 small onion, chopped
1 cup wild rice
3 cups chicken broth
Salt and pepper to taste
½ pound small crisp snow peas, stemmed
1 cup water chestnuts, drained and sliced
¼ cup soy sauce
1 tablespoon Toasted Sesame Seed Oil (page 238)
½ cup extra broth or water, if necessary

Wild Rice with Mushrooms and Rosemary

The little crunch from the celery that contrasts with the tender mushrooms.

❧

**Yields 6 servings;
serving size 5 ounces**

Calories: 165.74
Protein: 7.25 grams
Carbohydrates: 24.39 grams
Sugar: 1.2 grams
Fat: 5.22 grams

1 cup water
2 cups beef broth
1 cup wild rice
*2 tablespoons unsalted
    butter, cut in dice*
Salt and pepper to taste
*2 stalks celery, coarsely
    chopped*
1 tablespoon dried rosemary
*2 cups Italian brown or white
    button mushrooms, sliced*
*½ cup extra broth or water, if
    necessary*

1. Preheat the oven to 350°F. Put the water, broth, rice, butter, salt, pepper, celery, and rosemary in an ovenproof casserole dish.

2. Cover tightly and bake in the oven for 75 minutes.

3. Add the mushrooms. If the rice is dry, add more broth or water.

4. Cover and cook for another 30 minutes.

Chapter 16
Potatoes and Pasta

Garlic Mashed Potatoes. 224

Potato Skins Stuffed with Hot Barbecue 225

Stuffed Idaho Potatoes with Chives and Cheeses . . . 226

Crunchy Sautéed New Potatoes 227

Roasted New Potatoes with Carrots and Fennel 227

Pasta with Ricotta, Garlic, and Baby Peas. 228

Potatoes Sautéed in Olive Oil and Herbs 229

Pasta with Anchovy-Olive Sauce. 230

Pasta with Chicken, Green Olives,

    and Grape Tomatoes 231

Spaghetti with Shrimp 232

Ziti with Sausage and Ricotta Cheese 233

Rotini with Smoked Salmon

    and Cream Cheese Sauce 234

Warm Rotini Salad with Zucchini and Feta Cheese. . . 235

Tortellini with Basil and Walnuts 236

Garlic Mashed Potatoes

What's better than homemade mashed potatoes?
Homemade mashed potatoes with garlic!

⌒ↄ

Yields 4 servings;
serving size ⅔ cup

Calories: 274.97
Protein: 5.32 grams
Carbohydrates: 52.37 grams
Sugar: 4.00 grams
Fat: 5.50 grams

4 medium Idaho or Yukon
*   Gold potatoes*
1 teaspoon salt
2 teaspoons olive oil
3 cloves garlic, minced
1 tablespoon unsalted butter
¼–⅓ cup milk or half-and-
*   half*
¼ teaspoon pepper
⅛ teaspoon freshly grated
*   nutmeg*

1. Peel the potatoes and slice ½" thick. Place in a large pot and cover with cold water. Add salt and bring to a boil over high heat.

2. Reduce heat to a simmer. Cook, uncovered, for 15–20 minutes or until potatoes are fork-tender.

3. While the potatoes cook, heat the olive oil in a small pan over medium heat. Sauté garlic for 4–5 minutes or until just softened. Set aside.

4. Drain the potatoes and place in a bowl. Mash the potatoes with butter, milk, pepper, and nutmeg.

5. When the potatoes are smooth, stir in the garlic/oil combination. Serve hot.

Potato Skins Stuffed with Hot Barbecue

Buy spit-roasted barbecued chicken from the grocery store; just make sure the sauce is sugar-free. You could also go to the deli and get pre-roasted chicken, sliced and ready to shred.

Yields 4 servings; serving size ½ cup

Calories: 389.93
Protein: 19.75 grams
Carbohydrates: 64.17 grams
Sugar: 8.69 grams
Fat: 5.98 grams

1. Remove the tops from the baked potatoes. Cut potatoes in half lengthwise. Scoop out the insides and put them in a bowl, being careful to keep the skins intact. Mash potatoes and milk, adding salt and pepper to taste. Set aside.

2. Preheat the oven to 350°F. Prepare a baking pan with nonstick spray or cover with parchment paper.

3. Spoon half of the mashed potatoes onto the skins. Add the onion, pork, and barbecue sauce. Sprinkle with ground pepper. Place the stuffed potatoes on the baking pan.

4. Bake for 30 minutes. Serve with grated cheese and your favorite garnishes.

4 large Idaho potatoes, baked for 40 minutes at 400°F
¼ cup milk
Salt and pepper to taste
1 onion, minced
1 cup roasted pork tenderloin or roast chicken, shredded
½ cup Barbecue Sauce (page 243)
½ teaspoon freshly ground black pepper
4 tablespoons sharp cheddar cheese, grated

Potatoes are Good Food

Potatoes are very good for you, especially if you eat the skins. They are slow to digest and are a good source of fiber. However, some potato dishes are not health-friendly. Any processed and fried food is a rare treat, something you might have once every month or two, or never.

Stuffed Idaho Potatoes with Chives and Cheeses

You can serve this as a side dish or as a game-day snack. You can also make this the day before you plan to serve and then just bake them until they're hot.

❧

Yields 4 servings; serving size ½ cup

Calories: 398.38
Protein: 14.51 grams
Carbohydrates: 52.84 grams
Sugar: 5.01 grams
Fat: 14.88 grams

4 Idaho or Yukon Gold potatoes
⅓ cup warm 1% milk
2 tablespoons unsalted butter
⅛ teaspoon nutmeg
¼ cup fresh chives, rinsed and snipped
Freshly ground black pepper to taste
2 ounces grated Parmesan cheese
2 ounces grated white American cheese

1. Scrub the potatoes, prick them with a fork, and bake them at 400°F for 35–40 minutes.

2. Let cool until you can handle them. Slice off the tops. Remove the insides, leaving about ¼ inch of pulp inside the skin. Set the skins aside.

3. Put the potato innards and the rest of the ingredients in a bowl. Using an electric mixer, beat until fairly smooth. Return to the skins and bake for another 20 minutes at 300°F.

Excited Potato Starch

If you put your potatoes in a food processor or a blender to mash them, they will turn into a pasty, gluey mess. That's because the starch gets excited and separates. Instead, use a ricer or an electric mixer to mash your potatoes.

Crunchy Sautéed New Potatoes

Kids love this recipe! It's quick to make and very tasty. The potatoes get quite crisp as the water evaporates and cooks them through. Add fresh parsley just before serving for extra color and kick.

1. Add the oil and water to a nonstick pan over medium heat.

2. Place the potatoes in the pan, cut sides down. Cover and cook for 10 minutes. Remove the lid and continue to brown until the cut sides are crisp. Turn and sprinkle with salt and pepper.

Yields 4 servings; serving size 2 half-potatoes

Calories: 89.84
Protein: 1.00 grams
Carbohydrates: 13.00 grams
Sugar: 0 grams
Fat: 3.38 grams

1 tablespoon olive oil
2 tablespoons water
8 medium-sized new potatoes, scrubbed and halved
Salt and pepper to taste

Roasted New Potatoes with Carrots and Fennel

This potato dish is great with roasted meat, fish, or poultry. Serve it on the side or spread the seasoned, slightly oiled vegetables around pieces of meat.

1. Preheat the oven to 375°F. Prepare a baking sheet with nonstick cooking spray. Scrub and prepare the veggies, and place them on the baking sheet.

2. Whisk the chicken broth, olive oil, caraway seeds, thyme, salt, and pepper. Drizzle over the vegetables. Roast for 35–40 minutes or until the potatoes are fork-tender.

Roast Vegetables
Potatoes are just one of many great roasting vegetables! Try cauliflower, sweet peppers, onions, and celery. You can serve any of them over chilled salad greens for lunch.

Yields 4 servings; serving size ⅔ cup

Calories: 146.61
Protein: 2.66 grams
Carbohydrates: 18.18 grams
Sugar: 4.89 grams
Fat: 7.50 grams

4 golf-ball sized new potatoes, red, or purple, scrubbed and halved
4 medium carrots, peeled, ends trimmed, and cut in 3" lengths
1 fennel bulb, quartered
¼ cup chicken broth
2 tablespoons olive oil
½ teaspoon caraway seeds
1 teaspoon dried thyme
Salt and pepper to taste

Pasta with Ricotta, Garlic, and Baby Peas

*Make a great side of pasta for a buffet party, a big
family dinner, or kicked-back evening with friends.*

✃

**Yields 6 servings;
serving size 1 cup**

Calories: 386.09
Protein: 19.44 grams
Carbohydrates: 34.82 grams
Sugar: 3.81 grams
Fat: 19.58 grams

*1 pound short pasta, such as
    macaroni*
2 tablespoons olive oil
2 cloves garlic, chopped
*1 tablespoon dried thyme or 4
    tablespoons fresh thyme*
2 whole eggs
8 ounces ricotta
5 ounces frozen baby peas
4 ounces Parmesan cheese
*6 ounces sun dried tomatoes,
    packed in oil, drained,
    and cut in pieces*

1. Preheat the oven to 350°F. Cook pasta according to package instruc-
   tions. Heat the oil in a 3-quart ovenproof casserole dish over medium-
   low heat.

2. Sauté the garlic for 5 minutes, stirring constantly. Remove from the
   stove. Add the remaining ingredients, stirring to mix.

3. Drain the pasta and mix with the ingredients in the casserole dish.
   Bake for 40 minutes.

Potatoes Sautéed in Olive Oil and Herbs

This is ideal for a family dinner, but it works just as well for two.
You can eat half of it one night and the other half two days later. You can
also use the leftover potatoes and herbs to make a great potato salad.

❧

1. Prepare a nonstick pan with nonstick spray. Add the potatoes and water, cover, and cook for 15 minutes over medium heat.

2. Remove the lid. Toss the potatoes with olive oil, herbs, salt, and pepper. Reset heat to medium high.

3. Brown quickly and serve.

Cook Once, Eat Twice

Any of these recipes can be doubled, saved, and reheated for another night. Adjust the recipe if you are expecting a large number of guests. If you have leftovers, cover them tightly and refrigerate them.

Yields 4 servings;
serving size ⅔ cup

Calories: 123.79
Protein: 1.17 grams
Carbohydrates: 13.74 grams
Sugar: 0.04 grams
Fat: 6.89 grams

8 large new or fingerling
potatoes, scrubbed and
sliced ¼" thick
2 tablespoons water
2 tablespoons olive oil
¼ cup fresh Italian, flat-leaf
parsley, chopped
2 teaspoons dried rosemary
or 1 tablespoon fresh
rosemary
1 teaspoon dried sage leaves
or 1 tablespoon fresh
sage leaves, torn
Salt and pepper to taste

Pasta with Anchovy-Olive Sauce

This recipe, also called Pasta Puttanesca, was historically made by—and named after—the ladies of the evening. The idea was to attract clients with its irresistible aroma. Of course, it is also an extremely nutritious dish. Try it even if you insist you hate anchovies!

Calories: 478.62
Protein: 19.47 grams
Carbohydrates: 75.12 grams
Sugar: 8.73 grams
Fat: 12.57 grams

2 tablespoons olive oil
6 cloves garlic, chopped
4 anchovies, drained
1 teaspoon red pepper flakes
1 cup black Sicilian olives, pitted and chopped
28-ounce can crushed tomatoes, in their juice, no sugar added
6-ounce can tomato paste, no sugar added
½ cup fresh Italian flat-leaf parsley, chopped
1 pound thin whole wheat spaghetti
3 quarts boiling salted water
Freshly ground black pepper to taste
½ cup freshly grated Parmesan cheese

1. Heat the oil in a large sauce pot over medium heat. Sauté garlic and anchovies, stirring continuously with a wooden spoon until the anchovies melt.

2. Add the pepper flakes, olives, tomatoes, and parsley. Bring to a boil and reduce heat to a simmer. Cook the pasta to almost al dente, drain, and add to the pot of sauce. Let it simmer for a few minutes.

3. Sprinkle with pepper and cheese and serve.

Olives

Olives add an enormous amount of flavor to just about any sauce. The taste of cooked olives is more delicate than raw olives, almost sweet. Try different brands of olive. You'll find some are vinegary, others are lemony, and still others a combination of salty and smoky. The flavors depend on the region where they are grown and cured.

Pasta with Chicken, Green Olives, and Grape Tomatoes

You can buy chicken tenders fresh or frozen. Too often, they are used in fried chicken "nuggets," but they are excellent in any number of dishes and sandwiches. In fact, they are the top of the chicken breast—the filet—totally lean and excellent for a sugar-free menu.

∽

1. In a large frying pan, heat the olive oil over medium heat. Sprinkle the chicken with salt, pepper, and flour. Sauté and remove from the pan.

2. Add the garlic and shallots to the pan. Cook for about 3 minutes. Stir in the mustard, Splenda, olives, and broth. Cook for 5 minutes, stirring continuously. Return the chicken to the pot. Reduce heat to the barest simmer.

3. Cook the pasta until al dente. Add it to the pot with the chicken. Let cook for another minute or two to allow flavors to combine.

4. Garnish with the tomatoes and serve with a sprinkle of cheese.

Yields 6 servings; serving size 1½ cups

Calories: 432.86
Protein: 19.36 grams
Carbohydrates: 39.50 grams
Sugar: 2.56 grams
Fat: 21.44 grams

2 tablespoons olive oil
1 pound chicken tenders, cut in small pieces
Salt and pepper to taste
Dash of whole-wheat flour
2 cloves garlic, chopped
4 shallots, chopped
1 teaspoon Dijon-Style Mustard (page 241)
½ teaspoon Splenda
¾ cup green, pitted olives, stuffed with pimentos
1 cup chicken broth
1 pound thin spaghetti, cooked in 3 quarts boiling, salted water
Garnish of 1 cup grape tomatoes, halved
½ cup freshly grated Parmesan cheese

Spaghetti with Shrimp

Throw this together for a quick family or company meal. It's just as good as it is easy. Try it with artichokes or sun-dried tomatoes for extra sugar-free flavor.

◆

1. Toss the cooked shrimp in the oil over medium heat for 2 minutes. Add the sauce and parsley. Cook for 5 minutes.

2. Add the cooked linguine to the shrimp sauce. Sprinkle with lemon zest and serve immediately.

Storing Sauces

If you make a gallon of sauce, freeze leftovers in quart-sized containers so you always have a meal at hand. If you buy sauce, be sure it's sugar free. Most tomato sauce has sugar added.

Ziti with Sausage and Ricotta Cheese

Here's another quick and satisfying family meal. It's great for a cold night when you want to relieve yourself from the chill.

1. Preheat the oven to 350°F. Prepare a 3-quart casserole dish with non-stick spray.

2. Steam the sausage in ¼ cup boiling water in a frying pan over medium high heat.

3. Combine the Ricotta and Parmesan cheeses, eggs, salt, pepper, and oregano in a separate bowl. Stir in the sausage. Mix the cooked, drained pasta with the cheese mixture. Pour into the casserole dish.

4. Pour the tomato sauce over the top and bake for 35 minutes. Just before serving, spread the mozzarella over the top and let it melt. Serve the Parmesan cheese on the side.

Yields 6 servings; serving size 1¼ cup

Calories: 561.91
Protein: 41.75 grams
Carbohydrates: 26.74 grams
Sugar: 5.08 grams
Fat: 31.51 grams

½ pound Italian sausage, cut in small pieces
8 ounces ricotta cheese
½ cup Parmesan cheese
2 eggs, beaten
Salt and pepper to taste
1 tablespoon oregano
1 pound whole wheat ziti, cooked
8 ounces sugar-free tomato sauce
4 thin slices mozzarella cheese
Grated Parmesan cheese to taste

Rotini with Smoked Salmon and Cream Cheese Sauce

This is a good recipe for a brunch buffet. The sauce for the pasta can also be mounded on toast if you like.

❧

Yields 6 servings; serving size 1 cup

Calories: 208.85
Protein: 11.71 grams
Carbohydrates: 23.96 grams
Sugar: 5.03 grams
Fat: 7.04 grams

1 cup milk, heated
1 bunch green onions, chopped
6 ounces low-fat cream cheese at room temperature
4 ounces smoked salmon, cut in small pieces
1 teaspoon Splenda
Freshly ground black pepper to taste
1 pound rotini

1. Put a pot of water on to boil for the rotini. Meanwhile, beat the warm milk, green onions, and cream cheese together. Fold in the salmon and Splenda, and sprinkle with pepper.

2. Keep the sauce warm on a burner at a very low simmer until the rotini is cooked and drained. Mix and serve.

Smoked Salmon vs. Gravlax

Smoked salmon is pure salmon, cured by warm smoke. Gravlax is salmon that's been cured in a combination of salt and sugar, which actually cooks the fish. No matter how much you scrape off the coating, some of the sugar remains.

Warm Rotini Salad with Zucchini and Feta Cheese

The feta cheese gives this a great taste and extra protein.
It's easy and very good as a warm salad.

1. In a large bowl, mix the first six ingredients together. Cook the pasta, drain, and add to the bowl while still hot.

2. Stir in the cheese. Serve hot or warm, or chill to serve later.

Whole Grains

Eating a diet rich in whole grains may help lower your risk of developing diabetes and may lower your risk of developing vascular inflammation if you already have diabetes. Vascular inflammation contributes to your risk of heart attack and stroke. Choose whole grain pastas and breads to make sure you get enough.

Yields 6 servings;
serving size 1 cup

Calories: 434.39
Protein: 8.58 grams
Carbohydrates: 22.99 grams
Sugar: 2.59 grams
Fat: 35.68 grams

1 cup Basic Mayonnaise (page 238)
¼ cup white wine vinegar
2 small zucchini squashes, ends trimmed, finely diced
½ sweet red onion, minced
½ cup fresh Italian flat-leaf parsley, chopped
Freshly ground black pepper to taste
1 pound whole wheat rotini, cooked
1 cup crumbled feta cheese

Tortellini with Basil and Walnuts

*Frozen tortellini make a wonderfully quick meal for a week night.
This recipe is delicately tasty and very easy to cook after a rough day.*

და

1. Heat the oil and butter in a large sauce pan. Sauté the shallots over medium heat. Reduce to a simmer. Add the basil, pepper, walnuts, and cheese.

2. Cook and drain the pasta and add to the sauce.

3. Stir to coat pasta, add melted butter, and serve.

Filled Pastas

It's important to make sure the filled pastas you buy have no sugar. Some ravioli, tortellini, and other filled pastas have sugar hidden in the fine print. An alternative is to get wonton wrappers and make your own ravioli and tortellini.

Yields 2 servings; serving size 1½ cups

Calories: 938.18
Protein: 42.61 grams
Carbohydrates: 60.02 grams
Sugar: 3.22 grams
Fat: 71.67 grams

2 teaspoons unsalted butter
3 teaspoons olive oil
4 shallots, minced
1 cup fresh basil leaves, finely chopped
Freshly ground black pepper to taste
1 cup walnut pieces, toasted
½ cup finely grated Parmesan cheese
9-ounce box frozen cheese-filled tortellini
2 tablespoons unsalted butter, melted

Chapter 17
Dressings and Sauces

Toasted Sesame Seed Oil. 238

Basic Mayonnaise 238

Green Mayonnaise 239

Chili Sauce 240

Basic Mustard and Dijon-Style Mustard 241

Various Vinaigrettes 241

Roasted Red Pepper Sauce. 242

Asian Ginger Dipping Sauce 242

Barbecue Sauce 243

Dijon Dressing 244

Lemon-Herb Dressing. 244

Hot Lemon Sauce 245

Egg and Lemon Sauce 246

Fresh Tomato Sauce with Mushrooms and Herbs. . . . 247

Sweet Tea Sauce 248

Mustard Cream Sauce 248

Sweet-and-Sour Mustard 249

Mango Chutney 249

Tomato Salsa 250

Toasted Sesame Seed Oil

This couldn't be easier to make and will keep almost indefinitely.
It has a luscious taste and aroma essential to flavoring many Asian dishes.
Sesame oil is never used as a cooking oil because it's too strong.

Yields 7 ounces;
serving size ⅙ ounce

Calories: 11
Protein: 0.06 grams
Carbohydrates: 0.05 grams
Sugar: 0 grams
Fat: 1.25 grams

½ cup white sesame seeds
1 cup peanut oil

1. Toast the sesame seeds until golden in a large nonstick pan over medium heat. Add the oil and bring to a boil.

2. Turn the heat to low and simmer the oil for 10 minutes or until it takes on the color of honey. Pour through cheesecloth to remove seeds.

Basic Mayonnaise

If the eggs are cold, you'll get a very loose sauce, not a stiff mayonnaise.
Set the eggs out until they reach room temperature.

Yields 1 cup; serving
size 2 teaspoons

Calories: 68.12
Protein: 0.47 grams
Carbohydrates: 0.21 grams
Sugar: 0.07 grams
Fat: 7.28 grams

Juice of ½ lemon
1½ teaspoons dry English
*   mustard*
¼ teaspoon cayenne pepper,
*   or to taste*
1 egg white at room
*   temperature*
1 whole egg at room
*   temperature*
1 teaspoon Splenda
½ teaspoon salt
¾ cup olive oil

1. Blend all but the olive oil in a blender.

2. Add the oil a teaspoon at a time, and let the mayonnaise thicken slowly. When thick and creamy, refrigerate. This will keep for 4–5 days.

Green Mayonnaise

*This is a mayonnaise with many uses. You can dip
toasted bread in it, drop some into a soup, or use it cold
as a dressing. Green mayonnaise is a classic with salmon.*

1. Blend the lemon juice, mustard, salt, cayenne pepper, egg white, whole egg, and Splenda in a blender. Add the garlic, parsley, chives, dill, lemon zest, and black pepper.

2. Slowly add the oil one teaspoon at a time and blend until thick. Serve.

Homemade Mayonnaise

Homemade mayonnaise has a fresh taste and tastes good with just about everything. Just be sure to use very fresh eggs and don't use reconstituted lemon juice in a bottle or plastic lemon. It's worth the flavor to squeeze it fresh.

Yields 1¼ cups; serving size 2 teaspoons

Calories: 55.06
Protein: 0.41 grams
Carbohydrates: 0.29 grams
Sugar: 0.07 grams
Fat: 5.83 grams

*Juice of ½ lemon
1½ teaspoon dry English
    mustard
½ teaspoon salt
¼ teaspoon cayenne pepper,
    or to taste
1 egg white at room
    temperature
1 whole egg at room
    temperature
1 teaspoon Splenda
2 garlic cloves
¼ cup fresh parsley leaves,
    rinsed and dried
2 tablespoons chives, minced
2 tablespoons fresh dill or 1½
    teaspoon dried dill
½ teaspoon lemon zest
Freshly ground black pepper
    to taste
¾ cup olive oil*

Chili Sauce

If your garden is overflowing with tomatoes, you can blanch, peel, and throw them into the recipe.

∾

Yields 1 quart; serving size 1 teaspoon

Calories: 2.48
Protein: 0.12 grams
Carbohydrates: 0.58 grams
Sugar: 0.02 grams

2 28-ounce cans sugar-free whole Italian plum tomatoes, drained
1 6-ounce can sugar-free tomato paste
1 tablespoon garlic powder
1 tablespoon onion powder
1 tablespoon chili powder, or to taste
1 teaspoon ground cloves
½ teaspoon ground cinnamon
4 teaspoons Splenda
4 teaspoon DiabetiSweet Brown
1 teaspoon salt
1 teaspoon freshly ground black pepper, or to taste

1. Mix all ingredients in a large, heavy-bottomed pot. Bring to a boil. Reduce heat and simmer with the cover slightly cracked.

2. Stirring occasionally, simmer for about 3 hours or until the sauce is reduced by one-half. Cool, jar for storage, and refrigerate. Chili sauce will keep for 3–4 weeks.

Your Own Sauces

Once you have made a sauce base, you can taste and adjust the ingredients. Maybe you'd like more sour, spicy, salty, or sweet. Putting your own stamp on a recipe is the fun part of cooking. It puts you, the cook, in control!

Basic Mustard and Dijon-Style Mustard

*This basic recipe is the first mustard one learns to make.
Variations on this theme will follow.*

1. Whisk the mustard and cold water together. Let stand to develop for 15 minutes. Serve or mix into a sauce.

Yields ⅓ cup; serving size: ½ teaspoon

Calories: 8.18
Protein: 0.42 grams
Carbohydrates: 0.32 grams
Sugar: 0 grams
Fat: 0.55 grams

⅓ cup powdered English or
    Dijon mustard
⅓ cup cold water

Various Vinaigrettes

*You can make many differently flavored vinaigrette dressings by changing the
flavors of the vinegar. Various herbs also add different and exciting flavors.*

1. Blend all ingredients in the blender. Serve at your pleasure. This will keep for at least a week with good fresh flavor. Refrigerate after 2 days.

Exciting Vinaigrette Dressings

Take a look at the various vinegars on the shelves of your market. If you like raspberry, cider, or balsamic, use them in dressings and marinades. Add your own touch; use fresh raspberries as a garnish to a salad dressed in raspberry vinaigrette.

Yields 1 cup; serving size 2 teaspoons

Calories: 64.29
Protein: 0.1 grams
Carbohydrates: 0.2 grams
Sugar: 0.01 grams
Fat: 7.02 grams

1 clove garlic, smashed, plus
    extra to taste
½ bunch chives
½ teaspoon homemade
    Dijon-Style Mustard
    (page 241)
1 teaspoon anchovy paste
1 teaspoon Splenda
¼ cup of your chosen vinegar:
    Champagne vinegar,
    apple cider vinegar,
    raspberry vinegar, or
    balsamic vinegar
¾ cup olive oil or a mixture of
    olive oil and canola oil
1 tablespoon rosemary, basil,
    or thyme or 1 teaspoon
    dried herb
Salt and pepper to taste

Roasted Red Pepper Sauce

*This is delicious with crab cakes, crudités, and hard-boiled eggs.
Be sure to use within 4 days. This is an American version of
Maryrose sauce, which is very popular in Ireland.*

**Yields 1 cup sauce;
serving size 1 teaspoon**

Calories: 18.69
Protein: 0.18 grams
Carbohydrates: 0.31 grams
Sugar: 0.09 grams
Fat: 1.86 grams

4 ounces roasted red peppers
4 ounces Basic Mayonnaise
    (page 238)
1 tablespoon red pepper
    flakes
1 clove garlic
½ teaspoon Splenda
Salt and pepper to taste

1. Blend all ingredients in your blender. Spoon into a jar, cover, and refrigerate.

Sauce vs. Dressing
These are often interchangeable terms. Both can be hot or cold, but we think of dressings mainly as something to go on salad. Mayonnaise can be either a sauce or a dressing.

Asian Ginger Dipping Sauce

*You can make this sauce in advance and keep
it in a cool place for a week before using it.*

**Yields 5 ounces;
serving size ½ ounce**

Calories: 9.73
Protein: 1.04 grams
Carbohydrates: 0.86 grams
Sugar: 0.07 grams
Fat: 0.33 grams

½ cup Tamari
1 teaspoon fresh gingerroot,
    peeled and minced
1 garlic clove, minced
1 teaspoon Toasted Sesame-
    Seed Oil (page 238)
2 tablespoons lemon juice
½ teaspoon Splenda
½ teaspoon cayenne pepper,
    or to taste

1. Blend all ingredients in a blender. Pour into a jar. Use as needed.

Barbecue Sauce

This is spicy enough to cover for the extreme sweetness of many barbecue sauces. You may notice the flavor of molasses, but you won't miss the calories and sugar.

1. Heat the oil in a 1-quart pot over medium heat. Add the onions and garlic and sauté. Add the rest of the ingredients, stir, cover, and reduce heat.

2. Simmer for 45 minutes or until reduced to 2 cups of sauce. Cool and place in a jar. This will keep for two weeks when refrigerated.

Game Over
Get rid of the gamy flavor of venison and other popular game meats using one of two methods. Employ a slow cooker or soak the meat overnight in milk or tomato juice. Drain the meat and discard the soaking liquid.

Yields 16 ounces; serving size 1 ounce

Calories: 28.89
Protein: 0.75 grams
Carbohydrates: 4.07 grams
Sugar: 2.48 grams
Fat: 1.59 grams

2 tablespoons olive oil
3 cloves garlic, minced
¼ cup sweet white onion, minced
2 cups Chili Sauce (page 240)
½ cup sugar-free tomato juice
1 teaspoon Basic Mustard (page 241)
1 teaspoon liquid smoke
2 tablespoons cider vinegar
1 tablespoon orange zest
1 teaspoon lemon zest
⅛ teaspoon cinnamon
2 tablespoons DiabetiSweet Brown
1 teaspoon soy sauce
Cayenne pepper to taste

Dijon Dressing

This is a wonderful dressing for hot or cold fish and seafood.
It's also very good on a roast beef sandwich.

1. Blend all ingredients in a blender.
2. Pour into a jar or bottle and refrigerate.

Sugar-Free Salad Dressings

Just about any bottle of commercial dressing you pick up in the market has sugar in it. If you really want to eat sugar-free, make it yourself.

Lemon-Herb Dressing

This refreshing dressing is perfect on a crisp salad. Add an
ounce of Gorgonzola cheese for more oomph.

1. Place all ingredients in the blender and blend until very smooth. Pour into a bottle or jar and serve.

Yields 1 cup; serving size 2 teaspoons

Calories: 67.3
Protein: 0.33 grams
Carbohydrates: 0.15 grams
Sugar: 0.02 grams
Fat: 7.28 grams

2 teaspoons dry Dijon mustard
¼ cup white wine vinegar
1 teaspoon Splenda, plus extra to taste
1 teaspoon dried dill weed
½ teaspoon Tamari
1 whole egg
½ teaspoon salt
Freshly ground white pepper to taste
¾ cup olive oil

Yields 1 cup; serving size 2 teaspoons

Calories: 2.7
Protein: 0.1 grams
Carbohydrates: 0.69 grams
Sugar: 0.14 grams
Fat: 0.03 grams

¼ cup lemon juice
1 clove garlic
2 shallots
½ teaspoon soy sauce
1 tablespoon dried rosemary leaves
1 teaspoon oregano leaves
¼ cup fresh parsley leaves
1 teaspoon Splenda
½ teaspoon salt
Freshly ground black pepper to taste

Hot Lemon Sauce

This sauce is best served hot. You need a really good wire whisk to work this properly.

✦

1. Melt the butter and olive oil in a saucepan over medium heat. Stir in the flour and cook for three minutes.

2. Vigorously whisk in the broth and milk. When the sauce reaches the consistency of pancake batter, add the rest of the ingredients. Whisk to blend.

3. Remove from heat and serve warm.

Saucy Disasters

When sauces curdle or break, it looks like a disaster. Fortunately, there's an easy solution. Put the sauce into your blender and add 1 tablespoon of boiling water. Blend until the sauce is smooth.

Yields 1 cup; serving size 2 tablespoons

Calories: 89.22
Protein: 0.78 grams
Carbohydrates: 1.92 grams
Sugar: 0.15 grams
Fat: 8.95 grams

2 tablespoons unsalted butter
1 tablespoon canola oil or olive oil
1 tablespoon Wundra quick-blending flour
¼ cup chicken broth
¾ cup 2% milk or light cream
Juice of ½ lemon
½ teaspoon lemon zest
½ teaspoon Splenda
⅛ teaspoon cayenne pepper
Salt to taste

Egg and Lemon Sauce

This is delicious with fish. You can also serve it with cold shrimp or on a seafood salad. The homemade mayonnaise has enough of a sweet taste that you don't have to add any sugar to this recipe.

Calories: 95.15
Protein: 1.02 grams
Carbohydrates: 0.68 grams
Sugar: 0.23 grams
Fat: 9.86 grams

1 hard-boiled egg, mashed
⅞ cup Basic Mayonnaise (page 238)
1 shallot, minced
2 tablespoons fresh lemon juice
¼ cup fresh parsley leaves
Freshly ground black pepper to taste

1. Mash vigorously to blend all ingredients.

Egg Sauces

Raw or hard-boiled eggs are essential to certain sauces. If you are worried about getting sick from eating raw eggs, buy pasteurized eggs. The acid in jemon juice and vinegar neutralizes bacteria. If you're still skeptical, whisk the eggs and the other liquid ingredients in a double boiler until the eggs thicken. Cool and continue with the recipe.

Fresh Tomato Sauce with Mushrooms and Herbs

Since you can get fresh tomatoes year-round, you can get a summery taste without worrying about the sugar in commercial sauces.

❧

1. Heat the oil in a soup pot over medium heat. Sauté the garlic and onions. When soft, toss the mushrooms in the oil.

2. Blend the tomatoes in a blender and add to the sauce.

3. Stir in the rest of the ingredients. Reduce heat to low and simmer for 45 minutes.

Fresh Herb Conversions

If you substitute fresh herbs for the dried ones call for in a recipe, use three times the amount.

Yields 6 servings; serving size ⅓ cup

Calories: 191.17
Protein: 12.86 grams
Carbohydrates: 10.13 grams
Sugar: 7.91 grams
Fat: 11.32 grams

1 tablespoon olive oil
2 cloves garlic, chopped
½ cup sweet white onion, chopped
1 cup white or brown mushrooms, thinly sliced
1 pint fresh cherry or plum tomatoes, stems removed
11 tablespoon red vinegar
½ teaspoon salt
½ teaspoon Splenda
1 teaspoon dried rosemary leaves
1 teaspoon dried oregano leaves
Freshly ground black pepper to taste
Freshly grated Parmesan cheese to taste

Sweet Tea Sauce

*This sweet and sour sauce works well on pork, chicken,
or sorbet. The tea must be very strong for it to work.*

❧

Yields 1 cup; serving
size 1 tablespoon

Calories: 10.04
Protein: 0.19 grams
Carbohydrates: 2.69 grams
Sugar: 0.06 grams
Fat: 0.07 grams

*2 sachets Sunshine Lemon
Rooibos tea
2 teaspoons Splenda
2 tablespoons freshly
squeezed lemon juice
1 teaspoon lemon zest
1 teaspoon cayenne pepper
2 whole cloves (optional)
6 ounces boiling water*

1. Place all of the ingredients in a one-cup measuring cup. Steep for 15 minutes. Serve hot or at room temperature.

Tea as a Flavoring
The tea itself can produce wonderful flavorings. Tea with lemon, orange, or lime zest is quite delicious either to drink or to use in a sauce with a bit of Splenda.

Mustard Cream Sauce

*This is a fine basic mustard-cream sauce. You can use cream
if you aren't watching your cholesterol. Try this with broccoli,
asparagus, pasta, salmon, veal scallops, or seafood.*

❧

Yields 1 cup; serving
size 1 tablespoon

Calories: 18.13
Protein: 0.59 grams
Carbohydrates: 1.14 grams
Sugar: 0.51 grams
Fat: 1.29 grams

*1 tablespoon unsalted butter
1 shallot, minced
1 tablespoon Basic Mustard
(page 241)
1 tablespoon whole-wheat or
Wundra flour
½ teaspoon salt
½ teaspoon Splenda
⅔ cup whole milk, heated
Freshly ground nutmeg to
taste (optional)*

1. Heat the butter in a 1-quart saucepan over medium heat. Add the shallot and cook, stirring until softened.

2. Whisk in the mustard, flour, salt, and Splenda. Keep whisking until very smooth and thick.

3. Reduce heat to low. Slowly add the warm milk, stirring constantly. Add the nutmeg. Serve warm.

Sweet-and-Sour Mustard

This tastes like what you'd get commercially. It's lovely on hot dogs, meats, and poultry and in sauces and salad dressings.

1. Whisk all of the ingredients in the blender until smooth. Let stand for 15 minutes to develop. Place in a clean jar and use as needed.

Sugar in Sauces

Sugar is added to most sauces to bring out the flavors. The same is true of salt. When both are active ingredients, they enhance the flavor of sauces, cakes, cookies, and other dishes.

Yields ½ cup; serving size 1 teaspoon

Calories: 11.6
Protein: 0.62 grams
Carbohydrates: 0.78 grams
Sugar: 0.2 grams
Fat: 0.74 grams

⅓ cup powdered English or
    Dijon mustard
⅓ cup cider vinegar
¼ teaspoon salt or to taste
1 tablespoon Splenda
1 teaspoon cayenne pepper
    or to taste
¼ teaspoon freshly ground
    black pepper, or to taste

Mango Chutney

This is absolutely lovely with fish, shrimp, chicken, or other foods that you can grill or skewer. Using the Splenda leaves you with lots of natural flavor.

1. Place all ingredients in a food processor and pulse until they reach the texture of oatmeal. Serve chilled or at room temperature.

Makes 1¼ cups; serving size 2 teaspoons

Calories: 5.55
Protein: 0.06 grams
Carbohydrates: 1.5 grams
Sugar: 1.07 grams
Fat: 0.04 grams

1 large mango
1 tablespoon freshly grated
    gingerroot
1 teaspoon curry powder
½ teaspoon ground
    cardamom
2 teaspoons Splenda
Juice of one lime, freshly
    squeezed
½ teaspoon salt
1 teaspoon cayenne pepper

Tomato Salsa

Fresh salsa is easy to make and delicious with nachos and in dips, salad dressings, and soups. Using fresh ingredients and making your own gives you control over the sugar added to your salsas.

Yields 1½ cups; serving size 2 teaspoons

Calories: 10.38
Protein: 0.13 grams
Carbohydrates: 0.76 grams
Sugar: 0.36 grams
Fat: 0.82 grams

2 tablespoon olive oil
½ cup white onion, chopped
3 cloves garlic, minced
2 Poblemo or Serrano chilies, stems removed, minced
8 ounces fresh plum tomatoes, coarsely chopped
Juice of 1 fresh lime
¼ teaspoon ground coriander
1 teaspoon salt
½ teaspoon Splenda
1 teaspoon cumin powder
¼ cup fresh cilantro or Italian parsley, chopped

1. Heat the oil in a large saucepan over medium heat. Add the onions, garlic, and chilies. Sauté until soft, about 5 minutes.

2. Stir in the rest of the ingredients. Reduce heat and cover. Cook for 15 minutes. Remove from heat and let rest for another 15 minutes. Serve chilled or at room temperature.

The Ways of Salsa

You can make salsa with peaches, pineapples, mangos, yellow peppers, or whatever you like. The important thing is the spice level, which you can regulate yourself. For spicier sauce, leave the seeds in the chiles. For milder sauce, remove the seeds.

Chapter 18
Snacks

Hot Miniature Stromboli 252

Ham-Wrapped Asparagus 253

Tiny Italian Meatballs with Pine Nuts 254

Crispy Sesame Chicken Tenders 254

Barbecue Wings 255

Broiled Baby Chicken Drumsticks

    with Asian Flavors and Sesame 256

Smoked Turkey with Sour Apples 256

Miniature Crab Cakes 257

Zucchini, Feta, and Ricotta Pizza 258

Baked Cherry Tomatoes Stuffed

    with Three Cheeses 259

Cucumber Slices Piled with

    Mascarpone Cheese, Shallots, and Prosciutto . . . 259

Crunchy Mini Panini with Tomato,

    Basil, and Provolone Cheese 260

Middle-Eastern Black Bean Dip 261

Sweet-and-Spicy Toasted Nut Mix 261

Artichoke and Spinach Dip 262

Hot Miniature Stromboli

If you're using wooden toothpicks, soak them in water for 20 minutes prior to use. You could also use metal toothpicks, but stay away from plastic toothpicks, which will melt. Most imported Italian salami is sugar free, but ask a deli employee to check the label for you.

Yields 6 servings; serving size 3 pieces

Calories: 216.71
Protein: 15.04 grams
Carbohydrates: 2.12 grams
Sugar: 0.67 grams
Fat: 16.84 grams

16 very thin slices hard salami
16 very thin slices provolone cheese
16 basil leaves
16 toothpicks
Sugar-free Dijon-Style Mustard (page 241) or Vinaigrette (page 241)

1. Preheat oven to 475°F. Prepare a cookie sheet with nonstick spray. Lay the salami slices on the cookie sheet.

2. Place a piece of cheese and a basil leaf on each piece of salami. Roll them very tightly.

3. Skewer the rolls with toothpicks and bake for 6–8 minutes or until the salami is slightly brown and the cheese melts. Carefully cut into thirds to make 18 pieces.

4. Serve hot! Dip into mustard or salad dressing.

Soaking Wooden Instruments

Whenever you put wood in the oven or on the fire, it's important to soak the wood. Otherwise you can have a nasty fire, ruin the food, and be embarrassed by calling in the fire department.

Ham-Wrapped Asparagus

You can use any good melting cheese for this. Substitute cheddar, Gorgonzola, Monterey Jack, or Pepper Jack.

✧

1. Prepare a cookie sheet with nonstick spray.

2. Lay out the bread and spread butter on it. Place the ham on the bread. Thinly spread the mascarpone on the ham. Add a stalk of asparagus to each slice of bread.

3. Roll the asparagus, ham, and bread tightly. Put the seam facedown on the cookie sheet. Brush with melted butter. Freeze for 2 hours or overnight.

4. Preheat the oven to 375°F. Cut each frozen roll in 3 pieces. Bake until lightly browned, about 15 minutes. Serve hot.

Frozen Vegetables

Although most chefs prefer fresh vegetables, most of us can't get to a green market on a daily basis. Some of the best of the frozen vegetables are baby peas, asparagus, artichoke hearts, broccoli, and brussels sprouts. Frozen, chopped spinach is very useful for omelets and other dishes; just make sure to thaw it and squeeze all of the liquid out prior to using.

Yields 36 snacks; serving size 3 asparagus stalks

Calories: 139.01
Protein: 7.08 grams
Carbohydrates: 11.12 grams
Sugar: 0.68 grams
Fat: 8.39 grams

12 very thin slices sugar-free white or wheat bread, crusts removed
2 tablespoons unsalted butter at room temperature
12 slices sugar-free smoked ham
3 tablespoons mascarpone cheese at room temperature
12 stalks frozen asparagus, thawed
3 tablespoons unsalted butter, melted

Tiny Italian Meatballs with Pine Nuts

These doll-sized meatballs can also be fried, which does add to the calorie count. However, baking works well; just don't overcook them or they'll dry out.

**Yields 70 meatballs;
serving size 3 meatballs**

Calories: 66.24
Protein: 5.40 grams
Carbohydrates: 4.96 grams
Sugar: 2.19 grams
Fat: 2.23 grams

*1 pound lean ground sirloin
3 cloves garlic, minced
½ cup dried sugar-free bread
    crumbs
1 whole egg, beaten
1 teaspoon Splenda
½ teaspoon ground cinnamon
1 teaspoon salt
1 teaspoon dried oregano leaves
⅔ cup pine nuts
½ cup raisins with no sugar
    added (optional)*

1. Preheat oven to 375°F. Prepare two cookie sheets with nonstick spray. Mix all ingredients thoroughly with your fingers.

2. Roll into marble-sized meatballs, about ¾" in diameter. Bake for 8-10 minutes, turning the cookie sheets once to make sure they all get equal heat.

3. Serve on toothpicks, in sauce, or in mini-hero sandwiches.

Crispy Sesame Chicken Tenders

This gives you loads of flavor for very few calories. If you and your family are addressing problems of weight, serve this as a snack. High protein, very low fat, and no sugar!

**Yields 6 servings;
serving size 3 pieces**

Calories: 156.42
Protein: 7.06 grams
Carbohydrates: 9.14 grams
Sugar: 0.53 grams
Fat: 10.64 grams

*6 chicken tenders, cut into 18
    bite-sized pieces
¼ cup soy sauce
Juice of ½ lime
1 teaspoon Splenda
¼ teaspoon cayenne pepper
½ cup white sesame seeds*

1. Cut the tenders in bite-sized pieces. Mix the next four ingredients in a resealable plastic bag. Add the tenders and shake to coat the chicken. Let marinate for 20–30 minutes.

2. Preheat the broiler to 350°F. Prepare a cookie sheet with nonstick spray or coat it with aluminum foil.

3. Sprinkle the sesame seeds on a piece of waxed paper. Drain the tenders. Press the seeds into the chicken pieces. Discard the marinade.

4. Broil, turning occasionally, for 10 minutes. Reduce heat to 225°F and bake for another 5 minutes. Serve hot.

Barbecue Wings

Most of the time, wings are fried and dipped in a sauce of butter, vinegar, and hot sauce. This is more traditional, less fattening, and just as delicious. You have the option to either steam or boil the wings prior to adding barbecue sauce.

1. Remove the wing tips and halve the wings. Meanwhile, bring water to a boil.

2. Drop the wings into boiling water. Cover, reduce heat, and boil gently for 10 minutes. Preheat the broiler or indoor grill to 400°F.

3. Drain off the broth, reserving for stock. Prepare a broiler pan or indoor grill with nonstick spray.

4. Brush the wings with barbecue sauce and grill until browned. Serve hot with extra sugar-free barbecue sauce and Tabasco sauce on the side.

Healthy Snacks

Snacks should be an integral part of a good diet. They should have nutritional value, look appealing, be suitable for children and adults, and satisfy the need for "a little something."

Yield 10 servings; serving size 3 whole wings

Calories: 179.09
Protein: 12.63 grams
Carbohydrates: 7.20 grams
Sugar: 1.83 grams
Fat: 10.53 grams

30 whole wings
1 quart water
1 cup Barbecue Sauce (page 243)
Tabasco sauce to taste

Broiled Baby Chicken Drumsticks with Asian Flavors and Sesame

Up the number of servings for a quick supper. These are great hot or cold, so pack them for a school lunch, a family picnic, or just a good snack.

Yields 24 drumsticks; serving size 2 drumsticks

Calories: 307.56
Protein: 32.14 grams
Carbohydrates: 4.33 grams
Sugar: 0.20 grams
Fat: 17.26 grams

2 ounces Toasted Sesame
    Seed Oil (page 238)
1 tablespoon fresh lime juice
3 ounces soy sauce
1 teaspoon cayenne pepper
2 tablespoons cider vinegar
1 teaspoon Splenda
1 clove garlic, minced
1 inch fresh gingerroot,
    peeled and minced
24 very small chicken
    drumsticks

1. Whisk the first 8 ingredients together. Place in a nonreactive bowl. Add the chicken legs and turn to coat. Marinate for at least 60 minutes.

2. Preheat the broiler or grill to 500°F. Drain the chicken. Discard the marinade.

3. Prepare a broiler pan with nonstick spray or heat your charcoal grill to very high and set the grill well up from the coals.

4. Broil or grill the drumsticks, turning frequently, about 4 minutes per side. When nicely browned, serve with mango salsa or other chutney.

Smoked Turkey with Sour Apples

Add cheddar cheese if you want more sustenance. This is excellent for an after-school snack. It'll hold the kids over until dinner but not fill them up with a lot of simple sugars.

Yields 4 servings; serving size 2 pieces of turkey-wrapped apple

Calories: 44.13
Protein: 5.02 grams
Carbohydrates: 5.31 grams
Sugar: 3.98 grams
Fat: 0.60 grams

1 tart green apple, peeled,
    cored, and cut in eighths
Juice of ½ lemon
4 thick slices deli smoked
    turkey, halved

1. Core the apple and slice it. Sprinkle with lemon juice. Wrap each piece of apple in a smoked turkey slice. Use toothpicks if needed and serve.

Miniature Crab Cakes

Traditionally, crab cakes are fried in butter. This healthy alternative bakes them. It also takes advantage of panko, a type of bread crumb that adds a lot of crunch to a dish without adding a lot of fat.

1. Preheat the oven to 450°F. Prepare a baking sheet with nonstick spray.

2. Mix the first 8 ingredients together in a bowl. Spread the panko bread crumbs on a piece of waxed paper.

3. Make little burgers using about 1 tablespoonful of the crab mixture. Coat with panko.

4. Bake for 5 minutes. Turn and bake for another 5 minutes or until very crisp. Serve on slices of cucumber, leaves of romaine lettuce, or small pieces of bread.

Snacks vs. Treats

A snack is a small part of a healthy diet, something you can eat every day to maintain well-being. Snacks include fruit, raw veggies, cheese and crackers, even a half-sandwich. A treat is something you have rarely on special occasions. Treats include cookies, cakes, candy, and ice cream.

Yields 16 cakes; serving size 2 crab cakes

Calories: 116.95
Protein: 7.28 grams
Carbohydrates: 6.31 grams
Sugar: 0.82 grams
Fat: 6.89 grams

8 ounces crabmeat
¼ cup Basic Mayonnaise (page 238)
Juice and zest of ½ lemon
1 egg
1 tablespoon Chili Sauce (page 240)
2 tablespoons sweet white onion, minced
1 teaspoon dried dill weed or 1 tablespoon fresh dill, snipped
1 teaspoon dry Dijon-style mustard blended with 2 teaspoons water
½ cup panko

Zucchini, Feta, and Ricotta Pizza

*This snack has lots of calcium, and it's delicious
and easy to make for you and your team.*

✧

**Serves 10; serving size
two 2" x 2" squares**

Calories: 234.46
Protein: 7.87 grams
Carbohydrates: 26.92 grams
Sugar: 3.84 grams
Fat: 10.75 grams

1 pound sugar-free pizza
    dough
2 tablespoons olive oil
4 small zucchini, ends
    trimmed and thinly sliced
1 sweet red onion, cut into
    paper-thin rings
1 tablespoon dried oregano
Salt and pepper to taste
1 cup low-fat ricotta cheese
¼ cup feta cheese, crumbled
20 Sicilian or Greek black
    olives, pitted and
    chopped
2 tablespoons additional
    olive oil, placed in plastic
    spray bottle

1. Preheat the oven to 475°F. Prepare two cookie sheets with nonstick spray. Divide the dough in half and roll the dough into two 20" x 10" rectangles and place on the cookie sheets.

2. Place the dough on the cookie sheets. Turn over the edges to make a half-inch rim around the pizzas. Brush with olive oil.

3. Bake for 6–8 minutes. Remove from the oven and sprinkle lightly with salt and pepper.

4. Mix the oregano, pepper, ricotta, feta, and chopped olives. Spread evenly over the dough. Layer the zucchini and onions evenly atop the cheese mixture, pressing it down. Spray with additional olive oil.

5. Bake for 10–12 minutes. Cut, serve, and enjoy.

Sugar-free Pizza

Make sure you either prepare your own sugar-free pizza dough or scour your grocery store for sugar-free mixes or premade crusts.

Baked Cherry Tomatoes Stuffed with Three Cheeses

This fun, satisfying snack is loaded with calcium.

❧

1. Preheat oven to 375°F.

2. Prepare a baking sheet with nonstick spray. Cut the tops off the tomatoes. Use a melon ball cutter to scoop out the inside pulp and seeds.

3. Mix the ricotta, Parmesan, pepper, and chives. Stuff the tomatoes. Sprinkle the tops with the cheddar cheese. Bake for 10-12 minutes. Serve hot or warm.

Yields 12 tomatoes; serving size 3 tomatoes

Calories: 26.78
Protein: 1.75 grams
Carbohydrates: 1.02 grams
Sugar: 0.15 grams
Fat: 1.82 grams

12 cherry tomatoes
¼ cup ricotta cheese
2 tablespoons Parmesan cheese
Freshly ground black pepper to taste
1 tablespoon fresh chives, snipped
¼ cup grated aged cheddar cheese

Cucumber Slices Piled with Mascarpone Cheese, Shallots, and Prosciutto

This is fairly expensive and quite rich. You can substitute cream cheese for mascarpone and smoked sugar-free ham or smoked salmon for prosciutto.

❧

1. Mix the cheese and shallots together. Sprinkle with pepper. Place the cucumber slices on a plate.

2. Place a teaspoon of the cheese-shallot mixture on each cucumber slice. Cross the strips of prosciutto on top.

Yields 12 slices; serving size 2 slices

Calories: 63.76
Protein: 2.58 grams
Carbohydrates: 1.26 grams
Sugar: 0.79 grams
Fat: 5.40 grams

4 tablespoons mascarpone cheese at room temperature
2 shallots, minced
Freshly ground black pepper to taste
12 slices English cucumber
3 paper-thin slices prosciutto, cut in thin strips

Crunchy Mini Panini with Tomato, Basil, and Provolone Cheese

If you don't have a panini maker, use an indoor grill or a frying pan.
If you are using a frying pan, simply put another, heavy pan
on top of the sandwich with a weight in it.

∽

**Serves 4; serving
size ½ sandwich**

Calories: 245.96
Protein: 9.86 grams
Carbohydrates: 17.07 grams
Sugar: 2.30 grams
Fat: 11.96 grams

*4 slices sugar-free Italian
  bread*
*4 tablespoons oil and vinegar
  dressing*
4 slices ripe tomato
8 medium basil leaves
4 thin slices Provolone
*Sugar-free bacon or sugar-
  free prosciutto (optional)*

1. Prepare the grill or pan with nonstick spray. Brush both sides of each piece of bread with dressing. Stack the ingredients with pieces of cheese to "glue" them together. Heat the pan to medium.

2. Grill the sandwiches until one side is brown. Turn and grill the other side. Cut and serve.

Panini

These lovely Italian sandwiches enjoyed a recent surge in popularity in little restaurants all over the country. Some are like Philly cheese steaks, others filled with brie and roasted peppers. Be creative. They are wonderful either cut in small pieces as a snack or served whole for lunch. Vary the ingredients of the recipe based on what you have on hand.

Middle-Eastern Black Bean Dip

Black beans have a wonderful texture when puréed.
This dip can be used with chicken tenders, with sugar-free crackers,
chips or chunks of corn bread. You can make this in advance and
refrigerate it. Serve it chilled the next day or warm it in the microwave.

Yields 12 servings;
serving size 1 ounce

Calories: 112.15
Protein: 6.91 grams
Carbohydrates: 26.66 grams
Sugar: 4.37 grams
Fat: 0.42 grams

1 cup pineapple juice, no
  sugar added
1 tablespoon Splenda
1 tablespoon curry powder
1 teaspoon cayenne pepper
1 tablespoon almond paste
1 15-ounce can black beans,
  drained and rinsed
Salt and pepper to taste

1. In a small saucepan over high heat, whisk the first 5 ingredients together. Bring to a boil, reduce heat to medium, and cook until reduced by half.

2. Let the sauce cool slightly, place in the blender, add beans, and blend until puréed.

Sweet-and-Spicy Toasted Nut Mix

This is very easy and delicious, and it keeps for a couple of weeks in an airtight container.

Yields 18 servings;
serving size 8 nuts

Calories: 204.85
Protein: 4.63 grams
Carbohydrates: 4.70 grams
Sugar: 0.84 grams
Fat: 19.71 grams

¼ cup DiabetiSweet
½ cup unsalted butter, melted
2 teaspoons freshly ground
  black pepper
1 teaspoon coarse salt
½ pound blanched almonds
½ pound walnut halves

1. Preheat the oven to 400°F. Prepare a baking sheet with parchment paper or nonstick spray. Whisk the first four ingredients together in a large bowl.

2. Stir in the nuts. Turn until all are covered. Spread on the baking sheet. Bake for 10–12 minutes, checking often.

3. Cool at room temperature and store.

Nuts!

You can roast them, salt them, fry them, glaze them, and add them to all sorts of treats. Put them on desserts, add them to trail mix, salads, and even throw some toasted pine nuts into a salsa. Float them on top of soups or add them to cream cheese for some added crunch in your next sandwich.

Artichoke and Spinach Dip

*Serve this dip in a hollowed round loaf of bread. Surround the dip
with crackers or thinly sliced pieces of sugar-free sourdough baguette.
The only sugar in this dip comes from the lactose in the cheese.*

∽

**Serves 20–30; serving size
3 teaspoons on 3 crackers**

Calories: 51.61
Protein: 1.74 grams
Carbohydrates: 2.12 grams
Sugar: 0.93 grams
Fat: 4.18 grams

*10 ounces frozen chopped
    spinach, thawed*
*1 cup artichoke hearts,
    drained*
*8 ounces low-fat cream
    cheese at room
    temperature*
½ cup sweet onion, minced
Juice of ½ lemon
*¼ cup Basic Mayonnaise
    (page 238)*
¼ cup low-fat sour cream
½ teaspoon cayenne pepper
⅛ teaspoon nutmeg
1 teaspoon Splenda
*1 tablespoon Parmesan
    cheese*

1. Preheat oven to 350°F. Squeeze the moisture out of the spinach and press the oil out of the artichokes. Purée all ingredients except the Parmesan cheese in a food processor.

2. Prepare a 1 quart baking dish with nonstick spray. Turn the spinach dip into the dish. Sprinkle with Parmesan cheese. Bake for 30 minutes.

Dry vs. Prepared Mustard

Prepared mustards are generally mixed with sugar, vinegar, and sometimes spices. It's best to prepare your own mustard to make sure there is no sugar in it. You can also add all kinds of flavorings to it and make it very much your own invention.

Chapter 19
Desserts

Peach Parfait 264

Peach Melba with Sugar-Free Ice Cream 264

Baked Stuffed Apples 265

New York–Style Cheesecake 266

Apple-Blueberry Crisp 267

Banana Brownies 267

Pear Custard with Pecans 268

Spiced Poached Pears 268

Chocolate Fluff 269

Orange Mousse with Blueberries. 270

Grilled Pineapple 270

Raspberry Coulis with Sugar-Free

      Frozen-Yogurt Smoothie 271

Blackberry Clouds 271

Strawberry-Rhubarb Compote 272

Watermelon-Lime Sorbet 272

Fresh Fruit Sauces 273

Homemade Sugar-Free Chocolate Sauce 273

Homemade Sugar-Free Espresso Sauce 274

Not Your Grandmother's Citrus-Gelatin Ring 275

Joyous Gel 276

Peach Parfait

Parfait means "perfect" in French. You can lace a perfect parfait with lots of liqueurs; this recipe has plenty of flavor but avoids the alcohol.

✦

Yields 4 servings; serving size ½ cup

Calories: 157.91
Protein: 1.64 grams
Carbohydrates: 13.36 grams
Sugar: 10.62 grams
Fat: 11.81 grams

4 ripe peaches
4 teaspoons lemon juice
½ cup whipping cream
1 teaspoon Splenda
¼ cup Fresh Fruit Sauce (use raspberries) (page 273)
2 teaspoons slivered almonds, toasted

1. Bring 4 cups of water to a boil in a two-quart saucepan over medium heat. Add the peaches and cook for 3–4 minutes. Drain the water. Slip the skins off, then slice the peaches into a bowl.

2. Sprinkle the peaches with lemon juice. Whip the cream with the Splenda. Divide the peaches between four wine glasses. Add a teaspoon of Fresh Fruit Sauce.

3. Make a second layer and serve chilled with whipped cream.

4. Sprinkle the top of each parfait with almonds.

Peach Melba with Sugar-Free Ice Cream

Is company arriving on short notice? If you have berry coulis in your refrigerator and ice cream in your freezer, you're all set.

✦

Yields 4 servings; serving size 2 scoops

Calories: 132.17
Protein: 4.24 grams
Carbohydrates: 12.80 grams
Sugar: 6.56 grams
Fat: 7.60 grams

4 small scoops sugar-free vanilla ice cream
4 tablespoons walnut pieces, toasted
2 large peaches, blanched, peeled, and halved
4 tablespoons Fresh Fruit Sauce (use raspberries) (page 273)
Fresh raspberries and extra walnuts for garnish

1. Place one scoop of ice cream in each of four bowls. Sprinkle the nuts on top. Invert a peach half over the ice cream.

2. Drizzle with Fresh Fruit Sauce and sprinkle with fresh raspberries and extra walnuts.

Baked Stuffed Apples

This is delicious plain with whipped cream or ice cream.
It makes an excellent brunch dish.

ᴄⱱᴏ

1. Preheat the oven to 350°F. Prepare a baking dish with nonstick spray.

2. Using an apple corer or a grapefruit spoon, carve a channel down the center of each apple, leaving a base at the bottom to prevent the filling from falling out of the apple.

3. In a bowl, mix the DiabtiSweet Brown, cinnamon, raisins, walnuts, zest, and butter together. Fill the apples.

4. Place the apples in a baking dish. Add the juice to the bottom of the dish. Cover loosely with aluminum foil and bake for 40 minutes. Add water to the apple juice if the pan gets dry.

5. Serve hot or warm with whipped cream or sugar-free ice cream.

Filling Baked Apples

Experiment with the fillings. Use different citrus zests. Try currants instead of raisins or chop up some dried figs or apricots and substitute them for the raisins. Green apples are very low in natural sugar, so opt for them instead of the sweeter varieties.

Yields 4 servings;
serving size 5 ounces

Calories: 200.75
Protein: 1.18 grams
Carbohydrates: 39.17 grams
Sugar: 32.71 grams
Fat: 5.78 grams

4 large apples, rinsed and polished
2 teaspoons DiabetiSweet Brown
½ teaspoon ground cinnamon
4 teaspoons chopped raisins
4 teaspoons chopped walnuts
1 teaspoon finely grated lemon or orange zest
4 teaspoons unsalted butter, melted
½ cup apple juice with no sugar added, plus water if needed

New York–Style Cheesecake

The graham cracker crust is traditional, but simple dark chocolate wafers make a wonderful crust. If you can't find the wafers, use dry sugar-free bread.

ᴄᴠᴏ

Yields 16 servings; serving size 2 ounces

Calories: 296.08
Protein: 6.44 grams
Carbohydrates: 16.47 grams
Sugar: 2.22 grams
Fat: 23.50 grams

2 cups sugar-fee chocolate wafers or graham crackers
½ cup melted unsalted butter
5 egg whites
3 8-ounce packages low-fat cream cheese at room temperature
8 ounces sour cream
⅔ cup Splenda
4 egg yolks
¼ cup cake flour
1 teaspoon vanilla extract
½ teaspoon salt
1 tablespoon freshly squeezed lemon juice
1 teaspoon finely grated lemon zest

1. Preheat your oven to 325°F. Prepare a 9" spring form pan with nonstick spray. Grind the wafers in a food processor and add the melted butter.

2. Press the crumb mixture into the bottom and ½" up the sides of the spring form. Store in the freezer while you make the rest of the cake. Whip the egg whites into stiff peaks and set aside.

3. Mix the remaining ingredients with an electric mixer until smooth. Add egg whites and beat till just combined. Pour into the pan. Bake for 60 minutes or until cheesecake doesn't jiggle in the middle.

4. Turn off the oven and leave the cheesecake in for another 60 minutes. Cool, release the spring, and serve. Chill leftovers.

Apple-Blueberry Crisp

This is so old-fashioned, just what grandma used to make.

⌐⌐⌐

1. Preheat the oven to 350°F. Prepare an 8" x 8" glass pan with nonstick spray. In a bowl, mix the buttery spread, flour, walnuts, and ½ cup Splenda into a coarse, mealy consistency.

2. Spread the apples in the baking dish and sprinkle with blueberries. Sprinkle with remaining flour and Splenda. Spread the topping overall.

3. Bake for 35 minutes or until the topping has browned and the fruit is bubbling.

Apples in Desserts

You can mix apples with varieties of berry and other fruits. You can use different kinds of nuts according to what's available locally or what you have on hand in your kitchen when you are making the crisp.

Makes 6 servings; serving size 1 cup

Calories: 354.59
Protein: 5.31 grams
Carbohydrates: 39.03 grams
Sugar: 17.00 grams
Fat: 23.25 grams

½ cup buttery spread
½ cup plus 2 tablespoons all-purpose flour
⅔ cup walnut pieces
½ cup plus 2 tablespoons Splenda
5 apples, peeled, cored, and sliced
8 ounces blueberries
¼ cup all-purpose flour

Banana Brownies

These actually taste a lot richer than they are! They satisfy your sweet tooth and make use of your overripe bananas.

⌐⌐⌐

1. Preheat oven to 300°F. Prepare a 13" x 9" baking pan with nonstick spray. In a large mixing bowl, beat the bananas, Splenda, buttery spread, egg, water, and chocolate together.

2. Add the flour, salt, and cinnamon. Blend well. Pour into the pan.

3. Bake the brownies for 45 minutes.

Yields 36 brownies; serving size 1 brownie

Calories: 80.18
Protein: 1.43 grams
Carbohydrates: 9.24 grams
Sugar: 1.37 grams
Fat: 5.28 grams

2 mashed bananas
¾ cup Splenda
½ cup buttery spread
1 egg
¾ cup hot water
6 ounces unsweetened chocolate, melted
2 cups all purpose flour
½ teaspoon salt
1 teaspoon ground cinnamon

Pear Custard with Pecans

Fruit custards are a traditional dish. With a bottom crust, this would become a custard tart.

Yields 6 servings; serving size 1 cup

Calories: 169.38
Protein: 7.57 grams
Carbohydrates: 15.95 grams
Sugar: 9.63 grams
Fat: 9.85 grams

4 large pears, peeled, cored, and thinly sliced
2 tablespoons fresh lemon juice
4 whole eggs
1½ cups low-fat milk
1 teaspoon vanilla extract
¼ cup Splenda
½ teaspoon salt
½ cup coarsely ground pecans

1. Preheat the oven to 325°F. Prepare a baking dish with nonstick spray. Place the pears in the baking dish and sprinkle them with lemon juice.

2. Whisk the eggs, milk, vanilla extract, Splenda, and salt and pour over the pears. Sprinkle the top with ground pecans.

3. Bake for 35–40 minutes or until set.

Baking Custards and Cheesecakes
You absolutely must keep the oven well under 400°F or the custard will break, curdle, or become grainy. That is the only secret to making a silky custard.

Spiced Poached Pears

This is very good as a dessert and can also be served as a side dish with poultry or pork. It can be made spicier with coriander or extra cinnamon.

Yields 4 servings; serving size 1 pear

Calories: 94.98
Protein: 0.75 grams
Carbohydrates: 15.28 grams
Sugar: 8.60 grams
Fat: 0.34 grams

1 cup dry red wine
4 whole cloves
1" cinnamon stick
4 teaspoons Splenda, or to taste
4 sweet, ripe pears, peeled, cored, and halved

1. Mix the wine, cloves, cinnamon stick, and Splenda in a medium size saucepan over medium heat. Cover and let steep for 20 minutes.

2. Add the pears and cook, covered, at a simmer for 10 minutes. Turn off the heat and leave in the pan for another 10 minutes. Serve warm.

Poached Fruit
When you poach fruit in wine, be sure to add plenty of spices. You don't want too much sweetener. Serve the poached fruit plain or with cream or ice cream.

Chocolate Fluff

*This is a super easy version of Bavarian cream that is quite easy to make.
The addition of orange juice contributes a great deal to the flavor.*

∽

1. Melt the chocolate and set aside. Place the Splenda, gelatin, and water in a blender. Let it bloom. Meanwhile, heat the orange juice, but don't boil it.

2. Add the orange juice to the Splenda and gelatin. Blend until the gelatin has dissolved. Blend in the chocolate. Let cool to room temperature.

3. Beat the egg whites. Set aside and whip the cream. Pour the chocolate mixture into a large bowl.

4. Gently fold the egg whites into the chocolate mixture, then add the whipped cream.

5. Chill, mixing occasionally, bringing the chocolate up from the bottom of the bowl. Serve in wine glasses.

Whipping Egg Whites or Cream

When you whip egg whites they will not get stiff unless your bowl and beaters or whisk are immaculately clean. If there is a touch of fat or grease on them, your eggs will not puff up. If you are beating both egg whites and whipping cream, do the eggs first, rinse the beaters, and whip the cream.

**Yields 8 servings;
serving size 1 cup**

Calories: 151.87
Protein: 4.41 grams
Carbohydrates: 12.46 grams
Sugar: 8.60 grams
Fat: 11.43 grams

*3 ounces unsweetened
    baking chocolate
2 tablespoons Splenda
¼ ounce unflavored gelatin
2 ounces cold water
1 teaspoon salt
6 ounces orange juice
4 egg whites, beaten stiff
½ cup whipping cream*

Orange Mousse with Blueberries

The sharply orange flavor of this mousse is counterbalanced with the sweet-ness of the blueberries. You can also substitute lemon zest for the orange zest.

∽

Yields 8 servings; serving size ½ cup

Calories: 92.31
Protein: 3.56 grams
Carbohydrates: 10.33 grams
Sugar: 6.69 grams
Fat: 5.64 grams

½ ounce unflavored gelatin
¼ cup cold orange juice
1½ cups orange juice, heated
2 tablespoons finely zested orange peel
½ teaspoon salt
½ cup Splenda
3 egg whites, beaten stiff
½ cup whipping cream
1 pint blueberries
Thinly sliced orange for garnish

1. Place the gelatin and cold orange juice in a blender. Let the gelatin bloom for about 5 minutes. Add the hot orange juice, zest, salt, and Splenda. Blend until smooth.

2. Pour the orange mixture in a large bowl. Set aside.

3. Beat the egg whites. Rinse the beaters and beat the cream.

4. Gently fold the eggs and then the cream into the orange mixture. Refrigerate and stir occasionally.

4. Before serving, mix in the blueberries and garnish with orange slice.

Grilled Pineapple

This is best cooked outdoors on a gas or charcoal grill.
Serve it with sugar-free ice cream or sorbet.

∽

Yields 4 servings; serving size 1 piece of pineapple

Calories: 91.16
Protein: 0.33 grams
Carbohydrates: 11.91 grams
Sugar: 9.40 grams
Fat: 5.86 grams

4 thick slices fresh pineapple, core and skin removed
2 tablespoon butter, melted
2 tablespoons Splenda

1. Set your grill at medium high or wait until the coals turn white. Brush both sides of the pineapple rings with melted butter.

2. Sprinkle with sugar. Grill until you see grill marks and turn. Grill for a few more minutes.

Fruit on the Grill
Most fruit taste delicious grilled. With apples, peaches, pears, and apri-cots, it's best to leave the skins on and grill them flesh-side down.

Raspberry Coulis with Sugar-Free Frozen-Yogurt Smoothie

Adapt this recipe to your own tastes. Make it with your own favorite fruits.

∿

1. Place all ingredients in a blender. Blend and serve immediately.

Yields 2 servings; serving size 1 smoothie

Calories: 150.66
Protein: 3.12 grams
Carbohydrates: 28.11 grams
Sugar: 27.75 grams
Fat: 3.27 grams

¼ cup raspberry coulis
1 cup orange juice
¾ cup vanilla frozen yogurt

Blackberry Clouds

This is a very easy and delightful dessert with a smooth and luscious texture.

∿

1. Bring the berries, Splenda, and water to a boil over medium high heat in a small saucepan.

2. Mix the cornstarch and cold water together until smooth. Add to the blackberries, stirring vigorously. Cook until thick. Let cool.

3. Strain the mixture through a fine sieve into a large bowl. Beat the egg whites. Gently fold the slightly thawed ice cream into the berry mixture. Carefully fold in the egg whites. Chill and serve.

Blackberries

People worry about small blackberry seeds getting unattractively lodged in their teeth. Seeds are difficult to digest, but it's easy to strain them out. The texture of this recipe is excellent.

Yields 4 servings; serving size ½ cup

Calories: 119.67
Protein: 4.31 grams
Carbohydrates: 59.81 grams
Sugar: 7.77 grams
Fat: 3.83 grams

½ pint fresh blackberries
3 ounces Splenda
½ cup water
1 tablespoon cornstarch
2 tablespoons cold water
2 egg whites
8 ounces sugar-free vanilla ice cream or yogurt, slightly thawed

Strawberry-Rhubarb Compote

Splenda works beautifully with sour fruit such as rhubarb, grapefruit, and lemons or unripe fruit.

1. Place the rhubarb, Splenda, and water in a saucepan and cook over medium heat. Bring to a boil and reduce heat. Simmer for 15 minutes or until tender.

2. Mix cornstarch with cold water. Add the cornstarch-water mixture and then the strawberries. Bring back to a boil and cook for 2–3 minutes or until the compote is slightly thickened.

3. Serve plain or over pancakes, ice cream, crepes, or pie.

Yields 4 servings; serving size ½ cup

Calories: 34.49
Protein: 0.87 grams
Carbohydrates: 12.34 grams
Sugar: 4.17 grams
Fat: 0.12 grams

2 cups fresh rhubarb, red parts only, cut in ½" pieces
⅓ cup Splenda
1 cup water
1 tablespoon cornstarch
2 tablespoons cold water
1 pint strawberries, hulled

Watermelon-Lime Sorbet

If you don't have an ice cream maker, freeze this in your freezer.

❦

1. Combine the melon, Splenda, lime juice, and salt in your food processor.

2. Following the directions on an ice cream maker, freeze the sorbet. If you don't have an ice cream maker, freeze it in a baking dish in your regular freezer. Break it up with a fork every 30 minutes.

Unique Cocktail Sorbets

Any good fruit sorbet can be turned into a cocktail with the addition of some vodka. Citrus-flavored vodka imparts a particularly unique flavor. Pear and lemon are delightful, and the watermelon-lime sorbet is delicious with the addition of citron-flavored vodka.

Yields 6 servings; serving size ½ cup

Calories: 17.25
Protein: 0.33 grams
Carbohydrates: 4.98 grams
Sugar: 3.52 grams
Fat: 0.22 grams

2 cups sweet watermelon, seeds removed
Juice of 1 lime
2 tablespoons Splenda
½ teaspoon salt

Fresh Fruit Sauces

*Making fresh fruit sauces is a snap. They are a great alternative
to sugary sauces and toppings you find in the supermarket.*

1. Put berries and Splenda into your blender. Blend until smooth.

2. Put through a sieve if grainy. Pour into a jar and refrigerate. Use over
   any dessert that needs a fruit sauce.

**Yields 1 pint; serving
size 2 tablespoons**

Calories: 1.24
Protein: 0.02 grams
Carbohydrates: 0.69 grams
Sugar: 0.12 grams
Fat: 0.01 grams

*1 pint of raspberries,
    strawberries, or
    blueberries, hulled
2 tablespoons Splenda, or to
    taste*

Homemade Sugar-Free Chocolate Sauce

*This sauce will keep for weeks in the refrigerator. Use it as a base for other
desserts or spoon it over ice cream and frozen sugar-free yogurt.*

1. Whisk all ingredients together until all of the lumps are gone.

2. Place in a saucepan over medium heat. Bring to a boil, whisking until
   thickened. Taste and add more Splenda if necessary.

3. Let cool and pour into a jar for use as needed.

**Yields 1 cup; serving
size 2 tablespoons**

Calories: 3.72
Protein: 0.47 grams
Carbohydrates: 2.41 grams
Sugar: 0.05 grams
Fat: 0.33 grams

*⅓ cup Dutch process cocoa
2 tablespoons Splenda, or to
    taste
¼ teaspoon salt
1 tablespoon cornstarch
1 teaspoon instant espresso
1 cup cold water*

Homemade Sugar-Free Espresso Sauce

The cream makes this a very rich addition to any dessert. However, it's great with vanilla ice cream. This sauce will keep for weeks without the cream.

Yields 1 cup; serving size 2 tablespoons

Calories: 4.48
Protein: 0.00 grams
Carbohydrates: 2.53 grams
Sugar: 0.11 grams
Fat: 0.01 grams

¼ cup instant espresso powder
1 tablespoon cornstarch
¼ cup Splenda, or to taste
1 cup cold water
¼ cup heavy cream (optional variation)

∽

1. Whisk espresso powder, cornstarch, Splenda, and water until smooth. Place in a saucepan and cook over medium heat, stirring until the sauce comes to a boil and thickens.

2. Let cool and pour into a jar. Add cream, if desired.

Chocolate and Coffee Sauces

Chocolate and coffee sauces make great ingredients for mousses or soufflés. They are also tasty poured over ice cream, frozen yogurt, or as sauces for crepes. They will keep for a long time and are simple to make.

Not Your Grandmother's Citrus-Gelatin Ring

*You can fill the center of a ring mold with chicken salad,
shrimp salad, or berries frosted with Splenda.*

∾

1. Place the gelatin and cold water in a blender and let it bloom for 5 minutes. Turn on the motor and slowly add the Splenda and hot orange juice.

2. Add lemon juice, lime juice, salt, and cayenne pepper. Prepare a 3½-cup ring mold with nonstick spray. Pour the gelatin mixture into the ring mold and add the pieces of orange and grapefruit.

3. Chill for at least 3 hours in the refrigerator. Just before serving, invert mold on a large plate or platter. Apply hot, damp towels to the gel. It should drop right out of the mold.

Rings Filled with Goodies

You can use different juices and different fruits. Gelatin molds are a great dessert with berries in the center. The basic recipe can be varied in lots of ways. Be sure to prepare the mold with nonstick spray.

**Yields 6 servings;
serving size ⅓ cup**

Calories: 102.36
Protein: 2.45 grams
Carbohydrates: 26.77 grams
Sugar: 20.25 grams
Fat: 0.43 grams

*1 teaspoon unflavored
    gelatin
¼ cup cold water
¼ cup Splenda, or to taste
1¼ cup orange juice, heated
¼ cup lemon juice
¼ cup lime juice
½ teaspoon salt
½ teaspoon cayenne pepper,
    or to taste
1 cup mandarin orange
    sections
½ cup fresh pink grapefruit
    sections with their
    natural juice*

Joyous Gel

This is a berrylicious dessert that combines sour cream with sweet fruits.

Yields 6 servings; serving size ⅓ cup

Calories: 236.54
Protein: 2.82 grams
Carbohydrates: 46.56 grams
Sugar: 35.19 grams
Fat: 6.12 grams

1 teaspoon unflavored gelatin
¼ cup cold water
1½ cup sugar-free cranberry juice
¼ cup Splenda, or to taste
½ teaspoon salt
2 teaspoons fresh orange zest
1 cup fresh strawberries, hulled and sliced
1 cup fresh blueberries, stems removed
¾ cup sour cream, served on the side

1. Place the gelatin and cold water in a blender. Let stand until it blooms.

2. Bring the cranberry juice to a boil.

3. Turn the blender on low, add the boiling juice, and blend until smooth. Add the Splenda, salt, and zest.

4. Pour into a bowl and stir in the strawberries and blueberries.

5. Place in a 4-cup ring mold and set in the refrigerator until well gelled.

Chapter 20
Fun Family Snacks and Meals

Kiwi Balls with Frosted Strawberries 278

Frozen Grapes 279

Chocolate-Dipped Strawberries 279

Family Ice Cream 280

Popcorn with Hot-Pepper Butter 280

Kids' Favorite Meatloaf 281

Mini Pizzas with Broccoli and Cheese 282

Marinated Chicken Tenders on Toothpicks 283

Turkey Meatballs 284

Cranberry-Walnut Spread 285

Skewered Shrimp with Bacon 285

Chicken, Apple, and Celery Spread 286

Family-Style Hungarian Goulash 287

Deviled Eggs with Smoked Salmon 288

Deviled Eggs with Olives 289

Skewered Chicken Tenders with Sate 289

Cheese Soufflé with Artichokes and Spinach 290

Kiwi Balls with Frosted Strawberries

*Fixing a sweet and tasty icing for the berries
makes a very pretty and delicious presentation.*

∾

**Yields 4 servings;
serving size ¼ cup**

Calories: 40.22
Protein: 0.73 grams
Carbohydrates: 10.06 grams
Sugar: 5.74 grams
Fat: 0.38 grams

1 tablespoon Splenda
1 teaspoon cornstarch
½ teaspoon vanilla extract
*1 teaspoon freshly squeezed
lemon juice*
1 tablespoon cold water
2 kiwi fruit, halved
*12 medium-sized
strawberries, hulled and
halved*

1. Whisk the Splenda, cornstarch, vanilla extract, lemon juice, and water together to make frosting. Set aside.

2. Use a melon ball scoop to make balls of the kiwi fruit. Put kiwis and strawberries in a bowl.

3. Take a heavy-duty plastic bag and cut a tiny piece from the corner. Spoon the frosting mixture into the bag and drizzle over the fruit.

4. Chill and serve.

Favorite Tools

Every kitchen needs two tiny implements—a melon ball scoop and a grapefruit spoon. The melon ball scoop is great for more than melon balls; it scoops up tiny tastes of all sorts of goodies. The grapefruit spoon has a sharp point and is excellent for cutting out the insides of tomatoes, avocados, potatoes, and many other foods.

Frozen Grapes

This snack is very sweet but not at all fattening.

1. Prepare a cookie sheet with nonstick spray. Place the damp grapes on the cookie sheet, sprinkle with Splenda, and freeze. Use commercial lemon yogurt with no sugar as a dipping sauce for the frozen grapes.

Yields 1 pound grapes; serving size 4 ounces

Calories: 135.51
Protein: 4.75 grams
Carbohydrates: 29.65 grams
Sugar: 26.52 grams
Fat: 0.66 grams

1 pound grapes, rinsed
2 teaspoons Splenda
Lemon yogurt with no sugar added

Chocolate-Dipped Strawberries

Try to find strawberries with nice long stems so you don't have to use a fork. Some recipes call for a paraffin wax mixed with the strawberries, but the more natural, the better.

1. Mix the chocolate, Splenda, coffee, salt, and vanilla and melt in a double boiler over simmering water. If you don't have a double boiler, melt in the microwave for 10 seconds.

2. Dip the strawberries in the chocolate and lay on a piece of waxed paper. Refrigerate and serve.

Involving the Kids
If children can help prepare a snack or a meal, they will be much more interested in eating it than if you merely set it in front of them. That is one of the secrets of establishing healthy eating habits.

Yields 4 servings; serving size 4 strawberries

Calories: 140.20
Protein: 2.94 grams
Carbohydrates: 54.82 grams
Sugar: 4.21 grams
Fat: 12.03 grams

3 ounces unsweetened chocolate
3 ounces Splenda
2 tablespoons strong decaffeinated coffee
Pinch of salt
½ teaspoon vanilla
1 pint long-stemmed strawberries, rinsed and chilled

Family Ice Cream

*To make this ice cream, you must have immaculately clean
coffee cans. Remember, when the ice cream becomes aerated,
it will expand, so be sure to leave room in the container.*

ᴄᴚ

**Yields 16 ounces;
serving size 4 ounces**

Calories: 281.00
Protein: 6.89 grams
Carbohydrates: 52.72 grams
Sugar: 8.94 grams
Fat: 20.40 grams

*¾ cup half-and-half
6 tablespoons Splenda
½ cup Fresh Fruit Sauce (page
273)
1-pound coffee can with
plastic lid
2-pound coffee can with
plastic lid
Cracked ice
Kosher salt*

1. Mix the half-and-half, Splenda, and Fresh Fruit Sauce together and place in the 1-pound can. Close the lid tightly. Put it in the 2-pound can.

2. Fill the sides of the 2-pound can with alternating layers of cracked ice and salt until you get to the top. Close the top lid tightly. Seat the children on the floor and have them "churn" the ice cream by rolling the tin around, back and forth. Soon the ice cream will thicken and stop moving in the coffee can, and—WOW! Fresh ice cream! Enjoy!

Popcorn with Hot-Pepper Butter

*Try something a little different for a snack. You can substitute other
seasoned salts, such as garlic, onion, or lemon-pepper seasoning.*

ᴄᴚ

**Yields ½ cup of pepper
butter (for 4 cups of popcorn); serving size 1 cup
pepper-buttered popcorn**

Calories: 223.78
Protein: 0.73 grams
Carbohydrates: 4.18 grams
Sugar: 0.07 grams
Fat: 22.55 grams

*½ cup unsalted butter
½ teaspoon celery salt
1 teaspoon ground cayenne
pepper
1 package plain or low salt
microwave popcorn*

1. Mix the butter, celery salt, and cayenne pepper in a cup and heat them in the your microwave for just a few seconds.

2. Blend well. Then pop your corn and toss it in a bowl with the butter sauce.

If Variety Is the Spice of Life . . .
Seasoned salts and spicy peppers will help to vary your flavorings. Try different combinations, such as a mixture of celery salt, ground coriander seeds, orange zest, and garlic powder.

Kids' Favorite Meatloaf

Actually, this is much loved by grown-ups as well as children.

∽

1. Preheat the oven too 325°F. Whirl everything but the meat and bacon in your blender.

2. Prepare a bread pan with nonstick spray. Pour the ingredients in the blender into a large bowl, add the meat. Mix thoroughly. Pile into the bread pan without tamping it down.

3. Add bacon to the top, if desired. Bake the meatloaf for 60 minutes. Let cool slightly before cutting.

Loaf Pans

Your key to making unforgettable meatloaf lies in the pan you use to cook it. You need a pan that won't allow the meatloaf to stick to the sides or burn. Cast iron, though heavy, works well. You can use a traditional bread loaf pan or a specialized meatloaf pan with an insert to keep the meatloaf away from the excess fat.

Yields 16 ½-inch slices (Standard bread pan 4½" x 8½" x 2½"); serving size one ½-inch slice

Calories: 105.80
Protein: 5.70 grams
Carbohydrates: 6.35 grams
Sugar: 1.89 grams
Fat: 6.47 grams

2 whole eggs
2 ½-inch thick slices Hot Corn Bread with Cherry Peppers (page 19)
¼ cup Chili Sauce (page 240)
½ cup low-fat milk
½ teaspoon salt
¼ teaspoon pepper, or to taste
¼ cup grated Parmesan cheese
1 teaspoon dried oregano
1 pound ground meatloaf mix (beef, pork, and veal), or beef
1 slice sugar-free turkey bacon or regular bacon (optional)

Mini Pizzas with Broccoli and Cheese

*Pizza dough is available in most supermarkets, or you can go to your local pizza parlor and buy a pound of freshly made dough, **if** the pizza maker swears it's sugar-free. Or, you can make it yourself and freeze any extra.*

Yields 4 6" pizzas;
serving size ½ pizza

Calories: 181.10
Protein: 8.85 grams
Carbohydrates: 19.32 grams
Sugar: 2.86 grams
Fat: 7.45 grams

½ pound broccoli florets, chopped and blanched
1 pound package sugar-free pizza dough
2 teaspoons extra version olive oil
1 teaspoon dried oregano
1 teaspoon cayenne pepper, or to taste
6 thin slices mozzarella cheese
¼ cup finely grated Parmesan cheese

1. Preheat your oven to 450°F. Blanch the broccoli, drain it, and set it aside on paper towels.

2. Prepare a cookie sheet with nonstick spray, or use a pizza stone. Roll the dough out in a 12" x 12" square. Cut into 4 squares.

3. Turn the edges of the dough over by ½" to make a rim. Brush the dough with olive oil. Sprinkle with oregano and cayenne. Spread with broccoli, add the pieces of cheese cutting the 2 extra pieces to fill in gaps.

4. Sprinkle with Parmesan and bake for 15 minutes, or until the crust is nicely browned.

Endless Pizza Variations

You can make pizza with spinach, asparagus, peppers, or whatever you like. Try using oils infused with basil and/or garlic. Most kids will eat their veggies when incorporated into a pizza.

Marinated Chicken Tenders on Toothpicks

*This is an interesting marinade, both sweet and spicy
with a nutty undertone from the sesame seed oil. The snacks
can be made on a charcoal or gas grill, or under the broiler.
When you want to fill your family with energy, in the form
of good protein, try this as a snack, or lunch.*

1. Cut the tenders into one-inch pieces and put one or two on each pre-soaked toothpick. In a bowl whisk the rest of the ingredients together and coat each piece of chicken.

2. Cover the bowl and marinate, refrigerated for at least 60 minutes, or up to 3 hours. Preheat broiler or grill to 400°F.

3. Grill or broil the chicken tenders for about 5 minutes per side, depending on the thickness. Turn them often until nicely browned.

**Serves 6–8 as a snack;
serving size 2–3 tenders**

Calories: 166.36
Protein: 11.23 grams
Carbohydrates: 15.77 grams
Sugar: 3.25 grams
Fat: 6.57 grams

*1 pound chicken tenders, cut
    in bite-sized pieces, on
    toothpicks.*
*18 wooden toothpicks,
    soaked for 20 minutes in
    warm water*
*1 tablespoon Toasted Sesame
    Seed Oil (Page 238)*
*½ cup orange juice, no sugar
    added*
3 tablespoons tamari sauce
*3 tablespoons Chili Sauce
    (page 240)*
*1 teaspoon Basic Mustard
    (page 241)*

Turkey Meatballs

If you have a party or TV game night planned, you can make these in advance and either freeze them or fry at the last moment. Or prepare and refrigerate, then pop in the oven to re-heat.

1. Put all but the meat and oil into your blender. Whirl until well blended. Place the meat in a large bowl and pour the mixture from the blender over it.

2. Mix thoroughly and form into 32 meatballs. Heat the oil to 375°F in a frying pan. Fry the meatballs until brown. Drain on paper towels.

Family Food

Good food must always be nutritious, served with plenty of excellent baby veggies, such as grape tomatoes, little carrots, sticks of celery, rings of sweet peppers, and/or raw broccoli and cauliflower florets. Peppers are delicious and have the most nutrients in red, orange, and yellow.

Yields 32 tiny meatballs (in standard size bread pan); serving size 3 meatballs

Calories: 284.39
Protein: 8.13 grams
Carbohydrates: 3.55 grams
Sugar: 0.34 grams
Fat: 26.73 grams

2 cloves garlic, peeled
2 tablespoons chopped onion
2 slices sugar-free bread, such as Italian bread, cubed
1 egg
¼ teaspoon cinnamon
1 teaspoon oregano
Salt and pepper to taste
¼ cup grated Romano cheese
1 pound ground turkey
1 cup canola oil for frying

Cranberry-Walnut Spread

*This is excellent for an after-school sandwich, or spread on
cheese and crackers. The family needs constant fuel,
however, they all need fuel that will keep them going, not make
them logy and bloated with heavy sweets. If you make sandwiches
with this, add some shredded lettuce and serve them for tea.*

∽

1. Place all ingredients in a bowl and mix thoroughly. Use as a spread on
   sugar-free crackers or bread. This will keep in the refrigerator for four
   days.

**Yields 2 cups; serving
size 1 tablespoon**

Calories: 34.27
Protein: 0.79 grams
Carbohydrates: 1.05 grams
Sugar: 0.41 grams
Fat: 3.08 grams

*8 ounces cream cheese,
    softened to room
    temperature*
*¼ cup dried cranberries, no
    sugar added*
*¼ cup chopped walnuts,
    toasted*
¼ cup celery, minced
1 teaspoon Splenda
*Salt and freshly ground
    pepper to taste*

Skewered Shrimp with Bacon

*This is an excellent appetizer or snack that older
children love almost as much as grown-ups.*

∽

1. Dip each shrimp in a combination of melted butter, garlic powder, and
   pepper.

2. Set broiler at 375°F. Wrap the shrimp with bacon and secure with pre-
   soaked wooden toothpicks.

3. Broil the shrimp until the bacon is cooked and the shrimps are pink.
   About 4–5 minutes per side.

**Serves 6; serving size
4 jumbo shrimp or 6
extra large shrimp**

Calories: 314.84
Protein: 17.97 grams
Carbohydrates: 0.72 grams
Sugar: 0.03 grams
Fat: 26.03 grams

*1 pound fresh or thawed
    frozen, raw shrimp (about
    24 per pound)*
¼ cup unsalted butter, melted
½ teaspoon garlic powder
Pepper to taste
*8 strips of bacon, stretched,
    cut in thirds*

Chicken, Apple, and Celery Spread

Yields 2¾ cups Spread;
serving size 2 tablespoons

Calories: 115.33
Protein: 5.8 grams
Carbohydrates: 2.1 grams
Sugar: 1.35 grams
Fat: 9.37 grams

1 cup Basic Mayonnaise
    (Page 238)
1 teaspoon Sweet-and-Sour
    Mustard (page 249)
Salt and pepper to taste
½ teaspoon Splenda
½ teaspoon freshly squeezed
    lime juice
½ teaspoon curry powder, or
    to taste
¾ pound cooked chicken
    (leftovers are fine), diced
½ cup fresh apple, cored and
    diced
¼ cup white onion, minced
¼ cup celery, in small dice
¼ cup peanuts, chopped
Optional garnish: 1 cup green
    grapes or raisins

If you ever wonder what to do with leftover chicken, or how to use chicken breasts for a quick lunch or snack—this fits the bill. It is a fine after-school snack or quick lunch. And, you don't have to worry about filling your family with sugar.

❧

1. Whisk the first six ingredients together in a bowl. When well mixed, stir in the rest of the items. Chill and serve later, or serve right away.

Picnicking with Mayonnaise

Pack the chicken salad in a cooler with ice and leave it there until just before you're ready to eat it. Put it back in the cooler immediately after everyone has been served. If you are at all in doubt, throw it out. Food poisoning is not something to take chances with.

Family-Style Hungarian Goulash

This is an old fashioned crowd pleaser. Make a double recipe and serve a soccer team, or freeze for a future meal. There are two kinds of paprika—hot and sweet. There is no sugar added to the "sweet" paprika—it's made from a special breed of red peppers that are not hot. The hot paprika is made from red chili peppers. Adding just a bit of Splenda will give the goulash (stew) a lovely balance with the vinegar.

1. Preheat the oven to 325°F. Prepare a two-quart casserole with nonstick spray. In a large frying pan over medium heat, add one tablespoon of the oil and the butter. Add the onion, cook and stir until softened, but not browned.

2. Scrape the onions into the casserole. Add the second tablespoon of oil and stir in the beef. Brown the beef and add to the casserole with the onion.

3. Add all but the sour cream, one thing at a time, stirring to blend. Cover and set in the oven for 2 hours or until the veal is very tender. If the liquid dries out add some more broth or tomato juice.

4. Just before serving, add the sour cream. Serve over noodles.

Serves 6; serving size 1 cup

Calories: 491.62
Protein: 29.44 grams
Carbohydrates: 9.80 grams
Sugar: 3.20 grams
Fat: 36.78 grams

2 tablespoons peanut oil
1 tablespoon unsalted butter
3 yellow onions, peeled, cut into coarse dice
2 pounds stewing veal, boneless
1 tablespoon whole-wheat flour
1 teaspoon salt
½ teaspoon freshly ground black pepper, or to taste
1 tablespoon paprika
1 teaspoon Splenda
1 teaspoon caraway seeds
1 teaspoon dried marjoram leaves
1 tablespoon red wine vinegar
1 cup beef broth
1 cup tomato juice, no sugar added
1 cup sour cream (optional)

Deviled Eggs with Smoked Salmon

This is also a wonderful addition to brunch. It's got loads of protein and really no sugar! You can make extra or double the recipe and store them, covered, in the refrigerator for later, or the next day.

❧

Yields 6 eggs; serving size ½ egg with ½ ounce smoked salmon on top

Calories: 68.12 grams
Protein: 4.54 grams
Carbohydrates: 0.60 grams
Sugar: 0.36 grams
Fat: 9.93 grams

6 hard-boiled eggs, peeled
½ cup Basic Mayonnaise (page 238)
2 tablespoons green onions, minced
½ teaspoon Basic Mustard (page 241)
½ teaspoon white wine vinegar
Salt and pepper to taste
½ teaspoon Splenda
2 ounces smoked salmon cut in small matchstick pieces

1. Arrange the egg halves on a platter. Blend everything but the salmon in a bowl, using an immersion blender or a fork.

2. Stuff the eggs with the yolk mixture. Decorate the tops with strips of smoked salmon.

"Deviled"

The "deviled" in deviled eggs is actually a verb. Deviling an egg or another food means to heavily season it. Often, the seasonings make the food spicier or hotter. Because of the devil's obvious association with heat, these foods came to be known as deviled.

Deviled Eggs with Olives

Family food needs to be accessible, fresh, and ready to eat in a trice, tasty and easily digestible. There are so many options that take just a few minutes that avert the sugar addiction or highs of commercial, processed snacks.

1. Cut the peeled eggs in half. Arrange the whites on a plate, scooping the yolks into a bowl. Using an immersion blender, or a fork, beat in the rest of the ingredients, one by one until well blended.

2. Fill the eggs and either serve immediately or refrigerate, covered.

Serves 6; serving size 2 half-eggs

Calories: 216.35
Protein: 6.52 grams
Carbohydrates: 1.48 grams
Sugar: 0.64 grams
Fat: 20.37 grams

6 hard-boiled eggs, shelled and cooled
½ cup Basic Mayonnaise (Page 238)
1 teaspoon Sweet-and-Sour Mustard (page 249)
½ teaspoon garlic salt
Freshly ground pepper to taste
12 small black or green pitted olives, chopped

Skewered Chicken Tenders with Sate

High protein is what this snack, or light lunch, is all about. Or, you can chill it and eat it whenever someone in the family needs sustenance. Tenders make an excellent, healthy adjunct to any sugar-free diet. You can get them fresh or buy a big bag of frozen tenders that defrost in just a few minutes.

1. Preheat the broiler to 350°F. Dip the tenders in sauce. Broil for 4 minutes per side.

2. Whisk all of the sate ingredients in a small bowl. Using toothpicks for the chicken, dip as you go in the sauce.

Serves 6 as a snack, 3 for lunch; serving size 3 tenders

Calories: 171.04
Protein: 9.96 grams
Carbohydrates: 14.82 grams
Sugar: 1.79 grams
Fat: 8.63 grams

½ pound chicken tenders, cut in thirds (about 18 pieces)
1 cup Barbecue Sauce (page 243)

For the Sate:
¼ cup sugar-free peanut butter
Juice of ½ lime
½ teaspoon Splenda
2 tablespoons tamari

Cheese Soufflé with Artichokes and Spinach

*This makes an excellent family dinner or a delicious brunch.
Serve with chunks of toasted baguette, and a nice dessert. Lot's of
puff make this seem like a great deal more than it actually is!*

⌘

**Serves 6; serving
size 6 ounces**

Calories: 215.11
Protein: 9.12 grams
Carbohydrates: 8.42 grams
Sugar: 3.22 grams
Fat: 16.27 grams

1 tablespoon unsalted butter
1 tablespoon flour
*½ cup marinated artichokes,
    from the jar is fine,
    drained, chopped*
*10 oz. package frozen
    chopped spinach, thawed
    and moisture squeezed
    out*
1 tablespoon unsalted butter
1 tablespoon cornstarch
1 cup milk
½ cup grated cheddar cheese
Salt and pepper to taste
6 eggs, separated

1. Preheat oven to 375°F. Spread a two-quart soufflé dish or casserole with butter. Sprinkle with flour to cover.

2. Put the well drained vegetables in a bowl. In a saucepan, melt the butter and whisk in the cornstarch, let foam and slowly whisk in the milk. When thickened add the cheese, salt, pepper, and vegetables. Set aside.

3. Beat the egg yolks and add them to the vegetables and sauce. Using clean beaters and bowl, beat the egg whites until stiff.

4. Fold the egg whites into the vegetables and sauce. Bake in the middle of the oven for 35 minutes. Serve instantly. Don't open the oven door too soon, or your soufflé will sou-flop.

Appendices

Appendix A:
Resources

Appendix B:
Sugar-Free Menus

Appendix A
Resources

Products

Splenda Sugar substitute

Two Leaves and a Bud, specialty teas (available at fine stores and online)

DiabetiSweet Brown Sugar is totally sugar-free

Lucini Pasta Sauces are sugar-free

Jarlsberg Lite Cheese

Quaker Old Fashioned Oatmeal

John McCann steel cut Irish Oatmeal

Trader Joe's stores for all natural sugar-free cookies, crackers and cereals

Wild Oats stores for all natural and sugar-free cereals, bread, whole grains in bulk, cookies, and crackers

Whole Foods stores for all natural and sugar free cereals, breads, cookies, crackers, and grains

Books

Diabetes, Carbohydrates and Fat Gram Guide, Lea Ann Hotzmeister, American Diabetes Association, 2000.

American Diabetes Association Complete Guide to Diabetes (4th edition), American Diabetes Association, Bantam, 2006.

The New American Heart Association Cookbook (7th edition), American Heart Association, Clarkson Potter, 2007.

The Everything® Glycemic Index Cookbook, Nancy T. Maar, Adams Media, 2006.

The Ultimate Weight Solution, Dr. Phil McGraw, Pocket, 2005.

The Ultimate Weight Solution Food Guide, Dr. Phil McGraw, Pocket, 2003.

Web sites

U.S. Department of Agriculture Food and Nutrition
✍ *fnic.nal.usda.gov/nal_display/index.php?tax_level=1&info_center=4*

U.S. Food and Drug Administration
✍ *www.fda.gov*

Gluten-Free Mall
✍ *www.glutenfreemall.com*

American Heart Association
✍ *www.americanheart.org*

American Diabetes Association
✍ *www.diabetes.org*

American Stroke Association
✍ *www.strokeassociation.org*

Healthcastle.com
✍ *www.healthcastle.com*

Weight Watchers
✍ *www.weightwatchers.com*

Nutfactory.com
✍ *www.nutfactory.com*

Oprah.com
✍ *www.oprah.com*

Northwestern University
✍ *www.northwestern.edu/nucuisine/nutrition.html*

Mayo Clinic Nutrition Page
✍ *www.mayoclinic.com/health/food-and-nutrition/NU99999*

Appendix B
Sugar-Free Menus

Breakfast
Family Frittata with Onions, Potatoes, and Sausage
Baked Grapefruit
Hot Corn Bread with Cherry Peppers
Fresh Fruit
Coffee or Green Tea

Brunch
Coconut-Shrimp Soup
Grapefruit-and-Chicken Salad
Banana and Tart-Apple Bread
Chardonnay or Perrier

Hearty Lunch
Chicken and Wild Rice Soup with Cranberries
Baked Cherry Tomatoes Stuffed with Three Cheeses
Fresh Fruit
Perrier

Summer Lunch
Cucumber and Skimmed Buttermilk Summer Soup
Pasta Salad with Shrimp and Snow Pea Pods
White Wine or Sparkling Lemon Perrier

Game Party
Sweet-and-Spicy Toasted Nut Mix
Hot Miniature Stromboli
Crispy Sesame Chicken Tenders
Asian Ginger Dipping Sauce with a platter of raw vegetables
Banana Brownies

Elegant Cocktail Party

Smoked Turkey with Sour Apples
Ham-Wrapped Asparagus
Miniature Crab Cakes
Artichoke and Spinach Dip
Broiled Baby Chicken Drumsticks with Asian Flavors and Sesame
Middle-Eastern Black Bean Dip
Crunchy Mini Panini with Tomato, Basil, and Provolone Cheese
Asian-Style Baby Back Ribs

Sunday Dinner

Roast Whole Chicken with Apples and Celery
Marinated Mushroom Salad
Garlic Mashed Potatoes
Watermelon-Lime Sorbet

Quick Family Dinner for a Weeknight

Rotini with Smoked Salmon and Cream Cheese Sauce
Fennel with Orange Slices
Baked Stuffed Apples

Elegant Dinner for Company

Asparagus with Chopped-Egg Sauce
Baked Stuffed Shrimp
Pears and Walnuts over Mixed Greens
Chocolate Fluff

Feeding a Team

Turkey Chili
Jicama, Mandarin Orange, and Arugula Salad
Hot Corn Bread with Cherry Peppers
Family Ice Cream Served with Grilled Pineapple

Index

Almonds
    Sweet-and-Spicy Toasted Nut
        Mix, 261
Apples
    Apple-Blueberry Crisp, 267
    Baked Stuffed Apples, 265
    Banana and Tart-Apple Bread,
        22
    Brown Rice with Bacon and
        Apples, 215
    Chicken, Apple, and Celery
        Spread, 286
    Chicken, Apple, Celery, and Nut
        Salad, 165
    Curried Tart Apple and Rice
        Salad, 169
    Pork Burgers with Apples, 136
    Roast Whole Chicken with
        Apples and Celery, 78
    Sauerkraut with Apples and
        Ham, 208
    Smoked Turkey with Sour
        Apple, 256
Apricots
    Wild Rice Salad with Fresh
        Apricots and Water
        Chestnuts, 192
Artichokes
    Artichoke and Spinach Dip, 262
    Artichokes with Lemon Dipping
        Sauce, 197
    Braised Chicken with Green
        Olives and Artichokes, 85
    Cheese Soufflé with Artichokes
        and Spinach, 290
    Pork Chops Sautéed with
        Artichokes, 127

Tuna-Stuffed Artichokes, 196
Arugula
    Arugula Salad with Asparagus,
        186
    Jicama, Mandarin Orange, and
        Arugula Salad, 188
Asian Crab Soup with Cabbage
    and Sprouts, 75
Asian Ginger Dipping Sauce, 242
Asian-Style Baby Back Ribs, 134
Asparagus
    Arugula Salad with Asparagus,
        186
    Asparagus with Chopped-Egg
        Sauce, 197
    Ham-Wrapped Asparagus, 253
Autumn Muffins, 25
Avocados
    Avocado Soup, 64
    Avocado, Tomato, and Bacon
        Over Bib Lettuce, 183
    Shrimp-and Avocado Salad, 144

Bacon
    Avocado, Tomato, and Bacon
        Over Bib Lettuce, 183
    Braised Chicken Thighs with
        Bacon and Onion, 80
    Brown Rice with Bacon and
        Apples, 215
    Filet Mignon Grilled with
        Bacon, 98
    Green Bean and Bacon
        Salad with Hot Gorgonzola
        Dressing, 166

Oysters on The Half-Shell with
    Bacon and Green Onions,
    157
Skewered Shrimp with Bacon,
    285
Smoked Bacon Breakfast
    Sandwiches, 32
Bananas
    Banana and Tart-Apple Bread,
        22
    Banana Brownies, 267
    Lime-Banana Smoothie, 42
Barbecued Baby Back Ribs, 135
Barbecued Shrimp, 141
Barbecue Sauce, 243
Barbecue Wings, 255
Basque-Style Lamb Stew, 122
Beads and muffins, 15–30
Beans. See specific beans
Beef
    Asian-Flavored Burgers, 105
    Barbecue-Spice Rubbed Steak,
        103
    Beef Pot Roast with Winter
        Vegetables, 100
    Beef Sirloin Bites with Asian
        spices, 99
    Breakfast Sausage, 33
    Chili-Spiced Beef and Black
        Bean Soup, 48
    Filet Mignon Grilled with
        Bacon, 98
    Filet Mignon Stuffed with
        Gorgonzola Cheese, 96
    Filet Mignon Stuffed with Jack
        Cheese and Salsa, 97
    Kids' Favorite Meatloaf, 281

Marinated London Broil, 102

Mushroom Meatballs in Homemade Tomato Sauce, 106

New Orleans Black-and-Red Burgers, 104

Pumpkin Beef Harvest Stew, 101

Quick Italian Sausage for Soups, Meatballs, and Sauces, 49

Texas Burgers, 105

Tiny Italian Meatballs with Pine Nuts, 254

Beets

Red Salad, 189

Black beans

Chili-Spiced Beef and Black Bean Soup, 48

Middle-Eastern Black Bean Dip, 261

Blackberry Clouds, 271

Bloody Mary Tomato Aspic with Hardboiled Eggs, 174

Blueberries

Apple-Blueberry Crisp, 267

Blueberry Muffins, 24

Fresh Fruit Sauces, 273

Joyous Gel, 276

Mixed-Berry–Filled Omelet, 39

Orange Mousse with Blueberries, 270

Bran Muffins, 25

Broccoli

Baked Rice with Vegetables, 211

Broccoli and Pasta Salad, 178

Broccoli Stir Fry, 198

Creamed Broccoli and Cheddar Soup, 56

Mini Pizzas with Broccoli and Cheese, 282

Shrimp Stir-Fry with Broccoli and Almonds, 148

Brown rice. *See* Rice

Buttermilk

Avocado Soup, 64

Buttermilk Volcano Biscuits, 29

Corn-and-Ham Muffins, 27

Cucumber and Skimmed Buttermilk Summer Soup, 69

Hot Cornbread with Cherry Peppers, 19

Muffins with Sun-Dried Tomatoes and Pine Nuts, 26

Cabbage. *See* Napa cabbage; Red cabbage

Cannellini beans

French-Style Braised Lamb Shanks, 118

Caramelized-Onion and Gorgonzola Bread, 16

Caribbean Coconut Rice, 210

Carrots

Baked Chicken with Root Vegetables, 79

Beef Pot Roast with Winter Vegetables, 100

Chilled Spanish Vegetable Soup, 65

Cornish Game Hens in Red Wine Mushroom Sauce, 89

French-Style Braised Lamb Shanks, 118

Irish Stew, 121

Marinated Roast Leg of Lamb, 119

Roasted New Potatoes with Carrots and Fennel, 227

Salad with Nuts and Cheese Chunks, 176

Veal Stew with Roasted Vegetables, 110

Cashews

Baked Stuffed Tomatoes with Herbs and Cashews, 204

Celeriac

Celeriac Slaw, 194

Iced Celery and Celeriac Soup, 68

Celery

Beef Pot Roast with Winter Vegetables, 100

Chicken, Apple, Celery, and Nut Salad, 165

Iced Celery and Celeriac Soup, 68

Irish Stew, 121

Roast Whole Chicken with Apples and Celery, 78

Veal Stew with Roasted Vegetables, 110

Wild Rice Salad with Fruit and Nuts, 170

Cheddar cheese

Baked Cherry Tomatoes Stuffed with Three Cheeses, 259

Cheese-and-Herb Bread, 21

Corn-and-Ham Muffins, 27

Creamed Broccoli and Cheddar Soup, 56

Salsa-and-Cheddar Omelet, 40

Smoked Bacon Breakfast Sandwiches, 32

Spicy Cheese Twists, 62

Cheesecake, 266

Cheese Soufflé with Artichokes and Spinach, 290

Cheese Twists, 62

Cherries

Duck Breasts with Cherry Glaze and Black Cherries, 91

Chestnut Bread, 21
Chicken
  Baked Chicken with Root
    Vegetables, 79
  Baked Nut-Crusted Chicken
    Breasts, 81
  Barbecue Wings, 255
  Braised Chicken Thighs with
    Bacon and Onion, 80
  Broiled Baby Chicken
    Drumsticks with Asian
    Flavors and Sesame, 256
  Chicken and Wild Rice Soup
    with Cranberries, 47
  Chicken, Apple, and Celery
    Spread, 286
  Chicken, Apple, Celery, and Nut
    Salad, 165
  Chicken Breasts in Sicilian
    Olive Sauce, 83
  Chicken Breasts with Capers,
    84
  Chicken Breasts with Fennel
    and Orange Slices, 82
  Chicken with Egg and Lemon
    Over Baby Spinach, 81
  Crispy Sesame Chicken
    Tenders, 254
  Grapefruit-and-Chicken Salad,
    167
  Green Bean and Bacon
    Salad with Hot Gorgonzola
    Dressing, 166
  Marinated Chicken Tenders on
    Toothpicks, 283
  Pasta with Chicken, Green
    Olives, and Grape Tomatoes,
    231
  Risotto with Chicken Livers, 220
  Roast Whole Chicken with
    Apples and Celery, 78
  Skewered Chicken Tenders with
    Sate, 289
Chili, 137
Chili Sauce, 240
Chili-Spiced Beef and Black Bean
  Soup, 48
Chilled Spanish Vegetable Soup,
  65
Chocolate-Dipped Strawberries,
  279
Chocolate Fluff, 269
Clams
  Clam Hash, 156
  Clam-Poached Cod, 152
  Clam-Stuffed Tomatoes, 157
  Grilled Littleneck Clams with
    Homemade Barbecue Sauce,
    156
  Italian-Style Seafood Salad, 162
  Pan-Roasted Clams, 155
  Steamed Clam Bellies with
    Lemon-Butter Sauce, 154
Cockles over Linguini, 153
Coconut cream/coconut milk
  Caribbean Coconut Rice, 210
  Coconut-Shrimp Soup, 74
Cod
  Clam-Poached Cod, 152
  Creamy Fish Soup, 53
Coleslaw, 193
Corn
  Corn-and-Pepper Soup, 76
  Lobster-and-Corn Chowder, 55
Cornish Game Hens in Red Wine
  Mushroom Sauce, 89
Cornmeal
  Blueberry Muffins, 24
  Corn-and-Ham Muffins, 27
  Muffins with Sun-Dried
    Tomatoes and Pine Nuts, 26
  Polenta Griddle Cakes, 29
Crabmeat
  Asian Crab Soup with Cabbage
    and Sprouts, 75
  Miniature Crab Cakes, 257
  Picnic Breakfast Stuffed
    Hardboiled Eggs, 35
  Risotto with Seafood, 218
Cranberries
  Autumn Muffins, 25
  Chicken and Wild Rice Soup
    with Cranberries, 47
  Cranberry-Stuffed Pork
    Tenderloin, 131
  Cranberry-Walnut Spread, 285
  Duck Breasts Sautéed with
    Fresh Cranberries, 90
Cranberry-Walnut Spread, 285
Cream cheese
  Artichoke and Spinach Dip, 262
  Cranberry-Walnut Spread, 285
  New York–Style Cheesecake,
    266
  Spicy Cheese Twists, 62
Crown Roast Pork with Wild Rice,
  132
Crunchy Sautéed New Potatoes,
  227
Cucumber
  Cucumber and Skimmed
    Buttermilk Summer Soup, 69
  Cucumber Slices Piled with
    Mascarpone Cheese,
    Shallots, and Prosciutto, 259
  Dilled Shrimp Salad with
    Cucumbers, 173
  Radicchio, Cucumber, and
    Gorgonzola Salad, 185
Curried Lamb Stew, 120
Curried Rice with Nuts, 213
Curried Tart Apple and Rice
  Salad, 169

Desserts, 263–76
Dijon Dressing, 244
Dilled Shrimp Salad with
    Cucumbers, 173
Dressings and sauces, 237–50
Duck
    Duck Breasts Sautéed with
        Fresh Cranberries, 90
    Duck Breasts with Cherry Glaze
        and Black Cherries, 91

Eggplant
    Eggplant Rolls, 199
    Eggplant Soufflé, 200
    Eggplant, Tomatoes, and
        Peppers, 201
    Greek Lamb and Eggplant
        Casserole, 123
    Grilled Vegetable Salad, 168
Eggs
    Asparagus with Chopped-Egg
        Sauce, 197
    Bloody Mary Tomato Aspic with
        Hardboiled Eggs, 174
    Deviled Eggs with Olives, 289
    Deviled Eggs with Smoked
        Salmon, 288
    Egg-and-Cheese Wraps, 36
    Egg and Lemon Sauce, 246
    Family Frittata with Onions,
        Potatoes, and Sausage, 38
    High-Flying Poached Eggs in
        Tomato Sauce, 34
    Mixed-Berry–Filled Omelet, 39
    Picnic Breakfast Stuffed
        Hardboiled Eggs, 35
    Salsa-and-Cheddar Omelet, 40
    Smoked-Ham and Peach
        Omelet, 37
    Tomato-Basil Omelet, 41

Escarole
    Italian Escarole, Sausage, and
        Bean Soup, 51
Espresso Sauce, 274

Family Frittata with Onions,
    Potatoes, and Sausage, 38
Family snacks and meals, 277–90
Family-Style Hungarian Goulash,
    287
Fennel
    Baked Chicken with Root
        Vegetables, 79
    Chicken Breasts with Fennel
        and Orange Slices, 82
    Fennel with Orange Slices, 207
    Italian Escarole, Sausage, and
        Bean Soup, 51
    Roasted New Potatoes with
        Carrots and Fennel, 227
    Veal Stew with Roasted
        Vegetables, 110
Feta cheese
    Warm Rotini Salad with
        Zucchini and Feta Cheese,
        235
    Zucchini, Feta, and Ricotta
        Pizza, 258
Fish. *See specific fish*
French-Style Braised Lamb
    Shanks, 118
Fresh Fruit Sauces, 273
Fruits. *See specific fruits*

Garlic
    Garlic Mashed Potatoes, 224
    Spanish Garlic and Sausage
        Soup, 52
Gorgonzola cheese
    Filet Mignon Stuffed with
        Gorgonzola Cheese, 96

Green Bean and Bacon
    Salad with Hot Gorgonzola
    Dressing, 166
Pears and Walnuts Over Mixed
    Greens, 184
Radicchio, Cucumber, and
    Gorgonzola Salad, 185
Grapefruit
    Baked Grapefruit, 43
    Grapefruit-and-Chicken Salad,
        167
    Grapefruit and Romaine, 187
    Not Your Grandmother's Citrus-
        Gelatin Ring, 275
    Pork Chops Sautéed with
        Grapefruit, 126
Grapes, frozen, 279
Greek Lamb and Eggplant
    Casserole, 123
Greek Lamb-and-Pasta Casserole,
    124
Greek Lemon Soup, 66
Greek-Style Mussel Salad, 172
Green Bean and Tuna Salad with
    Romaine Lettuce, 164
Green Mayonnaise, 239

Ham
    Corn-and-Ham Muffins, 27
    Creamy Fish Soup, 52
    Ham-Wrapped Asparagus, 253
    Rice with Ham, Onions, and
        Rosemary, 214
    Sauerkraut with Apples and
        Ham, 208
    Smoked-Ham and Peach
        Omelet, 37
    Spicy Ham and Bean soup, 46
    Spinach, Pear, and Smoked
        Ham Salad, 183
Herb Crackers, 61

Herb Melange, 67
High-Flying Poached Eggs in
Tomato Sauce, 34
Hungarian Goulash, 287

Ice Cream, family, 280
Iced Celery and Celeriac Soup, 68
Iced Tomato-Basil Bisque, 73
Irish Leek-and-Potato Soup, 58
Irish Stew, 121
Italian Escarole, Sausage, and
Bean Soup, 51
Italian-Style Baby Pork Balls, 138
Italian-Style Seafood Salad, 162

Jack cheese
Filet Mignon Stuffed with Jack
Cheese and Salsa, 97
Jarlsburg cheese
Salad with Nuts and Cheese
Chunks, 176
Jellied Madrilène with Lemon,
Herbs, and Shrimp, 71
Jicama
Brown Rice with Bacon and
Apples, 215
Jicama, Mandarin Orange, and
Arugula Salad, 188
Shrimp Salad with Tomatillos,
Jicama, Grilled Peaches, and
Chimichuri, 147
Joyous Gel, 276

Kidney beans
Italian Escarole, Sausage, and
Bean Soup, 51
Pork Chili, 137
Spicy Ham and Bean soup, 46
Turkey Chili, 88
Kids' Favorite Meatloaf, 281

Kiwi Balls with Frosted
Strawberries, 278
Kolhrabi with Lemon, 206

Lamb
Baby Rack of Lamb with Zest
Crust, 115
Basque-Style Lamb Stew, 122
Braised Lamb Shoulder with
Lemon and Onions, 117
Curried Lamb Stew, 120
French-Style Braised Lamb
Shanks, 118
Greek Lamb and Eggplant
Casserole, 123
Greek Lamb-and-Pasta
Casserole, 124
Irish Stew, 121
Lamb Braised in Tomato Sauce,
116
Lamb Chops with Lavender
Buds, 114
Lamb Kabobs with Indian
Spices, 113
Marinated Roast Leg of Lamb,
119
Rosemary-Crusted Lamb
Chops, 115
Very Hot Lamb Kabobs, 112
Leeks
Irish Leek-and-Potato Soup, 58
Lemons
Braised Lamb Shoulder with
Lemon and Onions, 117
Egg and Lemon Sauce, 246
Greek Lemon Soup, 66
Hot Lemon Sauce, 245
Lemon-Herb Dressing, 244
Lentil Salad, 180
Lime-Banana Smoothie, 42
Lobster

Boiled Lobster, 149
Lobster-and-Corn Chowder, 55
Lobster on The Grill, 150
Lobster Salad, 171

Mandarin oranges
Jicama, Mandarin Orange, and
Arugula Salad, 188
Not Your Grandmother's Citrus-
Gelatin Ring, 275
Mango Chutney, 249
Mascarpone cheese
Cucumber Slices Piled with
Mascarpone Cheese,
Shallots, and Prosciutto, 259
Risotto with Lemons and
Mascarpone Cheese, 217
Mayonnaise
Basic, 238
Green, 239
Melon
Prosciutto with Melon, 43
Mexican Shrimp with Chipotles,
143
Middle-Eastern Black Bean Dip,
261
Mozzarella cheese
Mini Pizzas with Broccoli and
Cheese, 282
Mozzarella, Caper, and Olive
Salad, 186
Tomato and Mozzarella Salad,
191
Muesli, 41
Muffins. *See* Breads and muffins
Mushrooms
Broccoli Stir Fry, 198
Cornish Game Hens in Red
Wine Mushroom Sauce, 89
Creamy Pureed Mushroom
Soup, 57

French-Style Braised Lamb Shanks, 118

Fresh Tomato Sauce with Mushrooms and Herbs, 247

Marinated Mushrooms Salad, 190

Mushroom Meatballs in Homemade Tomato Sauce, 106

Sliced Turkey Breast with Mushroom Sauce, 87

Very Hot Lamb Kabobs, 112

Wild Rice with Mushrooms and Rosemary, 222

Mussels
Greek-Style Mussel Salad, 172
Italian-Style Seafood Salad, 162
Mussels with Tomato Balsamic-Vinegar Sauce, 159
Sicilian Mussel Soup, 54
Steamed Mussels with Fresh Tomatoes and Herbs, 161
Steamed Mussels with Lemon Butter, 160

Mustard
Basic Mustard and Dijon-Style Mustard, 241
Dijon Dressing, 244
Mustard Cream Sauce, 248
Sweet-and-Sour Mustard, 249

Napa cabbage
Cabbage Salad with Toasted Sesame Nuts, 190
Pork Tenderloin with Asian Spices, 128
Tri-Colored Coleslaw, 193
Wild Rice Salad with Fruit and Nuts, 170

New York–Style Cheesecake, 266

Not Your Grandmother's Citrus-Gelatin Ring, 275

Nuts. *See specific nuts*

Oatmeal-Walnut Bread, 20

Olives
Braised Chicken with Green Olives and Artichokes, 85
Chicken Breasts in Sicilian Olive Sauce, 83
Deviled Eggs with Olives, 289
Grilled Quail with Olive Condiment, 92
Mozzarella, Caper, and Olive Salad, 186
Pasta with Anchovy-Olive Sauce, 230
Pasta with Chicken, Green Olives, and Grape Tomatoes, 231
Rice with Tomatoes and Olives, 216
Veal Shanks Braised with Green Olives, 109

Onions
Braised Lamb Shoulder with Lemon and Onions, 117
Caramelized-Onion and Gorgonzola Bread, 16
Family Frittata with Onions, Potatoes, and Sausage, 38
Irish Stew, 121
Veal Stew with Roasted Vegetables, 110

Orange juice
Chocolate Fluff, 269
Not Your Grandmother's Citrus-Gelatin Ring, 275
Orange Mousse with Blueberries, 270

Oranges. *See also* Mandarin oranges
Chicken Breasts with Fennel and Orange Slices, 82
Fennel with Orange Slices, 207

Oysters
Fried Oysters, 158
Oysters on the Half-Shell with Bacon and Green Onions, 157

Panini with Tomato, Basil, and Provolone Cheese, 260

Parsnips
Baked Chicken with Root Vegetables, 79
Beef Pot Roast with Winter Vegetables, 100

Pasta dishes
Broccoli and Pasta Salad, 178
Cockles over Linguini, 153
Greek Lamb-and-Pasta Casserole, 124
Pasta Salad with Hot Peppers and Sweet Red Pepper Dressing, 177
Pasta Salad with Shrimp and Snow Pea Pods, 179
Pasta with Anchovy-Olive Sauce, 230
Pasta with Chicken, Green Olives, and Grape Tomatoes, 231
Pasta with Ricotta, Garlic, and Baby Peas, 227
Rotini with Smoked Salmon and Cream Cheese Sauce, 234
Shrimp Crunch Filling for Ravioli, 145
Shrimp Scampi, 146

Spaghetti with Shrimp, 232
Tortellini with Basil and
    Walnuts, 236
Warm Rotini Salad with
    Zucchini and Feta Cheese,
    235
Ziti with Sausage and Ricotta
    Cheese, 233
Zucchini and Sausage Soup, 50
Peaches
    Grilled Peaches with Cream
        Cheese, 44
    Peach Melba Smoothie, 42
    Peach Melba with Sugar-Free
        Ice Cream, 264
    Peach Parfait, 264
    Shrimp Salad with Tomatillos,
        Jicama, Grilled Peaches, and
        Chimichuri, 147
    Smoked-Ham and Peach
        Omelet, 37
    Wild Rice Salad with Fruit and
        Nuts, 170
Pears
    Creamy Pureed Mushroom
        Soup, 57
    Pear Custard with Pecans, 268
    Pears and Walnuts Over Mixed
        Greens, 184
    Pheasant with Fresh Pears, 93
    Spinach, Pear, and Smoked
        Ham Salad, 183
    Wild Rice with Pears and
        Pecans, 220
Peas. See also Snow peas
    Pasta with Ricotta, Garlic, and
        Baby Peas, 228
    Rice with Ham, Onions, and
        Rosemary, 214
Pecans

Baked Nut-Crusted Chicken
    Breasts, 81
Pear Custard with Pecans, 268
Swedish Coffee Bread, 18
Wild Rice with Pears and
    Pecans, 220
Pheasant
    Pheasant with Asian Marinade,
        94
    Pheasant with Fresh Pears, 93
Pineapple
    Caribbean Coconut Rice, 210
    Grilled Pineapple, 270
Pine nuts
    Muffins with Sun-Dried
        Tomatoes and Pine Nuts, 26
    Saffron Rice with Shrimp,
        Capers, and Pine Nuts, 212
    Tiny Italian Meatballs with Pine
        Nuts, 254
Pink Tomato Aspic with Shrimp,
    175
Pizzas
    Mini Pizzas with Broccoli and
        Cheese, 282
    Zucchini, Feta, and Ricotta
        Pizza, 258
Polenta Griddle Cakes, 29
Popcorn with Hot-Pepper Butter,
    280
Pork
    Asian-Style Baby Back Ribs, 134
    Barbecued Baby Back Ribs, 135
    Breakfast Sausage, 33
    Chili-Spiced Beef and Black
        Bean Soup, 48
    Crown Roast Pork with Wild
        Rice, 132
    Italian-Style Baby Pork Balls,
        138
    Kids' Favorite Meatloaf, 281

Marinated Pork Tenderloin on
    Skewers, 130
Oven-Braised Country-Style
    Spareribs, 133
Pork Burgers with Apples, 136
Pork Burgers with Asian Spices,
    136
Pork Chili, 137
Pork Chops in Homemade
    Barbecue Sauce, 127
Pork Chops Sautéed with
    Artichokes, 127
Pork Chops Sautéed with
    Grapefruit, 126
Pork Tenderloin with Asian
    Spices, 128
Quick Italian Sausage for
    Soups, Meatballs, and
    Sauces, 49
Roasted Citrus Pork Tenderloin,
    129
Potatoes
    Baked Chicken with Root
        Vegetables, 79
    Beef Pot Roast with Winter
        Vegetables, 100
    Clam Hash, 156
    Creamy Fish Soup, 53
    Crunchy Sautéed New Potatoes,
        227
    Family Frittata with Onions,
        Potatoes, and Sausage, 38
    Garlic Mashed Potatoes, 224
    Irish Leek-and-Potato Soup,
        58
    Irish Stew, 121
    Lobster-and-Corn Chowder, 55
    Potatoes Sautéed in Olive Oil
        and Herbs, 229
    Potato Skins Stuffed with Hot
        Barbecue, 225

Roasted New Potatoes with Carrots and Fennel, 227
Stuffed Idaho Potatoes with Chives and Cheese, 226
Poultry. *See specific bird*
Prosciutto
Cucumber Slices Piled with Mascarpone Cheese, Shallots, and Prosciutto, 259
Prosciutto with Melon, 43
Veal Scallops with Prosciutto and Cheese, 108
Pumpkin Soufflé, 208

Quail
Grilled Quail with Olive Condiment, 92

Radicchio, Cucumber, and Gorgonzola Salad, 185
Raspberries
Fresh Fruit Sauces, 273
Mixed-Berry–Filled Omelet, 39
Peach Melba with Sugar-Free Smoothie, 264
Raspberry Coulis with Sugar-Free Frozen-Yogurt Smoothie, 271
Red cabbage
Red Cabbage and Apple Salad, 193
Tri-Colored Coleslaw, 193
Red Salad, 189
Rhubarb
Strawberry-Rhubarb Compote, 272
Rice
Baked Rice with Vegetables, 211
Brown Rice with Bacon and Apples, 215
Caribbean Coconut Rice, 210

Chicken and Wild Rice Soup with Cranberries, 47
Crown Roast Pork with Wild Rice, 132
Curried Rice with Nuts, 213
Curried Tart Apple and Rice Salad, 169
Fried Rice, 215
Rice with Ham, Onions, and Rosemary, 214
Rice with Tomatoes and Olives, 216
Risotto with Cheese and Baby Spinach, 219
Risotto with Chicken Livers, 220
Risotto with Lemons and Mascarpone Cheese, 217
Risotto with Seafood, 218
Saffron Rice with Shrimp, Capers, and Pine Nuts, 212
Shrimp Stir-Fry with Broccoli and Almonds, 148
Wild Rice Salad with Fresh Apricots and Water Chestnuts, 192
Wild Rice Salad with Fruit and Nuts, 170
Wild Rice, Snow Peas, and Water Chestnuts, 221
Wild Rice with Mushrooms and Rosemary, 222
Wild Rice with Pears and Pecans, 220
Ricotta cheese
Baked Cherry Tomatoes Stuffed with Three Cheeses, 259
Eggplant Rolls, 199
Pasta with Ricotta, Garlic, and Baby Peas, 228
Ziti with Sausage and Ricotta Cheese, 233

Zucchini, Feta, and Ricotta Pizza, 258
Risotto. *See* Rice
Rosemary-Crusted Lamb Chops, 115

Saffron Rice with Shrimp, Capers, and Pine Nuts, 212
Salads
entree, 163–80
side, 181–208
Salmon
Deviled Eggs with Smoked Salmon, 288
Rotini with Smoked Salmon and Cream Cheese Sauce, 234
Salt-and-Sugar Cured Salmon, 34
Salsa-and-Cheddar Omelet, 40
Salt-and-Sugar Cured Salmon, 34
Sauerkraut with Apples and Ham, 208
Sausage
Breakfast Sausage, 33
Quick Italian Sausage for Soups, Meatballs, and Sauces, 49
Sausage, as ingredient
Family Frittata with Onions, Potatoes, and Sausage, 38
Italian Escarole, Sausage, and Bean Soup, 51
Spanish Garlic and Sausage Soup, 52
Ziti with Sausage and Ricotta Cheese, 233
Zucchini and Sausage Soup, 50
Seafood. *See specific seafood*
Shrimp
Baby Shrimp in Cream, 142

Baked Stuffed Shrimp, 140, 141
Barbecued Shrimp, 141
Coconut-Shrimp Soup, 74
Dilled Shrimp Salad with
    Cucumbers, 173
Grilled Shrimp with Asian
    Seasonings, 143
Italian-Style Seafood Salad, 162
Jellied Madrilène with Lemon,
    Herbs, and Shrimp, 71
Mexican Shrimp with Chipotles,
    143
Pasta Salad with Shrimp and
    Snow Pea Pods, 179
Pink Tomato Aspic with Shrimp,
    175
Risotto with Seafood, 218
Saffron Rice with Shrimp,
    Capers, and Pine Nuts, 212
Shrimp-and-Avocado Salad, 144
Shrimp Bisque, 72
Shrimp Butter For Hors
    d'Oeuvres, 144
Shrimp Crunch Filling for
    Ravioli, 145
Shrimp Salad with Tomatillos,
    Jicama, Grilled Peaches, and
    Chimichuri, 147
Shrimp Scampi, 146
Shrimp Stir-Fry with Broccoli
    and Almonds, 148
Skewered Shrimp with Bacon,
    285
Spaghetti with Shrimp, 232
Sicilian Mussel Soup, 54
Smoothies, 42, 271
Snacks, 251–62. *See also* Family
    snacks and meals
Snow peas
    Pasta Salad with Shrimp and
        Snow Pea Pods, 179

Wild Rice, Snow Peas, and
    Water Chestnuts, 221
Soups
    summer, 63–76
    winter, 47–62
Spanish Garlic and Sausage Soup,
    52
Spinach
    Artichoke and Spinach Dip, 262
    Cheese Soufflé with Artichokes
        and Spinach, 290
    Chicken with Egg and Lemon
        Over Baby Spinach, 81
    Risotto with Cheese and Baby
        Spinach, 219
    Spinach, Pear, and Smoked
        Ham Salad, 183
    Spinach Soup, 70
    Spinach-Stuffed Yellow
        Tomatoes, 205
Strawberries
    Chocolate-Dipped Strawberries,
        279
    Fresh Fruit Sauces, 273
    Joyous Gel, 276
    Kiwi Balls with Frosted
        Strawberries, 278
    Strawberry-Rhubarb Compote,
        272
    Strawberry-Stuffed French
        Toast, 30
Stromboli, 252
Sugar(s)
    kinds of, 2–3
    health and body functioning
        and, 1, 3–6
    exercise and 13–14
Sugar-free diet tips, 7–13
Sun-dried tomatoes
    Muffins with Sun-Dried
        Tomatoes and Pine Nuts, 26

Pasta with Ricotta, Garlic, and
    Baby Peas, 228
Swedish Coffee Bread, 18
Sweet-and-Sour Mustard, 249
Sweet-and-Spicy Toasted Nut Mix,
    261
Sweet Tea Sauce, 248

Tea
    Sweet Tea Sauce, 248
Toasted Sesame-Seed Oil, 238
Tomatillos
    Shrimp Salad with Tomatillos,
        Jicama, Grilled Peaches, and
        Chimichuri, 147
    Tomatillo and Tomato Salad
        with Salsa Dressing, 182
Tomatoes, fresh
    Avocado, Tomato, and Bacon
        Over Bib Lettuce, 183
    Baked Cherry Tomatoes Stuffed
        with Three Cheeses, 259
    Baked Stuffed Tomatoes with
        Herbs and Cashews, 204
    Clam-Stuffed Tomatoes, 157
    Crunchy Mini-Panini with
        Tomato, Basil, and Provolone
        Cheese, 260
    Eggplant, Tomatoes, and
        Peppers, 201
    Fresh Tomato Sauce with
        Mushrooms and Herbs, 247
    Mussels with Tomato Balsamic-
        Vinegar Sauce, 159
    Pasta with Chicken, Green
        Olives, and Grape Tomatoes,
        231
    Rice with Tomatoes and Olives,
        216
    Spinach-Stuffed Yellow
        Tomatoes, 205

Steamed Mussels with Fresh
Tomatoes and Herbs, 161
Tomatillo and Tomato Salad
with Salsa Dressing, 182
Tomato and Mozzarella Salad,
191
Tomato-Basil Omelet, 41
Tomato Bisque with Sour
Cream, 60
Tomato Salsa, 250
Tuna
Green Bean and Tuna Salad
with Romaine Lettuce, 164
Tuna-Stuffed Artichokes, 196
Turkey
Grilled Turkey Thighs with
Thyme, Basil, and Butter, 86
Sliced Turkey Breast with
Mushroom Sauce, 87
Smoked Turkey with Sour
Apple, 256
Turkey Chili, 88
Turkey Meatballs, 284
Turnips
Beef Pot Roast with Winter
Vegetables, 100
Veal Stew with Roasted
Vegetables, 110

Veal
Breakfast Sausage, 33
Family-Style Hungarian
Goulash, 287

Kids' Favorite Meatloaf, 281
Veal Scallops in Lemon Sauce,
108
Veal Scallops with Prosciutto
and Cheese, 108
Veal Shanks Braised with Green
Olives, 109
Veal Stewed in Tomato Sauce
with Garlic, 107
Veal Stew with Roasted
Vegetables, 110
Vegetables. *See specific vegetables*
Vinaigrettes, 241

Walnuts
Apple-Blueberry Crisp, 267
Baked Nut-Crusted Chicken
Breasts, 81
Baked Stuffed Apples, 265
Chicken, Apple, Celery, and Nut
Salad, 165
Cranberry-Walnut Spread, 285
Pears and Walnuts Over Mixed
Greens, 184
Swedish Coffee Bread, 18
Sweet-and-Spicy Toasted Nut
Mix, 261
Tortellini with Basil and
Walnuts, 236
Wild Rice Salad with Fruit and
Nuts, 170
Water Chestnuts

Wild Rice Salad with Fresh
Apricots and Water
Chestnuts, 192
Wild Rice, Snow Peas, and
Water Chestnuts, 221
Watermelon-Lime Sorbet, 272
White Bean and Tomato Soup, 59
Wild Rice. *See* Rice

Zucchini
Baked Rice with Vegetables, 211
Baked Yellow and Green
Squash, Dressed in Herbs
with Crumb Topping, 202
Grilled Vegetable Salad, 168
Savory Summer-Squash Bread,
17
Warm Rotini Salad with
Zucchini and Feta Cheese,
235
Zucchini and Sausage Soup, 50
Zucchini, Feta, and Ricotta
Pizza, 258
Zucchini-Spice Muffins, 28

THE EVERYTHING SERIES!

BUSINESS & PERSONAL FINANCE

Everything® Accounting Book
Everything® Budgeting Book
Everything® Business Planning Book
Everything® Coaching and Mentoring Book, 2nd Ed.
Everything® Fundraising Book
Everything® Get Out of Debt Book
Everything® Grant Writing Book
Everything® Guide to Foreclosures
Everything® Guide to Personal Finance for Single Mothers
Everything® Home-Based Business Book, 2nd Ed.
Everything® Homebuying Book, 2nd Ed.
Everything® Homeselling Book, 2nd Ed.
Everything® Improve Your Credit Book
Everything® Investing Book, 2nd Ed.
Everything® Landlording Book
Everything® Leadership Book
Everything® Managing People Book, 2nd Ed.
Everything® Negotiating Book
Everything® Online Auctions Book
Everything® Online Business Book
Everything® Personal Finance Book
Everything® Personal Finance in Your 20s and 30s Book
Everything® Project Management Book
Everything® Real Estate Investing Book
Everything® Retirement Planning Book
Everything® Robert's Rules Book, $7.95
Everything® Selling Book
Everything® Start Your Own Business Book, 2nd Ed.
Everything® Wills & Estate Planning Book

COOKING

Everything® Barbecue Cookbook
Everything® Bartender's Book, 2nd Ed., $9.95
Everything® Calorie Counting Cookbook
Everything® Cheese Book
Everything® Chinese Cookbook
Everything® Classic Recipes Book
Everything® Cocktail Parties & Drinks Book
Everything® College Cookbook
Everything® Cooking for Baby and Toddler Book
Everything® Cooking for Two Cookbook
Everything® Diabetes Cookbook
Everything® Easy Gourmet Cookbook
Everything® Fondue Cookbook
Everything® Fondue Party Book
Everything® Gluten-Free Cookbook
Everything® Glycemic Index Cookbook
Everything® Grilling Cookbook
Everything® Healthy Meals in Minutes Cookbook
Everything® Holiday Cookbook

Everything® Indian Cookbook
Everything® Italian Cookbook
Everything® Low-Carb Cookbook
Everything® Low-Cholesterol Cookbook
Everything® Low-Fat High-Flavor Cookbook
Everything® Low-Salt Cookbook
Everything® Meals for a Month Cookbook
Everything® Mediterranean Cookbook
Everything® Mexican Cookbook
Everything® No Trans Fat Cookbook
Everything® One-Pot Cookbook
Everything® Pizza Cookbook
Everything® Quick and Easy 30-Minute,
    5-Ingredient Cookbook
Everything® Quick Meals Cookbook
Everything® Slow Cooker Cookbook
Everything® Slow Cooking for a Crowd Cookbook
Everything® Soup Cookbook
Everything® Stir-Fry Cookbook
Everything® Sugar-Free Cookbook
Everything® Tapas and Small Plates Cookbook
Everything® Tex-Mex Cookbook
Everything® Thai Cookbook
Everything® Vegetarian Cookbook
Everything® Wild Game Cookbook
Everything® Wine Book, 2nd Ed.

GAMES

Everything® 15-Minute Sudoku Book, $9.95
Everything® 30-Minute Sudoku Book, $9.95
Everything® Bible Crosswords Book, $9.95
Everything® Blackjack Strategy Book
Everything® Brain Strain Book, $9.95
Everything® Bridge Book
Everything® Card Games Book
Everything® Card Tricks Book, $9.95
Everything® Casino Gambling Book, 2nd Ed.
Everything® Chess Basics Book
Everything® Craps Strategy Book
Everything® Crossword and Puzzle Book
Everything® Crossword Challenge Book
Everything® Crosswords for the Beach Book, $9.95
Everything® Cryptic Crosswords Book, $9.95
Everything® Cryptograms Book, $9.95
Everything® Easy Crosswords Book
Everything® Easy Kakuro Book, $9.95
Everything® Easy Large-Print Crosswords Book
Everything® Games Book, 2nd Ed.
Everything® Giant Sudoku Book, $9.95
Everything® Kakuro Challenge Book, $9.95
Everything® Large-Print Crossword Challenge Book
Everything® Large-Print Crosswords Book
Everything® Lateral Thinking Puzzles Book, $9.95

Everything® **Literary Crosswords Book, $9.95**
Everything® Mazes Book
Everything® Memory Booster Puzzles Book, $9.95
Everything® Movie Crosswords Book, $9.95
Everything® Music Crosswords Book, $9.95
Everything® Online Poker Book, $12.95
Everything® Pencil Puzzles Book, $9.95
Everything® Poker Strategy Book
Everything® Pool & Billiards Book
Everything® Puzzles for Commuters Book, $9.95
Everything® Sports Crosswords Book, $9.95
Everything® Test Your IQ Book, $9.95
Everything® Texas Hold 'Em Book, $9.95
Everything® Travel Crosswords Book, $9.95
Everything® TV Crosswords Book, $9.95
Everything® Word Games Challenge Book
Everything® Word Scramble Book
Everything® Word Search Book

HEALTH

Everything® Alzheimer's Book
Everything® Diabetes Book
Everything® Health Guide to Adult Bipolar Disorder
Everything® Health Guide to Arthritis
Everything® Health Guide to Controlling Anxiety
Everything® Health Guide to Fibromyalgia
Everything® Health Guide to Menopause
Everything® Health Guide to OCD
Everything® Health Guide to PMS
Everything® Health Guide to Postpartum Care
Everything® Health Guide to Thyroid Disease
Everything® Hypnosis Book
Everything® Low Cholesterol Book
Everything® Nutrition Book
Everything® Reflexology Book
Everything® Stress Management Book

HISTORY

Everything® American Government Book
Everything® American History Book, 2nd Ed.
Everything® Civil War Book
Everything® Freemasons Book
Everything® Irish History & Heritage Book
Everything® Middle East Book
Everything® World War II Book, 2nd Ed.

HOBBIES

Everything® Candlemaking Book
Everything® Cartooning Book
Everything® Coin Collecting Book
Everything® Drawing Book

Everything® Family Tree Book, 2nd Ed.
Everything® Knitting Book
Everything® Knots Book
Everything® Photography Book
Everything® Quilting Book
Everything® Sewing Book
Everything® Soapmaking Book, 2nd Ed.
Everything® Woodworking Book

HOME IMPROVEMENT

Everything® Feng Shui Book
Everything® Feng Shui Decluttering Book, $9.95
Everything® Fix-It Book
Everything® Green Living Book
Everything® Home Decorating Book
Everything® Home Storage Solutions Book
Everything® Homebuilding Book
Everything® Organize Your Home Book, 2nd Ed.

KIDS' BOOKS

All titles are $7.95

Everything® Kids' Animal Puzzle & Activity Book
Everything® Kids' Baseball Book, 4th Ed.
Everything® Kids' Bible Trivia Book
Everything® Kids' Bugs Book
Everything® Kids' Cars and Trucks Puzzle and Activity Book
Everything® Kids' Christmas Puzzle & Activity Book
Everything® Kids' Cookbook
Everything® Kids' Crazy Puzzles Book
Everything® Kids' Dinosaurs Book
Everything® Kids' Environment Book
Everything® Kids' Fairies Puzzle and Activity Book
Everything® Kids' First Spanish Puzzle and Activity Book
Everything® Kids' Gross Cookbook
Everything® Kids' Gross Hidden Pictures Book
Everything® Kids' Gross Jokes Book
Everything® Kids' Gross Mazes Book
Everything® Kids' Gross Puzzle & Activity Book
Everything® Kids' Halloween Puzzle & Activity Book
Everything® Kids' Hidden Pictures Book
Everything® Kids' Horses Book
Everything® Kids' Joke Book
Everything® Kids' Knock Knock Book
Everything® Kids' Learning Spanish Book
Everything® Kids' Magical Science Experiments Book
Everything® Kids' Math Puzzles Book
Everything® Kids' Mazes Book
Everything® Kids' Money Book
Everything® Kids' Nature Book
Everything® Kids' Pirates Puzzle and Activity Book
Everything® Kids' Presidents Book
Everything® Kids' Princess Puzzle and Activity Book
Everything® Kids' Puzzle Book
Everything® Kids' Racecars Puzzle and Activity Book
Everything® Kids' Riddles & Brain Teasers Book
Everything® Kids' Science Experiments Book
Everything® Kids' Sharks Book

Everything® Kids' Soccer Book
Everything® Kids' Spies Puzzle and Activity Book
Everything® Kids' States Book
Everything® Kids' Travel Activity Book

KIDS' STORY BOOKS

Everything® Fairy Tales Book

LANGUAGE

Everything® Conversational Japanese Book with CD, $19.95
Everything® French Grammar Book
Everything® French Phrase Book, $9.95
Everything® French Verb Book, $9.95
Everything® German Practice Book with CD, $19.95
Everything® Inglés Book
Everything® Intermediate Spanish Book with CD, $19.95
Everything® Italian Practice Book with CD, $19.95
Everything® Learning Brazilian Portuguese Book with CD, $19.95
Everything® Learning French Book with CD, 2nd Ed., $19.95
Everything® Learning German Book
Everything® Learning Italian Book
Everything® Learning Latin Book
Everything® Learning Russian Book with CD, $19.95
Everything® Learning Spanish Book with CD, 2nd Ed., $19.95
Everything® Russian Practice Book with CD, $19.95
Everything® Sign Language Book
Everything® Spanish Grammar Book
Everything® Spanish Phrase Book, $9.95
Everything® Spanish Practice Book with CD, $19.95
Everything® Spanish Verb Book, $9.95
Everything® Speaking Mandarin Chinese Book with CD, $19.95

MUSIC

Everything® Drums Book with CD, $19.95
Everything® Guitar Book with CD, 2nd Ed., $19.95
Everything® Guitar Chords Book with CD, $19.95
Everything® Home Recording Book
Everything® Music Theory Book with CD, $19.95
Everything® Reading Music Book with CD, $19.95
Everything® Rock & Blues Guitar Book with CD, $19.95
Everything® Rock and Blues Piano Book with CD, $19.95
Everything® Songwriting Book

NEW AGE

Everything® Astrology Book, 2nd Ed.
Everything® Birthday Personology Book
Everything® Dreams Book, 2nd Ed.
Everything® Love Signs Book, $9.95
Everything® Love Spells Book, $9.95
Everything® Numerology Book
Everything® Paganism Book
Everything® Palmistry Book
Everything® Psychic Book
Everything® Reiki Book
Everything® Sex Signs Book, $9.95

Everything® Spells & Charms Book, 2nd Ed.
Everything® Tarot Book, 2nd Ed.
Everything® Toltec Wisdom Book
Everything® Wicca and Witchcraft Book

PARENTING

Everything® Baby Names Book, 2nd Ed.
Everything® Baby Shower Book, 2nd Ed.
Everything® Baby's First Year Book
Everything® Birthing Book
Everything® Breastfeeding Book
Everything® Father-to-Be Book
Everything® Father's First Year Book
Everything® Get Ready for Baby Book, 2nd Ed.
Everything® Get Your Baby to Sleep Book, $9.95
Everything® Getting Pregnant Book
Everything® Guide to Pregnancy Over 35
Everything® Guide to Raising a One-Year-Old
Everything® Guide to Raising a Two-Year-Old
Everything® Guide to Raising Adolescent Boys
Everything® Guide to Raising Adolescent Girls
Everything® Homeschooling Book
Everything® Mother's First Year Book
Everything® Parent's Guide to Childhood Illnesses
Everything® Parent's Guide to Children and Divorce
Everything® Parent's Guide to Children with ADD/ADHD
Everything® Parent's Guide to Children with Asperger's Syndrome
Everything® Parent's Guide to Children with Autism
Everything® Parent's Guide to Children with Bipolar Disorder
Everything® Parent's Guide to Children with Depression
Everything® Parent's Guide to Children with Dyslexia
Everything® Parent's Guide to Children with Juvenile Diabetes
Everything® Parent's Guide to Positive Discipline
Everything® Parent's Guide to Raising a Successful Child
Everything® Parent's Guide to Raising Boys
Everything® Parent's Guide to Raising Girls
Everything® Parent's Guide to Raising Siblings
Everything® Parent's Guide to Sensory Integration Disorder
Everything® Parent's Guide to Tantrums
Everything® Parent's Guide to the Strong-Willed Child
Everything® Parenting a Teenager Book
Everything® Potty Training Book, $9.95
Everything® Pregnancy Book, 3rd Ed.
Everything® Pregnancy Fitness Book
Everything® Pregnancy Nutrition Book
Everything® Pregnancy Organizer, 2nd Ed., $16.95
Everything® Toddler Activities Book
Everything® Toddler Book
Everything® Tween Book
Everything® Twins, Triplets, and More Book

PETS

Everything® Aquarium Book
Everything® Boxer Book
Everything® Cat Book, 2nd Ed.
Everything® Chihuahua Book

Everything® **Cooking for Dogs Book**
Everything® Dachshund Book
Everything® Dog Book
Everything® Dog Health Book
Everything® Dog Obedience Book
Everything® Dog Owner's Organizer, $16.95
Everything® Dog Training and Tricks Book
Everything® German Shepherd Book
Everything® Golden Retriever Book
Everything® Horse Book
Everything® Horse Care Book
Everything® Horseback Riding Book
Everything® Labrador Retriever Book
Everything® Poodle Book
Everything® Pug Book
Everything® Puppy Book
Everything® Rottweiler Book
Everything® Small Dogs Book
Everything® Tropical Fish Book
Everything® Yorkshire Terrier Book

REFERENCE

Everything® American Presidents Book
Everything® Blogging Book
Everything® Build Your Vocabulary Book
Everything® Car Care Book
Everything® Classical Mythology Book
Everything® Da Vinci Book
Everything® Divorce Book
Everything® Einstein Book
Everything® Enneagram Book
Everything® Etiquette Book, 2nd Ed.
Everything® **Guide to Edgar Allan Poe**
Everything® Inventions and Patents Book
Everything® Mafia Book
Everything® **Martin Luther King Jr. Book**
Everything® Philosophy Book
Everything® Pirates Book
Everything® Psychology Book

RELIGION

Everything® Angels Book
Everything® Bible Book
Everything® **Bible Study Book with CD, $19.95**
Everything® Buddhism Book
Everything® Catholicism Book
Everything® Christianity Book
Everything® Gnostic Gospels Book
Everything® History of the Bible Book
Everything® Jesus Book
Everything® Jewish History & Heritage Book
Everything® Judaism Book
Everything® Kabbalah Book
Everything® Koran Book

Everything® Mary Book
Everything® Mary Magdalene Book
Everything® Prayer Book
Everything® Saints Book, 2nd Ed.
Everything® Torah Book
Everything® Understanding Islam Book
Everything® **Women of the Bible Book**
Everything® World's Religions Book
Everything® Zen Book

SCHOOL & CAREERS

Everything® Alternative Careers Book
Everything® Career Tests Book
Everything® College Major Test Book
Everything® College Survival Book, 2nd Ed.
Everything® Cover Letter Book, 2nd Ed.
Everything® Filmmaking Book
Everything® Get-a-Job Book, 2nd Ed.
Everything® Guide to Being a Paralegal
Everything® Guide to Being a Personal Trainer
Everything® Guide to Being a Real Estate Agent
Everything® Guide to Being a Sales Rep
Everything® **Guide to Being an Event Planner**
Everything® Guide to Careers in Health Care
Everything® Guide to Careers in Law Enforcement
Everything® Guide to Government Jobs
Everything® **Guide to Starting and Running a Catering Business**
Everything® Guide to Starting and Running a Restaurant
Everything® Job Interview Book
Everything® New Nurse Book
Everything® New Teacher Book
Everything® Paying for College Book
Everything® Practice Interview Book
Everything® Resume Book, 2nd Ed.
Everything® Study Book

SELF-HELP

Everything® **Body Language Book**
Everything® Dating Book, 2nd Ed.
Everything® Great Sex Book
Everything® Self-Esteem Book
Everything® Tantric Sex Book

SPORTS & FITNESS

Everything® Easy Fitness Book
Everything® **Krav Maga for Fitness Book**
Everything® Running Book

TRAVEL

Everything® Family Guide to Coastal Florida
Everything® Family Guide to Cruise Vacations
Everything® Family Guide to Hawaii
Everything® Family Guide to Las Vegas, 2nd Ed.
Everything® Family Guide to Mexico
Everything® Family Guide to New York City, 2nd Ed.
Everything® Family Guide to RV Travel & Campgrounds
Everything® Family Guide to the Caribbean
Everything® **Family Guide to the Disneyland® Resort, California Adventure®, Universal Studios®, and the Anaheim Area, 2nd Ed.**
Everything® **Family Guide to the Walt Disney World Resort®, Universal Studios®, and Greater Orlando, 5th Ed.**
Everything® Family Guide to Timeshares
Everything® Family Guide to Washington D.C., 2nd Ed.

WEDDINGS

Everything® Bachelorette Party Book, $9.95
Everything® Bridesmaid Book, $9.95
Everything® Destination Wedding Book
Everything® Elopement Book, $9.95
Everything® Father of the Bride Book, $9.95
Everything® Groom Book, $9.95
Everything® Mother of the Bride Book, $9.95
Everything® Outdoor Wedding Book
Everything® Wedding Book, 3rd Ed.
Everything® Wedding Checklist, $9.95
Everything® Wedding Etiquette Book, $9.95
Everything® Wedding Organizer, 2nd Ed., $16.95
Everything® Wedding Shower Book, $9.95
Everything® Wedding Vows Book, $9.95
Everything® Wedding Workout Book
Everything® **Weddings on a Budget Book, 2nd Ed., $9.95**

WRITING

Everything® Creative Writing Book
Everything® Get Published Book, 2nd Ed.
Everything® Grammar and Style Book
Everything® Guide to Magazine Writing
Everything® Guide to Writing a Book Proposal
Everything® Guide to Writing a Novel
Everything® Guide to Writing Children's Books
Everything® Guide to Writing Copy
Everything® **Guide to Writing Graphic Novels**
Everything® Guide to Writing Research Papers
Everything® Screenwriting Book
Everything® Writing Poetry Book
Everything® Writing Well Book